GETTING AWAY WITH MURDER

ON THE TEXAS FRONTIER

GETTING AWAY WITH MURDER on the TEXAS FRONTIER

— Notorious Killings & Celebrated Trials —

BILL ★ NEAL

Foreword by Gordon Morris Bakken

TEXAS TECH UNIVERSITY PRESS

This book is typeset in Monotype Waldbaum. The paper used in this book meets the minimum requirements of ANSI/NISO Z39.48—1992 (R1997).

Library of Congress Cataloging-in-Publication Data

Neal, Bill, 1936–
Getting away with murder on the Texas frontier : notorious killings and celebrated trials / Bill Neal ; foreword by Gordon Morris Bakken.
    p. cm.
Summary: "Longtime Texas prosecutor and defense attorney mines trial records and other primary sources to analyze murder trials from 1880 through WWI in West Texas and Oklahoma. Addresses not only legal and illegal ploys but also inherent pitfalls for a nascent criminal justice system in a frontier society. Historical photographs"—Provided by publisher.
    Includes bibliographical references and index.
    ISBN-13: 978-0-89672-579-9 (cloth : alk. paper)
    ISBN-10: 0-89672-579-0 (cloth : alk. paper) 1. Trials (Murder)—Texas. 2. Criminal justice, Administration of—Texas—History—Sources. 3. Frontier and pioneer life—Texas—History—Sources. I. Title.
    KF221.M8N43 2006
    364.152'309764—dc22   2006005618

Printed in the United States of America
07 08 09 10 11 12 13 14 / 9 8 7 6 5 4 3 2
MG

Texas Tech University Press
Box 41037
Lubbock, Texas 79409—1037 USA
800.832.4042
ttup@ttu.edu
www.ttup.ttu.edu

TO GAYLA—THE BEST THING THAT

EVER HAPPENED TO ME

CONTENTS

ILLUSTRATIONS

ILLUSTRATIONS

FOREWORD

Getting *Away with Murder on the Texas Frontier* is a significant contribution to a growing literature on the criminal justice system in the American West. Scholars have moved beyond the vigilance committees, lynch mobs, and popular tribunals that dominated the literature of previous western histories. More recently, scholars with legal and police backgrounds and experience have taken up the cases and controversies. With expertise in detection, prosecution, and criminal defense, these scholars have afforded readers insight into the criminal justice system in the West set within their particular times.

The cultural basis for the analysis of crime and punishment in the West is how Americans thought about crime, violence, law, and due process. John Phillip Reid's *Policing the Elephant: Crime, Punishment, and Social Behavior on the Overland Trail* cuts away the myths of crime and violence in the Wild West.[1] The average citizen crossing the plains in a wagon train carried traditions, customs, and laws. On the trail people lived by the rules, controls, and restraints of their recent past. Their lawmindedness was put to use in rare cases of criminality on the trail rather than the personal violence typically depicted in novels and films. People protected private property with violence if necessary, and, particularly, horse thieves were often shot without trial. Violence against American Indians was rare; fights among overlanders was the norm of violence on the trail. Most of the stabbings and shooting occurred between people who knew one another, and frequently these affrays were between business partners. A homicide, once discovered, led to a collective defense as ordinary people were ready to assist in the tasks of law enforcement.

Trials often proceeded in accordance with written constitutions crafted by company members. Although the constitutions were not instructions for how to conduct trials, the constitution and bylaw evidence clearly indicates a lawmindedness and a respect for procedure. The accused did not have the advantage of technical evidence rules, and hearsay and opinion evidence frequently found its way into trials. However, these overland trial courts demanded evidence of guilt and granted the accused the opportunity to be heard. A surprising number of the accused were exonerated at their trials on grounds of self-defense, provocation, or insufficiency of evidence. When someone was found guilty, punishment along the trail included whipping, banishment, or death.

Scholars also have focused on individual cases to tease out the legal and societal elements so important to understanding the western criminal justice system. John W. Davis Jr.'s *A Vast Amount of Trouble: A History of the Spring Creek Raid* is such a book. John W. Davis, a Worland, Wyoming, attorney, concentrated on a 1909 murder case in the Big Horn Basin.[2] The narrative is driven by the cattleman-sheepman conflict over range, the transition from frontier to twentieth-century social norms, and the law of the West. The actions were simple: three sheepmen crossed a deadline, a geographic point established by cattlemen across which a sheepman came only at his hazard, and seven cattlemen murdered them. A dark and bloody ground awaited the investigative arm of the law. Felix Alston, the sheriff of Big Horn County, arrived to collect forensic evidence and interrogate locals. Two deviants turned states evidence, and the trial of the alleged triggermen ended in guilty verdicts despite an ardent cattleman on the jury. Deals were made after the verdict, and five were sent to the state prison. Within five years, all of the felony murder convicts were out of jail.

One important element of Davis's book is the timeline of the criminal justice system. The murders took place in April 1909. Nine attorneys represented the defendants on trial on November 4, 1909. The state had four attorneys. Trial often continued until 6:00 p.m. On the final day, the judge gave jury instructions at 6:00 p.m., and they deliberated until midnight. Five votes enabled them to arrive at a verdict the next morning. Sentencing took place on Saturday, November 13, 1909. One prisoner died in jail of spotted fever in 1912, and another was released the same year. All were out of custody by 1914. Importantly, how and why the system was successful is part of the analysis, an analysis seldom attempted in other western historiographies.

Historians also have looked at criminal cases in terms of culture in a western place. Jill Mocho's *Murder and Justice in Frontier New Mexico, 1821–1846* inspects the fragmentary manuscript record of homicide and the legal system during the Mexican period in New Mexico.[3] Despite the paucity of official documents, Mocho exhumed eleven homicides, tracked down the historical culprits, deciphered the legal system, and solved the crimes of passion, culture, and greed. In the process she found that not a single confessed murderer suffered the death penalty, and for all of the incarcerated, freedom was less than six years away. But in Mocho's study, the process rather than the penalty was under scrutiny. The Hispanic players in the justice system took their duty seriously, although American expectations of speedy trial were not part of Mexican jurisprudence.

Instead, the criminal justice system followed Mexican forms. *Alcaldes* and *jueces de paz* were knowledgeable of legal procedure. They were prominent men in their communities, respected for their wisdom as well as for their social position. When a community member brought a crime to their attention, they acted with dispatch. Members of the community were brought to the crime scene to investigate and report on the homicide, a medical examination sought the cause of death, suspects gave statements as well as confessions, and evidence was set to paper. Legal procedure wound its way to judgment and exhibited an adherence to Spanish values, community traditions, and a clear sense of right and wrong.

When American-style justice came to New Mexico, there would be sixty-two official executions plus untold numbers of popular hempen cravats affixed over a thirty-year period. Times had clearly changed. Yet it is easy to see that the Anglo-Americans on the Overland Trail, Hispanic citizens in New Mexico, and lawmen in the Big Horn Basin of Wyoming all worked to identify enemy deviants, bring them into the criminal justice system, and allow the system to do justice in its time and place.

Race and justice is another theme scholars have used to gauge the fairness of the criminal justice system. Clare V. McKanna Jr.'s *The Trial of "Indian Joe": Race and Justice in the Nineteenth-Century West* focuses on an American Indian itinerant manual laborer caught up in a San Diego County, California, double murder.[4] McKanna makes it clear that racial prejudice was a major part of the proceedings that led to conviction. Even more certainly, McKanna's *White Justice in Arizona: Apache Murder Trials in the Nineteenth Century* found that justice for criminally accused Apaches was usually absent. Further, the native culture was at odds with the American criminal justice system.[5] This finding echoes Sidney L. Harring's *Crow Dog's Case: American Indian Sovereignty, Tribal Law, and United States Law in the Nineteenth Century.*[6] Harring's incisive analysis of tribal law and the case of a killing highlighted the divergent cultural approaches to punishment for homicide. Whether Hispanic or Indian, minority criminal defendants had a much different probability of conviction.

The probability of execution at the hands of a lynch mob was another matter. John W. Davis Jr.'s *Goodbye, Judge Lynch: The End of a Lawless Era in Wyoming's Big Horn Basin* uses his attorney's lens to analyze thirty years of criminality leading up to the 1902 case of *State v. Jim Gorman.*[7] The second trial of Gorman for killing his brother resulted in a conviction and a lynch mob attack on the Big Horn County jail. Two prisoners, including Gorman, and a deputy sheriff died in the attack. Yet this lawlessness resulted in the sobering establishment of law and order. This culture shift brought the Spring Creek raiders to justice as detailed in Davis's *A Vast Amount of Trouble: A History of the Spring Creek Raid.* Frederick Allen's *A Decent Orderly Lynching: The Montana Vigilantes* takes a closer look at vigilantes in Montana from 1864 to 1879, who executed over fifty men as a means of social control.[8] First committed to ending the reign of outlaw sheriff Henry Plummer and his gang, the vigilantes continued their hanging ways after Plummer and his gang tasted hemp. Despite the fact that courts were open, Paris

Pfouts directed the vigilantes to exterminate common thieves as well as social deviants. Yet in 1870 the hanging of two men in Helena drew the editorial criticism of newspapers, and the vigilantes melted away. Another culture shift had occurred.

As you read *Getting Away with Murder on the Texas Frontier,* note the resonance of legal procedure and changing cultural perspectives. This provocative book will excite the imagination and stand as a major contribution to our knowledge of the western criminal justice system.

GORDON MORRIS BAKKEN
California State University, Fullerton, 2006

PREFACE

YOU CAN'T hang out in country courthouses in West Texas for forty years or so, as I have, without hearing many tales of the sensational crimes and celebrated trials of bygone years. Having spent about half of my professional life as a prosecutor (a district attorney) and the balance as a country lawyer whose practice tilted heavily toward criminal defense work, I became fascinated with our criminal justice system and how our criminal laws, as well as the practice of criminal law, originated and evolved. Let other lawyers immerse themselves in much more lucrative specialties such as the esoteric intricacies of zoning law or in that great mother lode they call tax law, I (perhaps betraying a pronounced streak of masochism) persisted in wallowing around down in the trenches of the criminal courts. There was nothing pretty about that, nothing very pleasant; but, one thing's for sure, it was all damned real—and as serious as a heart attack. The outcome of every case was crucially important to everyone involved.

Some years ago my fascination with criminal law and its history led me to begin collecting and researching those old tales of criminal trials—murder cases in particular. I became convinced that many of these yarns were just too good to be left buried and forgotten. And so, between court appearances, I spent many hours digging into those old stories, rummaging through musty records in courthouse basements, and sifting through the dusty morgues of local weekly newspapers. County history books became an obsession. Now and then I found a local historian who helped me fill in the gaps. Once in a while I was even able to interview people with personal knowledge of the events. Finally, I decided to put all these tales together and make a book out of them.

When I did so, I discovered that in almost all of these tales of early-day murder trials, the accused, either by jury verdict or by some legal or extralegal highjinks, managed to skate home free. Why, I continued to wonder, and by what means? The stories themselves go a long way toward answering these questions, but a fuller understanding depends on an appreciation of the time, place, and culture in which they occurred. The time spanned from the 1880s through World War I (reaching occasionally into the 1930s). The place is that area of West Texas west of Fort Worth and north of Abilene (with a few exceptions reaching into western Oklahoma and northeast Texas.)

Acknowledgments

Many thanks are in order: to my wife, Gayla, for her encouragement, perceptive criticism, and many hours of secretarial duties; to my former legal secretary, Judy Payne, for many hours of research assistance; and to my longtime friend and college roommate of many moons ago, Dave McPherson, PhD, a retired English professor who, beyond the call of friendship, descended from the ethereal planes of Shakespeare to muck around and edit my pedestrian efforts.

Special thanks also to four real historians for their advice and encouragement: to the late A. C. Greene, my college journalism professor and a dear friend, the one who first encouraged me to follow my concept for this work; to Dr. Fred Rathjen; to Dr. Garry L. Nall; and to Wyman Meinzner.

Local historians who have generously shared their stories and material with me are greatly appreciated: the late Robert E. King of Seiling, Oklahoma; Marisue Burleson Potts of Motley County, Texas; Jack Jones of Seymour, Texas; Robert Kincaid, Leta Jo Haynie, and Clark Hitt of Crowell, Texas; Patsy Smart of Seiling, Oklahoma; and Myna Hicks Potts of Medicine Mound, Texas.

To those others who were kind enough to grant interviews I am also much obliged: Jim Lois Gafford of Amarillo, Texas; Betty B. Gafford of

Crowell, Texas; Foard County Judge Charlie Bell of Crowell, Texas; Billie Bell Gidney of Crowell, Texas; retired Childress County District Judge John T. Forbis; retired Baylor County District Judge Clyde Whiteside; A. J. Fires (grandson of the original Judge A. J. Fires) of Wellington, Texas; Carol Morse of Ardmore, Oklahoma; Jim Cloyd of Canadian, Texas; Stanton Brown of Benjamin, Texas; Frank McAuley of Knox City, Texas; and A. C. (Arb) Piper and Waylon (Toar) Piper, both of Paducah, Texas; and Ralph Powell of Matador, Texas.

Others who have helped one way or another are my mother-in-law, Opal Beall of Copperas Cove, Texas; lifelong friend Jean Hollowell Booziotis of Dallas; and Assistant State's Attorney Betty Marshall of Austin.

Thanks to the court clerks in Wichita Falls, Vernon, Quanah, Childress, Crowell, Benjamin, Seymour, Matador, Crowell, Canadian, Gatesville, and Clarendon, Texas, and Taloga, Oklahoma, for assisting me in my research of court records.

Also appreciated are personnel at the Southwest Collection Library at Texas Tech University, the Panhandle-Plains Archives Library, the University of Texas at Arlington Library, the Fort Worth Public Library, the Texas State Archives Library in Austin, the Oklahoma City Public Library, the Oklahoma State Archives Library, and the Hemphill County Museum at Canadian, Texas, all of whom were unfailingly patient and helpful.

GETTING AWAY WITH MURDER

ON THE TEXAS FRONTIER

PROLOGUE

A loyal son of Texas
Went out upon a spree—
Perpetrated six murders,
Some rape and burglaree.
They swung him from the gallows—
A proper end, of course;
But the reason that they hung him was—
That bastard stole a horse.

Texas' Uncommon Laws
By Corwin W. Johnson
University of Texas Law Professor
(Sung to the tune of "The Yellow Rose of Texas")[1]

DURING A 1916 jury trial in the tiny West Texas town of Benjamin, a gunman slipped into the crowded courtroom and touched off wall-to-wall pandemonium when he sneaked up behind the defendant (who was being tried for murder) and shot him in the back—fatally. For good measure he then proceeded to wound a witness and a defense attorney before being subdued. There was no doubt about the shooter's identity. He was not insane; he was not under threat of any immediate harm to himself. Yet he sailed through four jury trials with nary a conviction for murder, or for attempting to murder the witness or the attorney, or even for carrying a concealed weapon into a courtroom. He never served a day's time.

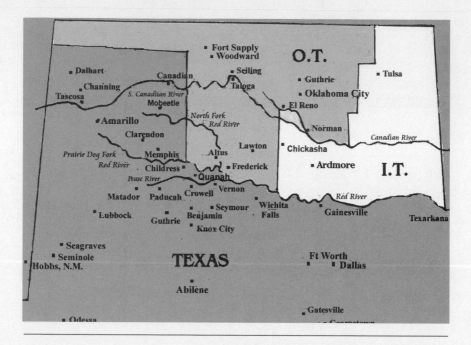

Where It All Happened

In 1912 in Fort Worth's finest hotel an esteemed pioneer cattleman and banker was chatting with a friend when an Amarillo wheeler-dealer half the age of the pioneer entered the lobby and, without a word, pulled a pistol and killed the old gentleman in the presence of an eyewitness—an eyewitness who just happened to be the son of a former Texas governor. The victim was unarmed and had made no prior threats to harm the shooter. The shooter was not insane. Yet after two trials a Fort Worth jury found him "not guilty." As the jury departed the courtroom, an astounded reporter cornered the foreman and asked the obvious question: "Why?"

"Well," the foreman shrugged, "because this is Texas."

Sufficient as that answer may have seemed to the jury foreman himself, if not the reporter, it did leave a few loose ends dangling—especially for today's readers.

So, how did they do it? How in the world did they get away with murder so flagrant?

THE COMING OF THE LAW

In That Time and That Place

UP UNTIL about a decade after the Civil War, no formal law existed in West Texas and western Oklahoma. The American criminal justice system as we know it was barely a seedling, struggling to take root in very rocky and arid soil. Even into the following decade, there was no judicial system to speak of, and lawmen were few and far between. By the 1890s cattle rustlers, claim jumpers, fence cutters, ruthless cattle barons, gouging railroad magnates, and vigilantes were still abundant. In somewhat of an overstatement, one pioneer jurist described the frontier as "a place inhabited by prairie dogs, coyotes, rattlesnakes, jackrabbits, bad men, and worse women."[1]

In that environment statutes passed by politicians in far-off Austin meant little to the westerners on the frontier. They were more accustomed to "self-help" justice as practiced in the courts of "Judge *Winchester*" or "Judge *Lynch*." Even when the first crude local courts were established, sagebrush justice still relied less on written statutes than on common sense, grassroots fairness, and rather vague notions of folk law derived in large part from the Old South's Victorian code of chivalry and honor, which I'll discuss in detail later.[2]

Although the seeds of our criminal justice system were planted during those turbulent times, none could be expected to mature overnight. Therein lies at least a partial answer to the failures in the frontier justice system you'll encounter in these pages. Causes of these failures may be divided into two categories: those relating primarily to the limitations under which prosecuting lawyers practiced during the first decades of the criminal justice system on the frontier, and those relating primarily to the values of society at large at that time and place.

Challenges Prosecutors Faced

Very few lawyers and judges of that day and place had extensive legal educations. Most had never even seen the inside of a law school. Customarily, aspiring attorneys simply apprenticed themselves to established practitioners for a few months and then applied to the local district judge for a law license. The district judge then appointed a committee of three local lawyers to "examine" the applicant and report back to the court. As often as not, their recommendation depended more on whether they liked the applicant than on his legal expertise or lack thereof. If they liked the candidate then one of the committee would usually take the applicant behind the woodshed for a pre-examination review of the questions the aspiring lawyer would encounter during the official examination.[3]

The economics of practicing law on the frontier was another factor that tilted the playing field in favor of defense attorneys and criminal defendants. Excepting a few criminal-defense veterans, few frontier lawyers made much money from their practice. Lucrative civil cases were few and far between on the frontier as there was very little commerce, no automobile accident cases, no medical malpractice suits, no big insurance companies to sue, few divorces, and probate estates that amounted to much were as scarce as hen's teeth. The most profitable civil practice cases involved land title disputes.[4] Even here attorney's fees were rarely paid in cash but instead with interest in lands recovered if the suit proved successful. Because land was plentiful and cheap (often a dollar or two per acre in Texas), such interests did not amount to much unless a wise counselor held on to the title, and then his descendants often became wealthy. Typically, in civil cases, a frontier lawyer had to take his fee in barter—a homemade quilt, vegetables, a hog, a chicken, or a cow. Some frontier lawyers who rode the circuit with a district judge took along irons to brand their newly acquired attorneys fees.[5] The largest cash fees in those days were derived from criminal defense cases,[6] but to command those fees, a lawyer had to have earned a reputation as a successful trial advocate.

Most prosecutors of the day, on the other hand, were ill-trained cub lawyers with freshly printed law licenses and little experience. Prosecution salaries barely met subsistence levels. Many young prosecutors had to *live* in the courthouse to make ends meet. Prosecutorial positions were viewed as stepping stones to future criminal defense practices or as rungs up the political ladder.[7] Consequently, in most murder (and livestock theft) cases, a prosecutor still wet behind the ears would find himself pitted against a lion of the defense bar—with predictable results.

Also tipping the scales in favor of the defense was the lack of modern crime detection methods and trained investigators, which meant scientific proof was largely unavailable. Forensic science was in its infancy—there were no means of matching fingerprints, hair, or fiber; no DNA testing or criminal history databases; and certainly no profiling of perpetrators. On top of that, only the most primitive forms of communication and transportation were available. The local sheriff—who typically had no law enforcement training—was about the only help the prosecutor had.[8]

One frontier lawyer, R. W. Hall, who later became chief justice of the Amarillo Court of Appeals, pointed out another handicap that burdened early-day lawyers in northwest Texas. He recalled that up until the end of the nineteenth century, "There was no such thing as a law library in all this broad expanse of country."[9] When Abilene lawyer J. F. Cunningham was elected district attorney of the thirty-plus-county 39th Judicial District in 1888, no one had case-law books or legal-form books. Here he recalls the details:

We had no form books in those days, there were no stenographers, no typewriters, everything was done in longhand—charges, indictments, facts, briefs, etc., had to be written out. . . . We simply wrote out what we wanted and trusted that it would stand the scrutiny of the higher courts.[10]

The district judge, making the multi-county circuit, usually carried a copy of the Texas statutes, which was all the written law available to practitioners out on the circuit. Of course most lawyers in the more settled eastern portions of Texas had access to law libraries. And soon after the Civil War some of those lawyers had impressive collections of law books.[11]

An even greater problem for prosecutors was the availability of witnesses—especially honest and cooperative witnesses. Plus, many folks on the frontier were rootless. With such a transient society and with prosecutors severely hampered by limitations in funding, transportation, and communication resources, when a key prosecution witness disappeared over the horizon, it was often *"adios amigo."* Even witnesses who could be located might not be retrieved by the time trials were called. And savvy defense lawyers, recognizing that time was very much on their side, made every effort to delay and continue trials.[12] In those violent times, especially when a vicious defendant was to be put in the dock, witness intimidation was a tremendous problem for prosecutors. Defendants and their associates would often make threats that not even the stout-hearted could ignore.[13]

Also, as the stories in the chapter on the 1890s Wells Fargo murder trials reveal, in those freewheeling times before bar associations and grievance committees, a laissez-faire attitude regarding permissible trial tactics prevailed in the courtrooms. All seemed fair in love, war, and criminal trials. As the ensuing tales demonstrate, defense lawyers, frequently and with little fear of adverse consequences, sponsored witnesses who they knew (or at least had good cause to believe) were going to perjure themselves, relied upon altered or forged documents, and knowingly misrepresented facts to the court and juries. Historian J. Evetts Haley in his biography of Charles Goodnight commented on dishonesty in the courtroom:

> The country was full of perjurers who almost made a business of going from court to court. . . . In regretting the difficulty, Goodnight simply observed that in court the dishonest had one decided advantage—he can swear whatever is necessary while the man of integrity is limited to the facts.[14]

And finally, if all else failed, the defense could pull out all the stops and try for a pardon—a righteous pardon, a bought pardon, or, as we shall see in another of the tales, a "funny" pardon. In those times, when there was much less media scrutiny of statehouse doings, this strategy seems to have worked even better than it does today.

Society at Large

An understanding of frontier society's prevailing beliefs, mores, and core values, as well as the public's general level of education and sophistication, goes far in explaining why, in many of the upcoming stories, juries exercised an early-day form of "jury-nullification" by simply ignoring the evidence or refusing to follow the written law as set out in the court's instructions.

What were some of the core beliefs, mores, and values that so viscerally influenced the early-day juror? The typical frontiersman's attitude toward, and acceptance of, violence in society is perhaps most salient.

The causes of violence in the West were myriad. Much blood was shed as a result of range issues such as cattle rustling, fence cutting, claim jumping, and boundary line disputes: ongoing feuds between cattlemen and sheepmen and between cattle barons and nesters (small family farmers). In Texas between 1875 and 1920 there were twenty-nine violent incidents between sheepmen and cattlemen resulting in the slaughter of 3,215 sheep, four sheepherders, and two cattlemen. However, the violence was even worse in Wyoming and Arizona. There were thirty-five confrontations during the same period in Wyoming, resulting in the killing of 16,305 sheep, ten sheepherders, and one cattleman. In Arizona twenty-three encounters killed 5,420 sheep, eleven sheepherders, and thirteen cattlemen.[15] Exact figures tallying deaths and injuries caused by confrontations between cattle barons and nesters are not available, but the toll does not appear to have been as great as films and dime novels might have led us to believe.

Not to be denied, however, is the fact that there were a number of violent episodes in the West that were screen-worthy, such as the famous 1878 Lincoln County war in the eastern New Mexico Territory, featuring Billy the Kid, Pat Garrett, and lesser shootists,[16] as well as the sensational 1892 Johnson County war in Wyoming.[17] West Texas, meanwhile, had its share of headline-capturing showdowns, including the 1878 lynching of a former county sheriff in Albany, Texas. John M. Larn was elected sheriff of Shackleford County in 1876, but he soon threw in with, and became the leader of, an agressive band of vigilantes known as the "Tin Hats." Then he went from bad to worse. Teaming up with the infamous John Selman, Larn became an arrogant outlaw and cow thief. Even his former vigilante compadres finally got enough of Larn, and on June 24, 1878, they broke into his jail cell and put a quick end to his career—and ensured his eternal silence.[18]

Another famous incident, which occurred near Graham, Texas, in 1889, served as the basis for the movie *The Sons of Katie Elder*, starring John Wayne and Dean Martin. Four Marlow brothers, all of whom were shackled prisoners, were being transported from Graham to Dallas to stand trial when they were ambushed by masked vigilantes who included some of the leading members of the community. Two of the Marlow brothers were killed outright, but brothers George and Charles, though badly wounded, heroically managed to arm themselves amidst a hail of gunfire and ultimately repeled the mob. Then, because the two surviving brothers were leg-ironed to their murdered siblings, they were forced to sever their deceased brothers' feet to free themselves.[19]

Another lynching occurred in Wichita Falls in 1896 when a large mob, again including prominent community leaders, broke into the local jail, dragged two outlaws down the street a few blocks, and hanged them from a telephone pole. That episode, and its aftermath, are described in "The 1896 Wichita Falls Bank Robbery."

Although all of the incidents depicted in this book occurred well to the north of the Rio Grande, it should be noted that a virulent strain of racially inspired violence was endemic throughout the Texas-Mexico borderland, and lasted well into the twentieth century.[20] Other causes of frontier violence included family feuds, blood soured by the Civil War and the bitter aftermath of Reconstruction, racial hatred, illicit sex, insulted honor, alcohol-inspired barroom brawls, and plain old greed— or any combination of the above.

Before traveling farther down that road, it is worthwhile to pause and note that most of the westerners were decent, honest, and hardworking folks with little capital but with large dreams. These settlers were very much absorbed in the unceasing daylight-to-dark struggle to survive and to carve out a niche for themselves and their families.[21] In general, in the time and place of these stories, neighbors helped neighbors and gave generously of their time and meager resources. A man's word was truly his bond. A hungry stranger was rarely turned away. It was a time when folks trusted one another and seldom bothered to lock the doors to their homes.[22] And, it was a time when prosecutions for burglary, forgery, and fraud seldom appeared on frontier court dockets.[23] And, except for those unfortunate settlers caught up in family feuds or ethnic frontier violence, the typical settler who stayed at home and minded his own business ran little risk of becoming a statistic of violence.[24] All that said, there was still violence aplenty in the Old West.

The extent of violence on the frontier continues to spark scholarly debates. Was the West really as violent as popularly depicted? We know the Hollywood myth is still alive and kicking in the psyche of the general public.[25] But, was the Old West more violent, for instance, than life in America's inner cities today?[26] In fact the history of violence and lawlessness in the West, including its causes, extent, and duration, differs from state to state[27] and even from region to region within each state— just as it does today from neighborhood to neighborhood within a city.[28] After all, Texarkana had about as much in common with El Paso as Peking does with Peoria.

It is nonetheless safe to hazard a few generalizations about the western experience. In no state or region did the establishment of a system of justice under duly enacted law come easy or with steady and uninterrupted progress. Although most newcomers were honest and hardworking folks, more than a few had no intention of burdening themselves with honest physical labor. As the frontier pushed westward, it typically outran the law. The frontier was a magnet that attracted desperadoes, thieves, killers, misfits, and other undesirables from all over the nation. Consequently the edge of any frontier went through an initial period of lawlessness followed by a corresponding period of mobocracy or vigilantism aimed at attaining some semblance of order and justice where none existed.[29]

When some semblance of justice under law began to take root, the settlers, even those of law-abiding persuasion, exhibited a curiously ambivalent attitude toward violent behavior as well as toward the prosecution of violent offenders—even killers. Homicide was considered "one of the probable contingencies of ordinary social life."[30] Indeed, it seemed most settlers not only accepted violence as a more or less normal way of life but enjoyed witnessing it in its most gruesome manifestations. Public hangings drew large crowds, and women and children joined the throngs of fascinated spectators. Parents wrote notes to their children's teachers seeking an excuse from class so the kids wouldn't miss the eagerly anticipated spectacle. One alert entrepreneur even cleared five hundred dollars by selling reserved seats to the macabre festivities—with a plate of barbecue thrown in for good measure. Photographers did a brisk business selling gruesome depictions of the dangling deceased for a dollar a piece at a time when a dime bought a pound of flour.[31]

That a large segment of Americans whose roots were south of the Mason-Dixon line seemed desensitized to violence in everyday life is hardly a wonder. After all, in the not too distant past they and their ancestors had suffered through the brutalizing effects of four years of horrific, wholesale slaughter during the Civil War followed by several more years of the violence, chaos, and bitterness that characterized the Reconstruction era. After four years of vicious fighting, when two massive armies marched back and forth across the South and completely ravaged it, there was a mass exodus from the scorched earth of the defeated land. Most of the survivors fled westward. And most of the late-nineteenth-century settlers who ended up in West Texas had Southern roots.

Yet there was more to it than the flight and lingering anger over the Civil War itself. Historian Edward L. Ayers attributes that "something more" to the pervasive southern influence on western frontier culture. He writes: "The violence that did erupt in western cattle towns and on the open range in post–Civil War years may well have been southern violence transplanted . . . especially by way of Texas."[32] Both before and after the Civil War, southerners flocked to Texas and other western states, and with them they brought their unshakeable dedication to the Old South's Code of Honor. Ayers elaborates:

Even after the South's fall in the Civil War, one thing remained constant. "Self-respect, as the Southerners understand it, has always demanded much fighting." . . . white Southerners' often-repeated explanation of why they killed each other with such frequency and regularity . . . [was] of course, . . . [that] they did it for honor's sake.[33]

In addition to killing for honor, the South's Code also held that no jury should convict a fellow who had dispatched another to vindicate an insult to that honor.[34]

While the typical West Texas settler in the late nineteenth century may have taken the prosecution of violent criminal offenses rather lightly, thefts of livestock were most assuredly taken seriously—very seriously. Trials of livestock thefts usually drew bigger crowds of spectators than murder trials. If you got caught stealing someone's cow, you were more likely to end up in the pen than if you shot someone. And if you got caught stealing a horse . . . well, you were powerful lucky if you even made it to the jailhouse, much less the courthouse.[35] In that agrarian frontier society where, for most folks, survival was always in question and hunger was a constant concern, livestock was indeed the family's treasure. Besides, a cowboy without a horse was in about as bad a fix as a sailor without a boat. One frontier editor no doubt summed up the feelings of most Texans when it came to the subject of horse thieves. Upon learning that the Texas legislature was considering lesser sanctions for the offense, he jeered, "Hang 'em first, then if they persist in their innocent amusement, cremate 'em!"[36]

One commentator on frontier justice, W. C. Holden, had this observation:

The public concerned itself little with an ordinary killing. . . . But horse stealing was another matter . . . every man caught was either shot on the spot or hung on the nearest tree. And no instance is yet recorded where the law paid the slightest attention to lynchers of this kind.[37]

When it came to the issue of the proper weight to be assigned to the value of human life, one of the first district judges in Dallas County, the colorful Nathaniel Macon Burford, did not suffer from a case of the mealy mouth when he delivered his opinion. While en route to the old wooden Dallas County Courthouse one fine morning in 1843, Judge Burford stopped off for a toddy or two. By the time he arrived to open grand jury proceedings, he was in fine fettle. "Gentlemen of the Grand Jury," he announced grandiloquently, "they tell us that more men are killed in Texas than in any other country in the world, and I guess that's a fact, but gentlemen of the Grand Jury, I tell you that more men need killing in Texas than in any other country in the world."[38]

Judge Burford sounded a chord that continued to resonate with frontier juries for many decades. To assure a defendant's acquittal, a lawyer usually needed only to convince the jury that the victim was a pretty sorry specimen of a human being. If he succeeded, then regardless of the circumstances of his demise, the evidence, or the law, the defendant was almost always assured of coming clear under the most popular of all defensive pleas of the day: the-sorry-son-of-a-bitch-needed-killing-anyhow.[39] Though this defense was rarely stated quite so explicitly by frontier lawyers, they seldom failed to get the message across to the jurors. In more than a few instances, if the victim was really worthless, popular opinion was strong enough to make a trial unnecessary in the first place.

Some of the early Texas criminal statutes evidence an almost callous disregard for human life. The law of self-defense, for example, was much more lenient, as reflected in the famous Texas "no duty to retreat" statute. Under English common law—the bedrock of American jurisprudence—a person who was assailed and in fear of death or great bodily injury was required, if at all possible, to flee the scene and thus avoid a confrontation. Failing that, he was further required "to retreat to the wall" behind his back before resorting to the use of lethal force to repel the attacker.[40]

But American pioneers had no use for that kind of thinking. The Texas law granted the assailed person the right to "stand his ground." A person who was "violently attacked"—or even a person "against whom hostile acts or demonstrations" were made—was not bound to retreat to avoid the necessity of killing his assailant.[41] And that philosophy was not limited to Texas boundaries. "A man is not born to run away."[42] Those were the words used by U.S. Supreme Court justice Oliver Wendell Holmes to explain the rationale of his 1921 Supreme Court opinion in *Brown v. United States*,[43] which rejected the English common law doctrine of "duty to retreat" in favor of a rule more in tune with the combative spirit of the American frontier—the "stand your ground" rule. In the Brown opinion, Holmes went on to explain that "detached reflection cannot be demanded in the presence of an uplifted knife."

Jim East was the sheriff in the now bygone town of Tascosa during the rough and rowdy 1880s. Although somewhat short on Holmesian eloquence, he, with typical West Texas directness, got straight to the point:

> Sentiment in the [Texas] Panhandle was strong against sending a man to the penitentiary who had killed a man in combat . . . it was hard to convict for manslaughter as they would generally plead self-defense.[44]

In later years, however, other observers viewed these early Texas laws and their popular application in a very different light. Perhaps without giving due weight to the exigencies and attitudes of the times, one scholar seems to have coated the butter a bit thick on the bun when (quoting from works by sociologist Henry P. Lundsgaarde and University of Texas criminal law professor George W. Stumberg) he observed:

> Both [Lundsgaarde and Stumberg] found an implicit system of legalized violent self-redress: so permissive were the Texas laws "pertaining to justifiable homicide" . . . that the need "for police, judges, juries and any form of third party authority [is practically eliminated] as long as one can convincingly establish that the killing was a response to a threat against person or property."[45]

The Texas law on self-defense has since reverted to the old common law "duty to retreat" standard. Under present Texas law, the assailed has a duty to retreat and thus avoid killing his adversary "if a reasonable person in his place would have believed he could safely retreat." A companion statute provides further that "the use of force against another is not justified in response to verbal provocation alone."[46]

At any rate, in early Texas jurisprudence, self-defense was almost a sure-fire answer to a murder indictment—especially if it could be coupled with that old frontier favorite, "the-SOB-needed-killing-anyhow" defense. Self-defense was often stretched to absurd lengths in a transparent effort to find some legal pretext for the desired not-guilty verdict.[47] In many such cases, the victim wasn't even armed. However, the defendant would simply testify that he feared the deceased, that somebody had told him the deceased had threatened to kill him, and that upon encountering the soon-to-be-deceased, he saw the victim make some furtive movement that appeared to be an attempt to draw a (usually nonexistent) pistol. The deceased, of course, was unable to take the stand and rebut this assertion. Even when bystanders testified they saw no weapon, nor any play for one, it was often enough for a jury if the defendant insisted he'd seen the deceased make a suspicious movement.

Ordinarily the defendant testified that he thought that the deceased was attempting to draw a pistol from his hip pocket. In one case, however, the defendant testified that he thought the (unarmed) deceased was attempting to draw a pistol from his vest pocket. This led the prosecutor, in his closing argument, to comment wryly: "Well, this is a new wrinkle! It is usually a hip pocket play."[48] As usual, however, the defendant was acquitted.

From the defense standpoint, it also helped that the jurors of those times, cut from a much coarser cloth than those of today, were considerably more credulous, unsophisticated, and gullible—and much more susceptible to the maudlin and the blatantly melodramatic appeals of the snake-oil salesman, the carnival barker, the hell-fire-and-damnation preacher, and the bombastic defense lawyer. Emotion trumped evidence nearly every time.

Sex, then as now, is a wild card in any deck. In that time your chances of walking away from a murder trial if you were a woman were almost assured (presuming, of course, that you were not "that kind of woman," in which event, all bets were off). In the afterglow of Southern Victorianism, respectable women were viewed as the gentler, kinder sex who had to be protected by their male champions and who were simply incapable of evil intent. Many early-day jurors candidly admitted that it would take much more evidence to convince them to convict a woman for murder than it would be to convict a man, and that under no circumstances could they vote to impose the death penalty on a woman.

However, if you were a male and had been foolish enough to participate in any kind of illicit hanky-panky with a woman—consensual or not—well . . . look out: hunting season was open, and you were fair game. If any member of the allegedly wronged woman's family (or even the wronged woman herself) nailed you, you could expect no sympathy from the courts or the juries of the day. If the written laws of Texas didn't clear the defendant, then, most assuredly, he or she would be exonerated by the Old South Code.[49] Even the early written laws of Texas went a long way down that path. Through 1973, by Texas statute, a husband was granted free shooting rights (no hunting license required) to kill any other man whom he caught *in flagrante delicto* with his wife.[50] Wives were not, however, granted reciprocal shooting rights.

Another peculiar Texas statute of the day went, in some respects, even further than the adulterer-killing statute. Under that one, the prosecutor didn't have to prove the soon-to-be-deceased had sexual contact with the woman—insulting words were enough. Nor was it necessary that the woman in question be the defendant's wife. The Texas statute provided that "insulting words or conduct of the person killed towards a female relative of the party guilty of homicide" constituted "adequate cause" to reduce the charge from murder to manslaughter.[51] Of course when defense lawyers got through massaging that statute before a jury, it was transformed into an adequate reason for killing that foul-mouthed insulter of Southern womanhood. Forget manslaughter, they would urge, find him "not guilty." The Texas legislature, in passing that statute, did not undertake to define which words were—and which words were not—insulting to one's female relative. One can only imagine the spirited debate that might occur on that point between opposing lawyers, particularly modern-day lawyers.

Until after World War I, ingrained notions of the purity of womanhood and the sanctity of the home were virtually immune from challenge in any court south (and even sometimes north) of the Mason-Dixon line, regardless of what the written law said.[52] How early Texans viewed the unwritten law of the Old South as opposed to the duly enacted written criminal laws and the value of human life came into sharp focus during jury arguments in one 1912 murder case wherein the defendant was tried for killing his wife's lover—the killing having occurred, mind you, months after the defendant learned of their affair.

> **Jordan Cummings for the state:** Regard for human life is the highest and ultimate test of a country's civilization.
> **W. P. McLean Jr. for the defense:** Human life is not the highest consideration of our laws, being less regarded by the law than domestic relations. . . . Every time there is a home broken up, there ought to be a killing of all who assisted in it.[53]

The early-day jurors found little difficulty in agreeing with McLean.

Race was always a factor—it helped a lot to be white if you hoped to get away with murder on the frontier. It is not necessary to cite cases or statistics to demonstrate that racism, unfortunately, did lead to the miscarriage of justice on the frontier. If you were white you stood little chance of being convicted for killing a non-white. If you were a non-white who killed a white person, you stood little chance of even getting to the courthouse. For example, on August 8, 1916, an African-American prisoner succeeded in overpowering and murdering Baylor County, Texas, Sheriff W. L. Ellis. A posse ran down and captured the prisoner the same day. That night a lynch mob, including all of the deputies and many leading citizens, hanged him on the courthouse lawn in Seymour. Not satisfied with that, they made a bonfire and burned the body.[54] No one even considered putting the mob members on trial.[55] This incident is just one example, and it is discussed in detail in ". . . And the Perpetrator Walked."

The successful establishment of the rule of law—not of men—depends upon the the public's confidence that, in most cases, justice will be best served by reliance upon criminal statutes enacted with the consent of the governed, and confidence that the courts will see to it honestly and fairly that justice is done under that law. In the early stages of our criminal justice system, while "Judge *Blackstone*" was struggling mightily to gain ascendancy over Judges *Winchester* and *Lynch*, it was most unfortunate that the Texas appellate courts seemed bent on undermining that public confidence.

Even into the first part of the twentieth century the ever-present threat of mob justice still smoldered mighty near the surface in West Texas, and those who participated in it were more often than not congratulated rather than prosecuted. Witness the absolute refusal of Wichita County citizens to prosecute the lynch mob leaders who murdered two bank robbers, as described in "The 1896 Witchita Falls Bank Robbery." Just before the lynching, District Judge George E. Miller stood on the steps of the courthouse and pleaded with the mob to desist, telling them that the law, in due course, would mete out justice—to which one of the mobsters yelled back, "Oh yes. There will be a continuance, and then an appeal, and then a reversal, and then a bond, and finally liberty."[56]

The mobster had a point. Although in contemporary society, many critics of the criminal justice system rail frequently against appellate courts for turning criminals loose on mere technicalities, the situation was much worse during the early years. There were two main reasons for this. First, unlike modern appellate review practice, review in those days occurred without the benefit of the harmless error doctrine. In that time, almost *any* trial court error was deemed reversible, whereas today appellate courts (in most cases) undertake an evaluation of the error to determine whether it is of such magnitude as to warrant overturning the trial court's guilty verdict. Second, frontier appellate judges seemed to delight in showing off their superior learnedness by making frog's hair distinctions invisible to average Texans.[57] (The Court of Criminal Appeals once reversed a murder conviction on a faulty indictment. The indictment alleged that the defendant killed the victim "with malice aforethought by poisoning him with strychnine." The evidence clearly showed that the victim had, in fact, died of strychnine poisoning and that there was little doubt that the defendant was the culprit. Still, opined the Court of Criminal Appeals, a reversal was mandated because the thoughtless prosecutor didn't allege in the indictment whether the defendant put the strychnine in the victim's coffee or his tea or his buttermilk or perhaps he poisoned the victim's oatmeal—and if so, no doubt the careless district attorney should have alleged which *brand* of oatmeal.)[58] These actions resulted in an inordinate number of reversals of jury convictions in cases where the defendant was obviously guilty. The too frequent and highly visible reversals by appellate courts on hypertechnical grounds served to undermine public confidence in a fledgling and vulnerable judicial system.

An editorial in the *Dallas Morning News* made the point succinctly:

Civilization demands that mob violence be suppressed, but it demands with just as much emphasis that the law punish the guilty. Justice has failed so often through petty technicalities that public confidence in the machinery of the law is at a low ebb.[59]

Frequent appellate reversals played into the hands of the defense attorneys in yet another way—bogging down the judicial progress for months or even several years, often making retrial impossible.

Part and parcel with the public's general distrust of the system were, as we shall discover in the stories ahead, the jurors themselves (even those not bribed), who often took decidedly pragmatic and extralegal views of their duties.[60] For example, one obviously guilty defendant was set free by a frontier jury when one of its members, a bootmaker by trade, told his fellow jurors that he had just made a pair of boots for the defendant and that if he were sent to prison then the juror would never collect his fee.

Although some of the best criminal defense lawyers of that day, such as A. J. Fires, were noted for collecting hefty fees, others, such as Temple Houston, often undertook representation for little or no financial gain if the defendant's plight struck his fancy or if the case was sensational. Few of the defendants in the following stories had much money, yet most were able to obtain quality representation. Either the defendant or the crime was sufficiently notorious to attract a born showman such as Houston or third parties (relatives or others with a personal interest in the case) were willing to bankroll the defense. Taking into account the immaturity of Texas's criminal justice system, the general public's rather callous disregard for the life and limb of fellow citizens, as well as all the problems and impediments burdening frontier prosecutors, one wonders how anyone was ever convicted of anything (except, that is, of stealing a cow or a horse). Yet occasionally, even with celebrated attorneys, a few slayers found themselves nailed by the same social mores, beliefs, and core values that permitted so many others to slip through the prosecutorial net. If, for instance, it was the defendant instead of the deceased who was "the sorry SOB who deserved a damned good killing," the prosecutorial outlook brightened considerably. Or if the defendant was a man who'd killed a woman, his remaining days on earth were likely to be few and dark—even if he was a minister of the Gospel.

In 1899 the Reverend G. E. Morrison was the pastor of a church in the little village of Panhandle, Texas. His wife, who had been in good health, suddenly got sick and died. Shortly before her death she had complained of stomach cramps, but the cause of death was unknown. The congregation extended its sympathy to the pastor. Still, the preacher's actions just before, and just after, her death seemed strange to some of his wife's close friends, and somehow his unctuous and ostentatious lamentations seemed a tad off-key. Finally, an autopsy was ordered.

An indictment for murder was eventually returned against the reverend, and the venue was changed to Vernon in Wilbarger County, Texas. Reverend Morrison hired the two best criminal defense lawyers in all West Texas to defend him, Temple Houston and A. J. Fires. In his day, the reverend had led some soul-soaring revivals and hallelujah-shoutin' choruses, but the shoutin' was all over when the jury learned that strychnine poisoning was the cause of his wife's death and read some of the preacher's torrid love letters to his girlfriend. And neither Temple Houston's spellbinding oratory nor A. J. Fires's exhaustive witness coaching and perspicacity in jury selection could save that preacher. On October 27, 1899, in Vernon, Texas, they hanged the Reverend G. E. Morrison.[61]

The Lawyers in Society

Despite its growing pains, the infantile Texas criminal justice system matured rather quickly. As Wayne Gard pointed out in his book *Frontier Justice,* "In the short span of two generations, settlers witnessed a rise from savagery to social stability that in some parts of the world, took several thousand years . . . as history goes, the transition from the bloody tomahawk to the polished gavel of the black-robed judge came with bounding speed."[62]

The heroes of these tales were, of course, the pioneer lawyers—admittedly a pretty coarse bunch of rambunctious, boisterous, and often besotten individualists bearing little resemblance to today's tall-building corporate counselors whose fees would bankrupt Australia. It would be a mistake to judge these frontier lawyers by today's legal standards of performance or ethical conduct. Bear in mind that just a few years before these tales, there were no courthouses in this land, no lawyers, and no law to speak of except that of vengeance and vigilante. These lawyers were the product of the land where they hung out their shingles—a land populated by the coarse, the crude, and the violent. They were a rough-hewn lot who came of age in a time when courtroom battles were bare-knuckle, no-holds-barred affairs. Still, warts and all, and despite the physical hardships of months on the road traveling by horseback or buggy from one remote county seat to the next, and despite having to brave the ever-present risk of violent assault inside or outside the courthouse, these advocates alone stood as a phalanx battling for the establishment of law and its supremacy.[63]

They had little money, they lacked library facilities, they were ill-trained and poorly paid, they were torn between the "unwritten" folk laws of the frontier and the crude legislation passed in distant Austin, and they were largely without legal precedent to guide them. The astonishing thing, however, is not how poorly they performed but, considering all these handicaps, how well they filled the void and laid the foundation for a lawful and ordered society. They were able, for the most part (but, admittedly, with some glaring lapses), to adjust the law to the facts with conscience, reason, and analogy as guides in an undeveloped field. Basically, they were thinkers and orators rather than disciplined students of the law.[64] That, however, resulted in an original and unique blend of wit, philosophy, and wisdom that enriches our history—a historical treasure, the veins of which, to date, have only been surface-mined.

In West Texas some wag derisively assigned to this cadre the distinctively inelegant handle of "prairie dog lawyers," undoubtedly meant to connote such unenviable attributes as common, uncouth, unwashed, and unlearned. Well, at least in that part of the state, the label stuck, and not in any small measure because the subjects of the derision, in a typical display of frontier grit and humor, eagerly grasped the thorny crown and claimed it as their own, wearing it with perverse pride.[65]

Common sense was considerably more abundant and more valued than a talent for making fine legal distinctions. One pioneer jurist noted that, while the prairie dog lawyer was "sorter weak on the law occasionally, he made up for it by being pretty strong and long and awfully loud on the facts, so he didn't need much written law in his business, though he frequently had to appeal to unwritten law in behalf of his client."[66]

The prairie dog lawyer had a distinct distaste for musty law books—just give him a living, breathing jury and turn him loose! Florid oratory, liberally spiced with random quotations from the Bible and classical literature as well as analogies to Greek mythology, was his choice of weapons on the legal battlefield. Dispassionate appeals to logic or law came in a sad second. Judge Thomas F. Turner, the dean of Amarillo lawyers and the first president of the Panhandle-Plains Historical Society, summed up the spirit and essence of these prairie dog lawyers in an article he wrote for that society's journal in 1929 when he observed:

> Let no one think that these lawyers of the early days were inferior in point of intellect or ability to those of the present time. They were strong men, rugged, forceful, powerful before the juries of their country. . . . They were carefree, generous and convivial, poor business men; in fact they would scorn to think of business. They were professional men. Let the tradesmen dwell on the prosaic matter of making money. . . . "On with the dance; let joy be unconfined" was their motto. So long as they had the wherewithal to pay their hotel bills . . . and to settle the score when they stood with one foot on the brass rail, that was enough. . . . [Theirs was a courtroom forum in which] personal magnetism and eloquence were the chief forces used to win.[67]

The first, and perhaps the foremost, of the prairie dog lawyers was

Judge Frank Willis was the first district judge of the new 31st Judicial District, which covered twenty-nine counties in the Texas Panhandle. His appointment in 1881 was a vital factor in establishing law and order in a wild and outlaw-infested land.
(Courtesy of the Panhandle-Plains Historical Museum, Canyon, Texas.)

Judge Frank Willis, who was appointed in 1881 as the first district (trial) judge of the newly formed 31st Judicial District, a huge district that included twenty-nine counties and just about the whole Texas Panhandle, a mighty tough territory teeming with outlaws who hung out in such well known haunts as Tascosa and Mobeetie. Judge Turner described Willis as "large of girth, large of intellect, large of heart, [whose] friends were legion."[68]

An anecdote about Judge Willis captures the spirit of frontier justice. In Judge Willis's day, it was necessary for the district judge and the district attorney to make the rounds of every organized county in their district at least once a year. They would then spend a week or more in each county seat, whatever it took to catch up on pending legal matters. During Willis's time and for many years afterward, until roads and automobiles made travel fast and easy, the lawyers in multi-county judicial districts traveled by horseback or horse-and-buggy. Customarily, the district judge and the district attorney, along with several defense attorneys, caravanned together across the district, often camping out on the prairie or staying overnight at a friendly rancher's home during their wanderings.[69]

As the only law book in the whole Panhandle was an 1879 edition of

Texas statutes, Judge Willis and his district attorney, W. H. Woodman, carried this volume with them from county to county. On one trip through the circuit Judge Willis, Woodman, and their judicial entourage were traveling to the next county seat when they were forced to cross a rain-swollen Canadian River. Short and stocky, Willis stripped to his underwear and began wading across. Woodman, much taller, was in charge of the precious 1879 Texas statutes, which he held on top of his head. As they progressed the water got deeper and deeper, and Judge Willis, who couldn't swim, began to sink into the mud or, more likely, a pocket of quicksand for which the Canadian River is famous. He yelled for Woodman to help. Woodman, however, was clinging tenaciously to the treasured legal tome.

"I can't let go of the law," Woodman yelled back.

Judge Willis, in a deep voice that boomed across the prairie rejoined, "To hell with the law, Woodman, save the court!"[70]

It thus appears that "the law"—then as now—is sometimes secondary to other considerations.

We have just explored some of the more significant reasons for judicial misfires on the western frontier, which might explain how so many culprits slipped through the law's net and "got away with murder." Argument begs validation, hence the actual cases that follow—each of which stands on its own as a fascinating and dramatic study of murder and justice (or injustice) on the frontier.

But before launching into the stories, I have a few suggestions for the reader. Remember that successful prosecutors and defense attorneys are always among the best students of human nature and the most attuned to the nuances of the society in which they practice. So listen to how they played to the juries of that day—what chords did they strike in their jury arguments? And not only what they said to the jury, but how they phrased it, and, maybe even more importantly, what they did not say to the jury. What did the witnesses say, and how did they phrase their testimony? Their open and unguarded expressions tell much, not only of their own biases, beliefs, and assumptions, but also those of their society. How did the judges and jurors react to the cases under scrutiny, and what were their comments?

How the press covered the trial is even more instructive. Typically, editors of the day were not at all bashful about inserting their own and very strongly expressed opinions in their accounts of the trials. Hence, it is not necessary to do much reading between the lines to find out what the editor's take was on the proceedings, the parties and the outcome of the trial, as well as how the public perceived the issues and the outcome.

David v. Goliath in a West Texas Courthouse

THE PROSECUTION'S SLAM DUNK—THAT WASN'T

MORE THAN a century has passed since Thomas J. Fulcher waylaid Old Man Beemer on September 10, 1887. Even though Fulcher was a killer, it would seem that in view of the notoriety of the case and with all the time that has passed, somebody would have said something good about the man. Yet the only favorable reference to him that history has recorded is a passing observation that "he was a handsome sort of fellow."[1]

Handsome, maybe—*sorry* and *vicious* and *vindictive* and *violent,* for sure. Hearing the tale of Thomas J. Fulcher's crimes is quite sufficient to catch almost anyone's attention, but the crimes are not half again as fascinating as the story of the resulting trials—a yarn with more unexpected twists and turns than an O. Henry short story. And the final twist was a dandy. It caught everyone in the courtroom flatfooted. Everyone, that is, except the twister himself.

Fulcher's first appearance in recorded history occurred sometime in 1886 when he and his wife, Minnie, showed up—dead broke—in the West Texas counties of Dickens and Motley, a land of rolling, almost treeless prairies and unbroken skies that, even today because of the scarcity of human inhabitants, they call "the Big Empty." The Fulchers took advantage of the hospitality of three pioneer homesteaders: B. F. Brock, F. M. Wells, and J. A. Askins and their families. Brock even got Fulcher a job in the summer of 1887 with a haying outfit working on the Spur Ranch in Dickens County.

At some point Fulcher got into a bitter dispute with A. Beemer, a Civil War veteran who worked as a blacksmith on the sprawling Matador Ranch in Motley County.[2] A bachelor, Beemer lived in his blacksmith shop at the ranch headquarters just outside of the present village of Matador, the county seat. Exactly what the dispute involved is not now clear except that Fulcher somehow ended up with some of Beemer's possessions, including a pistol, and Beemer demanded that Fulcher return them. Fulcher refused. Beemer consulted a lawyer and, being advised that he was on sound ground, wrote Fulcher a letter threatening to file theft charges against him if he failed to return the property. This demand was rewarded with at least partial compliance. Fulcher returned everything except the pistol; however, the threats and demands threw Fulcher into a towering rage.

September 10, 1887, had been a hot day, so when Beemer retired that evening shortly after sundown, he dragged his cot just outside the door of the blacksmith shop. Shortly thereafter Matador cowboy Nat John, who happened to be at the ranch headquarters, heard two gunshots coming from the direction of the blacksmith shop. When John arrived Beemer was lying on the ground, face down and resting on his hands. The cot was overturned. Beemer was wounded but still alive and conscious. John noted that Beemer "was in his right mind."

Nat John asked Beemer who shot him, and without hesitation he replied, "Tom Fulcher." He had struggled with Fulcher before the shooting, he said, and even though it was pretty dark, he knew Fulcher's voice and recognized Fulcher's very large and prominent front teeth. Beemer added, "I am bound to die; my insides are torn all to pieces."

J. M. Campbell was the next to arrive on the scene. Campbell also lived at the Matador headquarters. Campbell said that soon after he retired that evening he heard the two pistol shots and got up to investigate. As he approached the shop he heard Beemer ask, "Are you going to let me lie here and die?" Campbell asked him what was the matter. "I am shot twice" was the reply.

"Who shot you?"

"Tom Fulcher," Beemer gasped.

"How do you know it was Fulcher?"

"How do I know you, Mr. Campbell?"[3]

Campbell then returned to his house for brandy and water. The drink cleared Beemer's throat of blood, and he was better able to talk. After about fifteen minutes, Beemer got up and urinated, passing blood with his urine. Seeing that, Beemer exclaimed: "Mr. Campbell, I am bound to die; I have seen many such wounds in the army, and they always die."

Campbell echoed Nat John's opinion that Beemer was perfectly lucid when he gave the following detailed account of what happened:

> I was lying on my cot in front of my shop asleep, with my left hand over my head. I heard him twice call my name, "Beemer! Beemer!" I looked up and saw Fulcher holding his pistol a short distance from my head. I grabbed the pistol with my left hand. He pulled backward, yanking the pistol out of my hand, and then shot me through the throat and tops of my shoulders. I fell back into my cot. The cot then fell over. I fell on my face, and then he shot me in the back and ran off. I had hold of the pistol. It was in bad keeping and was rusty. You can easily identify it by that.[4]

On the day after the shooting, Deputies Jeff Boone and Tom Stewart arrested and lodged Fulcher in the brand new Motley County jail. Fulcher had the dubious honor of being the jail's first inmate. He promptly earned another dubious distinction—he was the first inmate to escape from the new jail. However, he was soon recaptured and returned to his accommodation. (Deputy Jeff Boone, a Matador Ranch cowboy and wagon boss, later earned a dubious distinction of his own. Some five years after the Fulcher arrest, Boone died as a result of a gunshot wound sustained in a shootout with Motley County's first elected sheriff, Joe Beckham.)[5]

J. M. Campbell later testified that after Fulcher was arrested he was taken before Beemer, and that Beemer, face-to-face with Fulcher, identified Fulcher as the man who shot him. Three days elapsed after the shooting before the ranchers and townsfolk finally managed to find a doctor to treat Beemer. On the fourth day after the shooting, Beemer sent for a notary public to take his formal "dying declaration." The notary public recorded Beemer's sworn statement, reduced it to writing, and Beemer signed it. The statement reiterated the tale Beemer had told Campbell and Nat John just after the shooting. Beemer also declared in his statement that he was sane and that he believed he could not recover and was about to die. However, Beemer lingered on, clinging to life for almost two months before he expired on November 4, 1887.

Within a few days after Beemer died, an examining trial was held. During this proceeding the state was required to put on a skeleton case to convince a magistrate (the local justice of the peace) that Fulcher should be held in custody until the case could be presented to a grand jury. At the examining trial (with Fulcher present), the state presented several important witnesses, including George Walker, who identified Fulcher as the man he saw riding toward the Matador Ranch headquarters just before the shooting. He added that Fulcher was riding a roan horse, wore a red scarf around his body, and had a pistol belt with red thread woven through it.

It came as no surprise that after the examining trial the justice of the peace bound Fulcher over for the grand jury. Motley County was not organized for judicial purposes at that time, but it was attached to neighboring Crosby County for jurisdiction. The Crosby County grand jury promptly indicted Fulcher for the murder of A. Beemer in Motley County, Texas. However, in the first of a series of blunders, the indictment (prepared by the prosecution) proved defective and had to be dismissed on objection by the defense.[6] It wasn't until May 22, 1889, that the Crosby County grand jury got around to re-indicting Fulcher.[7] A delay of more than a year and a half in getting the indictment right probably didn't seem important to anyone at the time.

The trial venue was then set for Anson in Jones County, and the date was set for September 2, 1889—almost two years after the shooting. When the case was called for trial, the courtroom was populated by some larger-than-life players. The prosecutor was young J. F. Cunningham of Abilene, district attorney of the recently formed 39th Judicial District. The huge district stretched from Anson on the south to the Oklahoma border on the north, and sprawled across West Texas from Seymour on the east all the way to the New Mexico line on the west. Cunningham

Thomas Fulcher was tried and convicted during his first trial under his second (Crosby County) indictment. Note this indictment, Cause No. 50 on the docket of the District Court of Crosby County, was returned on May 22, 1889. However, before Fulcher was retried, this indictment was dismissed and a third indictment was obtained out of the newly formed Motley County. Note the names of the grand jury witnesses on left, and note the jury's death sentence verdict on the right. It was customary in those days for the jury to note its verdict on the reverse side of the indictment.

(Official court records of Crosby County, Texas.)

was the county's first district attorney (1888–1890) and an able prosecutor. However, his real talent lay on the defense side of the docket, and after serving out his term as D.A., he soon became the premier defense lawyer in the area. The Matador Ranch hired another able attorney, C. M. Cristenberry, to assist Cunningham in the prosecution. Fulcher somehow managed to employ the formidable and high-spirited Felix G. Thurmond of Sweetwater, Texas, as defense attorney. But the star of the show was none other than the trial judge himself, the Honorable Jeremiah Vardeman Cockrell, the first judge of the 39th Judicial District.

Judge Cockrell didn't limit the scope of his activities to judicial matters. He was also a self-styled, old-time, fire-and-brimstone preacher. At the time of the trial, a district judge (along with the district prosecutor and two or three regular defense lawyers) customarily traveled around his district by horseback or buggy, servicing the judicial needs of the many counties in the district. They were on the road most of each year. Given his dual interests, Cockrell could be found on the bench in one of the county seat towns on most days, and behind one of the local pulpits most nights.[8] Furthermore, Cockrell didn't envision a judge's role to be that of a passive umpire of judicial proceedings. When a defendant in a criminal case came before him, he needn't expect a level playing field. Cockrell considered himself a coach for the prosecution team, and when he called a criminal case for trial, he invariably looked to the district attorney and inquired, "Mr. District Attorney, are *we* ready for trial?"[9]

Worse yet, Judge Cockrell was incapable of keeping a poker face during the trials, and his every thought and emotion seemed to be reflected on his countenance. Many defense lawyers (and defendants) complained that his facial expressions and demeanor invariably telegraphed to the jury his undeniable bias against criminal defendants, thus making it impossible for them to receive a fair trial.

Cockrell's trial demeanor once led to a hilarious episode wherein a defendant indicted for murder got away with the perfect crime right before Judge Cockrell's eyes. After the jury had found the defendant guilty of murder and assessed punishment at life imprisonment, it was left to Judge Cockrell to pronounce the sentence. As is prescribed by Texas law, the judge, before formally pronouncing sentence, must inquire of the defendant whether he has anything to say as to why sentence should not be pronounced against him. On this occasion the condemned's reply to this query was as follows.

"I don't think I got a fair trial. You used your influence to convict me."

"Tut! Tut!" Cockrell clucked. "I'll have to send you to jail for contempt of court."

To which the prisoner (with total immunity) retorted, "All right, send me to jail, you old son-of-a-bitch, I have already been sent up for life."[10]

When Cockrell called the Fulcher matter for trial, the prosecution presented a straightforward and compelling case. J. M. Campbell and Nat John gave their testimony, including the statements Beemer made immediately following the shooting. Beemer's sworn "dying declaration" was also introduced into evidence. George Walker, the examining trial witness who had identified Fulcher as the man he saw riding toward the Matador Ranch headquarters immediately before the shooting, had died shortly after the examining trial. But his examining trial testimony was admitted into evidence via an exception to the hearsay evidence rule.

The general rule is that hearsay evidence is not admissible because it violates the constitutional right of the accused under the Sixth Amendment of the U.S. Constitution to confront and cross-examine any witnesses called to testify against him. However, there are exceptions to the hearsay evidence rule in instances when hearsay evidence, because of its nature and the surrounding circumstances, is deemed sufficiently reliable to be considered by the jury even though the defendant is denied the right to confront and cross-examine the declarant.

The Fulcher case featured three exceptions to the hearsay evidence prohibition. First, another witness was allowed to repeat George Walker's testimony at the examining trial. This is permitted when, although the original witness is dead (or otherwise unavailable), his prior testimony was nevertheless under oath and given in a proceeding where the issues involved were the same, and where the defendant was present and had the opportunity to cross-examine the original witness at that prior proceeding. Next, J. M. Campbell and Nat John were allowed to tell what Beemer said just after being shot. Their statements fell under the "excited utterance" exception to the hearsay rule, which allows another witness to tell what someone said while he was still under the immediate influence of a traumatic event. The underlying rationale is that under those circumstances the declarant would not be likely to fabricate a falsehood. Finally, Beemer's "dying declarations" (both written and oral) were allowed because it was shown that Beemer, when he made the statements, knew his death was certain and imminent. The rationale in this instance is that a man who knows he is about to die is unlikely to lie or go to his grave with a false accusation on his lips.[11]

But there was plenty more to the prosecution's case. Fulcher's three benefactors, Brock, Askins, and Wells, all testified about the threats Fulcher had made against Beemer shortly before the shooting. Fulcher told Brock that he had been trying to "get old man Beemer out . . . that if he could not catch him out, then he was going to go where Old Man Beemer was . . . and Goddamn him, when they met he would make Beemer bite the earth." Fulcher also told Askins that he'd been "trying to catch Beemer out," and that when he did "Beemer will bite the dust." Askins also testified that Beemer rode a roan horse.

F. M. Wells, however, had even more damaging evidence to give. He testified that Fulcher told him that he intended to kill Beemer. Fulcher said that he had heard that Beemer was going to get out a warrant for his arrest on a charge of theft but that Beemer had better "be damned quick about it, for his last days on earth are . . . dark and short." Wells also stated that shortly before the shooting Fulcher had given him a dollar and requested that Wells buy some .45 caliber pistol cartridges, but Fulcher asked him not to tell anyone. Wells then testified that at the time of the shooting, Fulcher and his wife were staying at Wells's home. On the night of the shooting, however, only Fulcher's wife spent the night there. Worse yet, Wells said that on the day after the shooting, Fulcher returned riding a roan horse and wearing a red scarf around his waist and a pistol belt that had red thread woven through it.

The state then elicited from Wells a bit of testimony that, compared to the overwhelming evidence of Fulcher's guilt already on the record, must have seemed rather trivial and insignificant. But it would prove to be very significant indeed. Continuing his story, Wells testified that he was present when the two deputies, Jeff Boone and Tom Stewart, arrived at his home the day after the shooting and arrested Fulcher. Wells was permitted to testify, "I heard Stewart say to Fulcher, 'We have arrested you for killing Beemer last night,' whereupon Fulcher seemed agitated and turned pale."[12]

Defense attorney Thurmond objected to this testimony on the ground that it violated Fulcher's Fifth Amendment right against self-incrimination because the arresting officers, following Fulcher's arrest but prior to the time he "got agitated and turned pale," had failed to properly "caution" Fulcher about his Fifth Amendment rights not to do anything that might tend to incriminate himself. Judge Cockrell overruled the objection and allowed Wells's testimony.

Fulcher's only defense was alibi. Thurmond paraded eight fellow Spur Ranch cowboys to the stand who, in turn, swore that on the night Beemer was shot, Fulcher was with them on the Spur Ranch in Dickens County. But the jury wasn't having any of that, and quickly returned with a unanimous verdict: guilty. Sentence: death by hanging.

Thurmond successfully appealed the conviction, and the case was remanded for a new trial. The Texas Court of Criminal Appeals agreed with Thurmond that Wells's testimony to the effect that Fulcher "got agitated and turned pale" when informed he was under arrest for murdering Beemer amounted to an "uncautioned confession," in violation of his Fifth Amendment rights. The appellate court explained:

> . . . where the confessions of a defendant under arrest are inadmissible against him because made while he was uncautioned, his acts, if tantamount to such a confession and done under similar circumstances, are likewise inadmissible.[13]

"Cautioning" the defendant, as used by the 1889 Court of Criminal Appeals, was roughly equivalent to what we commonly call "Mirandizing" the defendant today. The term derives from the famous U.S. Supreme Court decision of *Miranda v. Arizona*[14] whereby law officers, before questioning a suspect under arrest, must first warn the defendant, pursuant to the Fifth Amendment, that he has a right to remain silent, that he doesn't have to make any statement, and that any statement he does make can and will be used against him, and so on.

The hypertechnical appellate decision in the Fulcher case was then, and is now, just plain wrong—wrong from a legal standpoint and wrong from a logical and common sense standpoint. In the first place, this is just not the type of evil that the Fifth Amendment is intended to address. The Fifth Amendment is designed to prevent police, after an arrest, from pressuring the defendant to involuntarily confess guilt either by force, threats, intimidation, trickery, or other devious means, none of which were employed by Deputies Stewart and Boone.[15] Second, the amendment is aimed at *verbal* confessions. Indeed, today's standard Miranda warning starts out with, "You have the right to remain silent, and not make any statement at all. Any statement you do make can and will be used in evidence against you. . . ." Clearly, only words uttered from the defendant's mouth—not physical acts or facial expressions—are protected.

There is yet another ground for admitting Wells's testimony. Fulcher's reaction to the traumatic event (his arrest and accusation of murder), was tantamount to an "excited utterance," akin to the "excited utterance" exception to the hearsay evidence rule. Even though a suspect is under arrest and has not been warned, if he blurts out some exclamation that is not in response to police interrogation, it is admissible. For instance, if Fulcher, when told he was under arrest for killing Beemer, had blurted out, "I should have known I couldn't get away with it!" his exclamation would have been admissible because it was an "excited utterance" and not a response to police interrogation. The witness's observation of Fulcher's physical reactions should fall under the same ruling.

The next problem with the appellate court's conclusion comes from a simple question. Was the fact that Fulcher "got agitated and turned pale" when told he was under arrest for murder really incriminating and "tantamount to a confession"? How many innocent folks might become agitated and then turn pale if two cops showed up at their front door, slapped the cuffs on them, and told them they were under arrest for murder? Most, if not all, one would suppose. "Getting agitated and turning pale" under such circumstances is as likely to be observed in the innocent as in the guilty.

Finally—forgetting all of the above—even if it was an error to let Wells tell the jury that Fulcher "got agitated and turned pale," when considered and weighed against the mountain of damning evidence against Fulcher, wasn't this revelation a relatively inconsequential bit of evidence? Wasn't it a relatively harmless error, one not rising to the level of a reversible error? If this bit of testimony had been excluded, could it really have been argued with any degree of credulity that the jury would have found the defendant not guilty?

Despite these arguments against the appellate court's decision, Fulcher's conviction was reversed, and the case was sent back to the trial court arena.

Between the first and second Fulcher trials, the whole judicial landscape changed, and with it, the cast of players for the upcoming drama. At the time of the murder and the first trial, unorganized Motley County had

Fulcher was retried on October 31, 1893, based on this third (Motley County) indictment. The second murder trial found him not guilty of murder but guilty of assault with intent to murder A. Beemer. This indictment was returned by the Motley County District Court grand jury in Cause No. 12 on the criminal docket of the newly formed county. It was returned on March 28, 1893, more than five years after Fulcher shot Beemer—a fact that had enormous significance in the final disposition of the case.
(Official court records of Motley County, Texas.)

been attached to Crosby County for judicial purposes and was a part of the multicounty 39th Judicial District. However, on February 2, 1891, Motley County became officially organized and thereafter had its own district court.[16] In addition, the county was placed in a newly formed judicial district—the 50th Judicial District.[17] With the formation of the new judicial district, new officials were elected. Instead of Judge Cockrell presiding over the second trial, Judge W. R. (Billy) McGill would man the bench, and instead of J. F. Cunningham prosecuting, it would be new district attorney L. S. Kinder.

Something else happened between the two Fulcher trials that, while seemingly insignificant at the time, would prove to be very significant indeed at the second trial. Recall that the Crosby County grand jury had already returned two murder indictments against Fulcher. The first was dismissed because of a defect in form. The trial was then held under the second Crosby County indictment. After Motley County was organized and placed in the 50th Judicial District, the new D.A. could have obtained a court order transferring the second Crosby County indictment and other official documents in the Fulcher case to the Motley County District Court. For some reason, however, Kinder elected to dismiss the second Crosby County indictment and obtain a new indictment against Fulcher from the Motley County grand jury. He succeeded in this endeavor on March 28, 1893.[18]

The venue was then changed from Motley County to Benjamin, county seat of Knox County, which was also located within the new 50th Judicial District. The stage was set for the retrial of Thomas J. Fulcher.

If the defense thought Judge Jeremiah Vardeman Cockrell was a terror . . . well, it hadn't seen anything yet. Judge W. R. (Billy) McGill was something else again. Judge McGill himself was no stranger to violence. In fact, before coming to West Texas, McGill had been indicted for murder in Wood County in east Texas. At that time, the Wood County district attorney was none other than James Stephen Hogg, destined to be elected governor of Texas. Hogg prosecuted McGill for murder, but McGill was acquitted. In light of that background, one would expect that McGill would have been sympathetic to the defense in criminal cases and that he would have harbored a lasting grudge against Governor Hogg. Wrong. Wrong on both counts. Surprisingly, he and Hogg

Charles E. Coombes, pioneer West Texas attorney, served as both district attorney and district judge of the 50th Judicial District, and later became a preeminent defense attorney. However, he had yet to obtain his law license when, in 1893, serving as deputy district clerk of Knox County, Texas, he witnessed the second trial of Thomas J. Fulcher. After his retirement he penned an account of the trial in his memoir, *The Prairie Dog Lawyer*.
(From the *Abilene-Reporter News*, April 12, 1981.)

became lifelong friends, and later, in 1891, when the new 50th Judicial District was formed, Governor Hogg appointed McGill as the first district judge. However, McGill's outspoken populist views had not endeared him to groups like cattle barons and railroad executives, so the Texas senate refused to confirm Hogg's appointment of McGill. Not to be denied, McGill, in the November 1892 election, ran for and won the judgeship.[19] And that's how, when the second Fulcher trial was called on October 31, 1893, in the Knox County courthouse, Billy McGill came to be perched on the bench.

The judicial career of the fearsome Judge McGill might well be summed up by a remark often made by trial lawyers (but always beyond the hearing of the judge referred to): "He's often wrong but never in doubt." The colorful character of Judge Billy McGill was accurately captured by Charlie Coombes, who was a frontier West Texas lawyer and a contemporary of all the lawyers and judges in the Fulcher case.[20] Following his retirement Coombes penned his memoirs and thus preserved invaluable snapshots of the participants in this drama as well as some behind-the-scenes commentary.

Charlie Coombes recalled McGill as a "severe" judge who "brooked no interference from anyone. I have seen him make a lawyer sit down with such force and suddenness as to break an arm chair."[21] Coombes elaborates:

Judge W. R. McGill was by nature a prosecutor. Reversals had no terror for him. His theory as a judge was to bring about the conviction of the criminal or to so terrorize him that in the event of an acquittal, or in the event his conviction was reversed on appeal, he would flee the country.[22]

To make matters worse for Thomas J. Fulcher, the new prosecution team was as mean as a junk-yard dog. While the previous prosecutor, J. F. Cunningham, was a skilled trial lawyer and a forceful advocate, he was no courtroom bully. Such could not be said about the new team, District Attorney L. S. Kinder and Special Prosecutor J. J. Brents. Charlie Coombes had this to say about them:

L. S. Kinder, while one of the finest men I have ever known, when once convinced of the righteousness of his cause was extremely vigorous and overbearing. Whoever met J. J. Brents in the courtroom met an arrogant and uncompromisingly bitter foe.[23]

But there was still more bad news for the defense!

Veteran defense lawyer F. G. Thurmond would not be representing Thomas J. Fulcher in the upcoming trial. Instead, Fulcher would be represented by an inexperienced cub lawyer named J. E. Yantis, Thurmond's young associate. Moreover, in contrast to the attack dogs of the prosecution, Yantis was mild-mannered and soft-spoken.

There was a good reason why Thurmond couldn't represent Fulcher in the upcoming trial. For openers, McGill and Thurmond were two entirely different breeds of cat: McGill stern, staid, severe, intolerant, humorless . . . and a teetotaler; Thurmond, none of the above. McGill was not only a teetotaler, he was also steadfastly intolerant of anyone who was not a teetotaler. Still, Thurmond might have managed to effectively represent Fulcher had he not let his rambunctious nature get the best of him.

Shortly after McGill assumed the mantle of district judge, a comical incident (at least it was funny to almost everyone except McGill) occurred in Crosby County. A farmer was coming down a country road one day when he encountered two strangers who appeared to be joyously suffused in spirits. In fact, the farmer formed the opinion that both were rip-roaring drunk. One of the celebrants, in a grand theatrical gesture, swept off his hat, bowed from the waist and introduced himself to the farmer as "Judge McGill."

Although nowadays grand juries don't often concern themselves with minor (misdemeanor) offenses, limiting their judicial scrutiny to felony-grade offenses, it was not uncommon in those times for grand juries to stray far afield in their inquiries. Meanwhile, the farmer felt compelled to do his duty as a good, sober, law-abiding citizen and report this scandalous incident to the grand jury. And that's why the Crosby County grand jury indicted Judge McGill for the misdemeanor offense of drunkenness in office. One can only imagine the thunderous outrage of the pompous, teetotaling Judge W. R. McGill when the grand jury foreman came before him and returned *that* indictment! When McGill finally regained coherency, he ordered the sheriff to drag the farmer into court for an explanation.

"Have you ever seen me before?" he demanded of the bewildered farmer.

"No sir," the farmer stuttered.

"Then, why in hell did you swear that I was guilty of drunkenness in office?"

The witness apologized abjectly and told what had happened. The grand jury, of course, recalled the indictment, but this did not appease Judge McGill. He pursued the matter, grilling the farmer to give him an exact description of the McGill impersonator—a description that fit lawyer F. G. Thurmond, head to toe.[24] McGill barely tolerated defense lawyers in the first place, especially if he suspected they were not teetotalers, but this prank was an outrage that the grudge-holding McGill was not about to tolerate. Charlie Coombes commented:

> McGill felt that Thurmond had done him a great injustice in impersonating him as a drunk, and he could never free himself from the idea that the fact that Thurmond defended Fulcher was overpowering evidence of Fulcher's guilt. In his eyes, therefore, Yantis was of an ilk with Thurmond. Actually, Yantis was modest, respectful, gentlemanly, courteous, and diplomatic—a real actor in the courtroom.

He assumed for himself, in the defense of Fulcher, the attitude of injured innocence, in the hope that the jury would attribute some of that spirit to his client.[25]

Thurmond knew McGill would seek revenge against him during the Fulcher trial if he represented Fulcher, so he sent J. E. Yantis to present the case. At the outset it appeared to everyone, including the jury, that Yantis was hopelessly outclassed. Yet he protected his client's rights by "pleasing repartee" coupled with timely and correct objections when the prosecution overreached. As the trial progressed the bitterness and arrogance of the prosecution became more pronounced, as did the obvious bias of the trial judge. But Yantis maintained his composure and countered with courtesy and diplomacy. And the jury didn't miss it. Jury sympathy began to develop for the mild-mannered little David and against the roaring giant, Goliath.

Meanwhile, apparently unnoticed by the prosecution, Yantis was constructing another dimension to Fulcher's defense—one not properly pursued during the first trial. At the conclusion of the presentation of evidence in the first trial, Thurmond requested the trial judge, in his jury instructions, to permit the jury the alternative of finding Fulcher guilty, not of murder, but of the lesser offense of "assault with intent to murder." This alternative was advanced by Thurmond on the theory that, even if the jury found that Fulcher had indeed shot Beemer, Fulcher's wound was not the cause of Beemer's death. The real cause of Beemer's death was the failure to promptly and properly treat his wound. Thurmond pointed out that nobody had even bothered to send for a doctor for more than three days after Beemer was shot. In the first trial, however, Judge Cockrell refused Thurmond's request to allow the jury the choice of making this less serious alternative finding. After the jury in the first trial found Fulcher guilty of murder, Thurmond pursued this point on appeal. The appellate court did reverse Fulcher's conviction, but it did so, as we have seen, on a completely different point of error—the "uncautioned" confession. However, in so doing, the appellate court commented that Judge Cockrell properly refused Thurmond's request to give the jury the alternative of finding Fulcher guilty of assault with intent to murder since Thurmond had failed to produce any evidence to substantiate his theory that had Beemer received proper and timely medical treatment he probably would have survived.[26]

The prosecution in the second trial apparently paid no heed to the rather obscure point in the appellate court's opinion for reversing Fulcher's conviction, namely, the appellate court's remark that the trial court was not obliged to give the jury the option to find the defendant guilty of the lesser offense of "aussault with intent to commit murder," since the defense, in the first trial, had failed to produce any evidence that Beemer's wounds were not necessarily fatal and that had he received prompt medical attention he probably would have survived. That obscure point might have failed to catch the attention of the prosecution, but it certainly didn't escape Yantis's notice. Therefore, in the second trial Yantis advanced alternate, and conflicting, defenses for the jury's consideration. First, *I didn't shoot him—I was on the Spur Ranch at the time of the shooting; but if I did shoot him, he didn't die as a result of my acts but as a result of a failure to obtain proper medical treatment.* And to that end, Yantis, unlike Thurmond in the first trial, did present some expert medical opinion testimony to support his alternate theory. To support his first theory, Yantis did trot out the same eight Spur Ranch cowboys to testify that Fulcher spent the night of the shooting on the Spur Ranch, although we may speculate with some assurance that Yantis seriously doubted that the jury would buy into that alibi. Since Yantis managed to get the requisite medical opinion testimony into the record, McGill was obligated to grant Yantis's demand that the court's instruction permit the jury the option of finding Fulcher guilty of the lesser offense of assault with intent to murder. McGill probably didn't give it much thought, convinced that this jury, like the first, would not hesitate to convict Fulcher of murder.

Meanwhile, the prosecutors huffed and puffed and blustered and plowed ahead, full steam.

At the time of this trial, Charles Coombes had not yet acquired his law license. He was, however, the deputy district clerk of Knox County, and he watched with fascination as this most unusual trial progressed.

Toward the end of the trial, Coombes had occasion to visit with Yantis at a social event one evening. Coombes, who was absolutely convinced of Fulcher's guilt, later reflected:

To my mind the evidence was conclusive as to the defendant's guilt of murder in the first degree. There were no extenuating circumstances. The question of identity of the slayer was likewise conclusive. The defense, based on alibi, was extremely weak and thoroughly overcome by testimony of several credible witnesses in the best position to know the facts. That the defendant had threatened to kill the deceased was not seriously disputed.[27]

Yet Coombes was much in sympathy with Yantis, who, in his view, was himself being unjustly persecuted by the McGill-Kinder-Brents team. At the social event, Coombes asked Yantis how he viewed the case—how he assessed his chances for success. Yantis, according to Coombes, replied that his only hope was that the "over-prosecution" would result in sympathy for the defendant "and his conviction for an offense from which he would ultimately be freed."

Coombes admitted that he "didn't get it" when Yantis made that remark. "I was not lawyer enough then to understand his point."[28] But neither did the prosecutors—who should have been.

The next day, an extraordinary incident occurred during Yantis's final jury argument, an incident that must have worked to Yantis's benefit in the eyes of the jury—a jury that undoubtedly had already begun refocusing much of its attention on the judicial abuse Yantis was enduring rather than keeping its focus on Fulcher and his misdeeds. In obvious disdain of Yantis's presentation to the jury, McGill got up off the bench and walked over to the side of the courtroom, rolled a cigarette, and began to enjoy a smoke. At that point in the solemn legal proceedings a new player suddenly appeared and took center stage. The new player was . . . a dog, a bird dog. McGill owned a very well trained bird dog that he took with him everywhere, including into the courtrooms where he presided. And so, when McGill vacated the bench for a smoke during Yantis's final argument, the bird dog hopped up on the bench and proceeded to seat himself in the judge's chair. Amid much chuckling by the jury, Judge McGill smirked that a dog was good enough to preside over the court while Yantis was arguing. Nonplussed, Yantis, according to Coombes, "quoted some poetry about a dog which fitted the occasion." But McGill was not amused by this impudence. In fact, he was enraged and in the presence of the jury, imposed a twenty-five-dollar fine against Yantis for contempt of court.[29] This also, as we shall see, did not sit well with the jury.

In the end the jury found Fulcher not guilty of murder but guilty *only* of the lesser offense of assault with intent to murder and sentenced him to a seven-year term in the state penitentiary. Moreover, the jury took up a collection and paid the twenty-five-dollar contempt fine that McGill had assessed against Yantis.

Yantis was now set to unveil his final surprise—a blockbuster that completely freed his client. It all had to do with provisions of law known as "statutes of limitations." That is, all criminal offenses must be charged (by indictment, if a felony) against a defendant within a certain amount of time after the commission of the crime—after which prosecution is forever barred. The only exceptions are murder and manslaughter. But, the jury did not convict Fulcher of murder or manslaughter—it convicted him of "assault with intent to murder." That offense had a five-year statute limitation, meaning that unless the indictment under which Fulcher was tried was returned by a grand jury within five years of the date of offense, prosecution was thereafter barred. Recall that the shooting occurred on September 10, 1887, that the first two (Crosby County) indictments had been dismissed, and that Kinder had obtained the third (Motley County) indictment on March 28, 1893. So, when the prosecution blundered and dismissed the second indictment against Fulcher (the Crosby County indictment upon which Fulcher was first tried), the only crime for which Fulcher could therefore have been convicted of in the second trial was murder, a crime for which the Knox County jury found him not guilty when they opted to convict for "assault with intent to murder." Yantis's brilliant strategy of winning-by-losing had paid off, and Fulcher was free as a wild goose.

Of course, when Yantis pointed this out to the infuriated McGill in his "motion of arrest of judgment," the latter refused to back down and overruled Yantis's motion. Yantis took it to the appellate court, which had no difficulty in agreeing with him:

Upon the plainest principle of law, supported by an unbroken line of authority, the defendant's motion should have been sustained. Murder being charged, a motion to quash [dismiss the indictment] was not available, but when the verdict for assault to murder was returned, murder being eliminated, the motion in arrest of judgment was then properly invoked [because of the statute of limitations].

Then the appellate court added a final comment that no doubt sent the volatile, dictatorial McGill into vein-popping rage:

Why the trial court overruled the defendant's motion in arrest of judgment, thus forcing the defendant to appeal to this court, is past our comprehension. That the assault was barred [by the statute of limitations] cannot be questioned.[30]

After he was cleared, Fulcher freely confessed that he had, in fact, murdered Beemer. (The constitutional prohibition [in both the Texas and U.S. constitutions] against double jeopardy barred any subsequent prosecution.) One day he even accompanied District Attorney Kinder to the murder scene, Beemer's blacksmith shop. He took Kinder to a clump of trees behind Beemer's shop and showed him the tree to which he had tied his horse before the fatal shooting. Fulcher told Kinder that when he shot Beemer, his frightened horse reared back on the reins and pulled the knot so tight that he couldn't untie it, and so, in his haste to escape, he drew his pocket knife and cut the reins. Kinder related that they then found the abandoned remnants of the reins there, and, although shriveled and decayed, they were still tied tightly around the tree.[31]

And so Thomas Fulcher walked. Yet he was still a violent and troubled man whose freedom couldn't have brought him very much happiness. His wife left him during the midst of all this legal skirmishing, and shortly after Fulcher was finally cleared of all charges connected with the Beemer shooting, he filed for divorce in the Motley County District Court in Matador on December 24, 1894. He alleged that he and his wife, Minnie E. Fulcher, had been married in Haskell County, Texas, in 1885, but that she had "abandoned" him in March 1889 (about a year and a half after he shot Beemer), and her present whereabouts were unknown to him.[32]

After his first conviction was reversed, Fulcher was released from custody on a six-thousand-dollar bond while awaiting retrial. It didn't take Tom Fulcher long to get into more trouble. On July 26, 1893, he was indicted for assaulting and falsely imprisoning one J. L. Moore in Motley County.[33] It just so happened that J. L. Moore was the acting sheriff of Motley County. Why Fulcher captured and imprisoned the sheriff is unclear, and the Motley County District Court records do not reflect any disposition of this indictment.

Less than two years after he skated free on the Beemer killing as well as the charge of falsely imprisoning Sheriff J. L. Moore, he was indicted again for still another violent offense. On August 14, 1895, the Motley County grand jury indicted Fulcher for assault with intent to murder one Jim Turner. He was tried before a jury. Result: a hung jury. He was retried, and that time the jury found him guilty of a lesser included assault offense. He again avoided imprisonment—the jury assessed no prison time, only a fine of fifty dollars.[34] However, the irrepressible Tom Fulcher was not satisfied with getting off with even that token punishment. He had his lawyer file a motion for a new trial and succeeded in persuading the trial court to grant it, thus overturning the conviction. With that, the exasperated district attorney threw up his hands and surrendered. He filed a motion to dismiss the prosecution, citing "insufficient evidence" as the ground. The court granted it, and the elusive Tom Fulcher once again got away with (attempted) murder.[35]

What then happened to Thomas Fulcher is not of record, at least any found by this writer, except the old "prairie dog lawyer," Charles Coombes, ends his account of the Fulcher case with the comment that several years later he heard Fulcher was "shot and killed with his boots on," somewhere in New Mexico.[36]

Off the Record

The appellate court that reversed the death-penalty conviction of Thomas J. Fulcher on a hypertechnical distinction in a singularly ill-reasoned opinion was one of his "unlikely saviors" as were the obviously biased district judge W. R. McGill and the arrogant and overreaching prosecutors L. S. Kinder and J. J. Brents—all of whom were those most dedicated to slipping a noose around Fulcher's neck. And Yantis, Fulcher's astute young attorney, cleverly crafted an understated defense that played well with the jury in contrast to the overbearing and over-confident bluster of his antagonists. Plus, as we have seen, he detected and took full advantage of a chink in the prosecution's legal armor.

The Fulcher story then illustrates several of the reasons for "Getting Away with Murder"—pre-eminent of which was the tendency of early appellate courts to advocate the absurd.

THE 1896 WICHITA FALLS
BANK ROBBERY

The Case of the Clairvoyant Cashier

AND JUDGE LYNCH TRUMPS JUDGE BLACKSTONE

NEARLY EVERYONE in Wichita Falls, Texas, knew and respected Frank Dorsey—knew him to be a solid citizen, a family man, and a trusted employee as cashier of the City National Bank. He was not an unduly superstitious man, nor had he ever been known to dabble in the supernatural. Yet one night in late 1895, Dorsey had such a terrifying premonition that he awoke trembling in a cold sweat. He had vividly envisioned the bank being robbed and himself being murdered during the course of the robbery. He slept not another wink that night, and in the morning he related the whole nightmare to his wife, who tried to calm and reassure him. But the bone-chilling presentiment was just too real to ignore. Frank went straightaway to bank president J. A. Kemp and tendered his resignation. Kemp remonstrated with him at length and finally persuaded Dorsey to remain at his post. Nevertheless, that indelible, blood-splattered imprint was branded on Frank Dorsey's psyche.[1]

There was, however, some legitimate concern about a possible bank robbery. Bank officials were alarmed at rumors that Indian Territory outlaws had targeted a Wichita Falls bank to rob—alarmed enough that Kemp wired Texas gover-

Frank Dorsey, a cashier of the City National Bank, was a popular family man and a well-respected citizen of Wichita Falls, Texas, in the 1890s. He had premonitions that his bank would be robbed and that he would be killed, which everyone assured him were unfounded.
(From the *Wichita Falls Times Record News*,
December 2, 2005.)

nor C. A. Culberson for Ranger support. Culberson, in turn, wired Texas Ranger captain Bill McDonald. McDonald dispatched Sergeant W. J. L. Sullivan and four of his men to provide protection for the town's two banks.[2] As it turned out, the rumors were valid. Two Indian Territory outlaws had, in fact, been laying plans to rob the City National Bank.

Elmer "Kid" Lewis, although only eighteen years old, was already a hardened criminal and soon to be a stone-cold killer. A native of Missouri, he migrated to Montana, where he first began his life of crime. Lewis cut his teeth on highway robbery and taking the pots at poker games with a pistol instead of an ace.[3] He departed Montana just ahead of the law and drifted down to Burk Burnett's ranch in north Texas, just west of Wichita Falls, where he hired on as a cowboy. In addition to his Texas ranch, Burnett also leased (with the assistance of Comanche Indian chief Quanah Parker) about 280,000 acres across the Red River on the Ft. Sill (Kiowa-Comanche) Indian Reservation. In that outlaw-infested land, Kid Lewis fit right in with the other inhabitants—long riders such as "Red Buck" Weightman, Hill Loftis, Joe

Beckham, and another Burk Burnett cowboy named Foster Crawford. Crawford, then thirty-five years old, came from a good family in the Waco area in central Texas. He briefly hooked up with the notorious (though notably unsuccessful) Al Jennings bandit gang in northern Oklahoma Territory. Jennings later said he kicked Crawford out of his gang because Crawford was too "high-tempered." He added that when Crawford got "delirious" he began quoting poetry "in some foreign language"—Latin, Jennings thought.[4] Apparently it was about this time that Crawford and Lewis, in order to supplement their meager cowboy wages, began some illicit moonlighting. It was also about this time that Burk Burnett kept coming up a few head shy when he counted his herd at the annual fall roundup. Crawford's excessive brawling and whiskey consumption led Burnett to fire him about a year prior to the events in this tale.[5]

This petty thievery was not enough for Lewis and Crawford. Less than two months after Lewis barely escaped death in a December 28, 1895, Indian Territory shootout with a posse led by Texas Ranger W. J. L. Sullivan (which resulted in the killing of ex–Motley County sheriff turned renegade Joe Beckham), Lewis and Crawford decided they would go big time and rob a bank—the City National Bank of Wichita Falls. Someone told them that there was often more than a quarter of a million in cash lying around that bank.[6] Of course the bank never had anything close to that in its vault, but then nobody ever accused Crawford or Lewis of being very bright.[7]

It looked easy. The two of them would simply swoop down from Indian Territory, scoop up a few hundred thousand bucks, and then hightail it back across the nearby Red River to their safe haven. They even went around bragging about their upcoming adventure, and Wichitans began hearing the rumors.

Meanwhile, Sergeant Sullivan and his men spent ten uneventful days hanging around Wichita Falls before deciding there was nothing to this bank robbery talk. Frank Dorsey, however, continued to be convinced that his fears were real. He even related his premonition to Sergeant Sullivan, who assured Dorsey he had nothing to worry about. Yet, in the early morning hours of February 25, 1896, Dorsey was again awakened by the dreadful dream. That morning he tried again to tender his resignation, but President Kemp once again managed to assuage Dorsey's fears.[8] Kemp then left the bank to attend to other business matters. It was the last time he would see Frank Dorsey alive.

At noon that day the Rangers gave up their watch and caught the train headed southeast toward Fort Worth. Captain McDonald joined his Rangers to leave on the same train. A small crowd assembled at the Wichita Falls railroad depot to wave goodbye to the Ranger force. One account has it that Crawford and Lewis were in that crowd.[9] Whether true or not, the pair undoubtedly was aware that the Rangers had departed, because shortly thereafter (about mid-afternoon the same day) Crawford and Lewis tied up their stolen horses (one of which was stolen from Burk Burnett's 6666 Ranch) behind the City National Bank and implemented their get-rich-quick scheme.

It turned out to be a badly botched affair. In the first place, even though Crawford was well known around Wichita Falls, including by at least one bank employee, neither Crawford nor Lewis bothered with a mask or disguise.[10] Second, the pair had fortified themselves with a few shots of whiskey before tackling the bank job. Perhaps due to the whiskey, a bad case of the jitters, pure accident, or a combination thereof, they had hardly entered the bank when shooting broke out. Exactly who did what is still unknown. However, historians believe Crawford approached bookkeeper P. P. Langford and commanded, "Up! Up!" Langford, concentrating on a column of figures at the time, did not immediately realize what was happening and failed to respond. Crawford therefore cracked him on the head with his pistol, and it is surmised that his pistol accidentally discharged into the ceiling. Although the shot didn't hit anyone, it set off a fusillade, with both bandits firing away. One or the other (probably Lewis) then shot and killed Frank Dorsey, who was going for a pistol. One of the bandits then shot Dr. O. J. Kendall, a prominent physician and a vice president and director of the bank. Even though Dr. Kendall was unarmed, the bandit aimed for his heart and didn't miss. But it was Dr. Kendall's lucky day, for the shot hit a metal hypodermic case he was carrying in his vest pocket and was deflected. Dr. Kendall wisely fell to the floor and feigned death. Meanwhile, the addled bookkeeper, Langford, partially recovered. He staggered to his feet, jumped over the counter, and headed for the door. The

City National Bank of Wichita Falls, Texas, as it appeared on February 25, 1896, when Indian Territory outlaws Foster Crawford and Elmer "Kid" Lewis entered, robbed it of $416, and killed cashier Frank Dorsey. *Left to right* are Wiley Robertson, an assistant cashier and later president of the bank; Lovik P. Webb, a collection clerk; an unidentified customer; P. P. Langford, the bookkeeper who was wounded during the robbery; and O. E. Cannon, a collection clerk. (From the *Wichita Falls Record News,* March 21, 1944.)

bandits fired three shots at the departing bookkeeper. Two missed, but the third hit him in the buttocks. Still, he managed to get out the door and yell, "Robbers!"

All this shooting and commotion commenced before the outlaws ever got around to the business of looting. They didn't do much of a job of that either. They eventually sacked up $416 from one teller's cash drawer. An adjacent cash drawer held about $1,000, but they didn't find it. They tried, briefly but unsuccessfully, to open the unlocked door to the vault where the big bucks were stashed. However, by this time, a clamor was growing outside in the street and all hell was breaking loose. The robbers realized they could not afford to tarry any longer.

Rushing out the back door, they ran headlong into unarmed city marshal J. D. (Madge) Davis, who demanded to know what they were doing. The outlaws simply pushed him aside and mounted their horses. Deputy Sheriff Frank Hardesty arrived on the scene, and shots were exchanged as the pair put steel to their mounts. Lewis or Crawford managed to shoot Hardesty, but once again, as luck would have it, the shot hit a large, round pocket watch in Hardesty's pants pocket and had no effect.

However, the inept pair's fate was already sealed. Someone in the crowd (possibly Deputy Hardesty) fired back at Kid Lewis. Although the Kid was not hit, his horse was fatally wounded. Lewis was forced to dismount, slip the bridle from his dying steed, and climb aboard Crawford's horse. Riding double slowed the outlaws down even more and thwarted their plan for a swift retreat to the safety of Indian Territory.

At the time of the robbery, Will Skeen, the editor of the *Wichita Daily Times*, was at his desk several blocks away pounding out an editorial that, ironically, he had entitled "The Peaceful Wichita Valley."[11] Hearing all the commotion, he ran into the street, and upon discovering what had happened, armed himself, borrowed a horse, and started off as one of the first to pursue the robbers. City Marshal Davis, meanwhile, also armed himself and began rounding up a citizens' posse. Someone sent a telegram to Captain McDonald, which intercepted him and his Rangers at Bellevue, some thirty-five miles southeast of Wichita Falls.[12] Informed of the situation, McDonald and Rangers Lee Queen, Jack Harwell, Bob McClure, W. J. McCauley, and W. J. L. Sullivan immediately commandeered a special car and engine from the Fort Worth and Denver Railroad and headed back to Wichita Falls. They arrived before dark that afternoon to find fresh, saddled horses awaiting them. Meanwhile, a burgeoning posse of one hundred or more outraged citizens under the leadership of City Marshal Davis and Editor Skeen was pursuing the two beleaguered desperadoes, who were experiencing serious transportation problems.

Wichita County sheriff C. M. Moses and a deputy were over in Oklahoma Territory on Burk Burnett's 6666 Ranch, where (in another twist of rich irony) they were searching for Foster Crawford, who they suspected of having stolen one of Burnett's horses. As it turned out, the horse Crawford and Lewis were then riding in their desperate flight from the determined posse was, in fact, that stolen 6666 horse. (Lewis's mortally wounded horse was supposedly stolen from a Methodist circuit-riding preacher.)[13] The pair eventually had to abandon their exhausted

Company B, Frontier Battalion of the Texas Rangers was commanded by Captain W. J.
(Bill) McDonald. This picture was made in 1893 at Amarillo. Back row (*left to right*):
Jack Harwell, Sergeant W. John L. Sullivan, Bob Pease, Arthur Jones, Ed Connell, and
Lee Queen. Front row (*left to right*): Billy McCauley, Bob McClure,
Wes Carter, and [first name unknown] Owens.
(Courtesy of the Panhandle-Plains Historical Museum, Canyon, Texas.)

mount and commandeered a couple of plodding farm horses. But these
steeds simply were not up to the task of leaving the posse behind; the
farm horses were not built for speed, plus they had been pulling a plow
all day before the race commenced. Although McDonald, in his biography, tried to take sole credit for running down the outlaws and capturing
them, it actually was the rag-tag mob of Wichita Falls citizenry who
finally cornered the robbers in a thicket just south of the Red River.[14]
However, daylight was failing, and no one was anxious to confront the
desperate pair in that thicket, or, as a writer of the time phrased it, no
one wanted to charge in and "bell the buzzards."[15]

At about that time the Rangers arrived on the scene. Never short of
courage, McDonald and his Rangers did not hesitate to charge in and
bell the buzzards. They approached the thicket, and McDonald made
himself known. The robbers agreed to surrender if the Rangers would

agree to protect them from mob vengeance.[16] McDonald agreed and ordered them to come out with their hands up "and damned high, too!"[17] Lewis and Crawford did as ordered and were taken into custody without further incident. All $416 of the cash loot was recovered.

At this point, the tale took an unexpected turn. According to his biographer, McDonald claimed he first considered taking the prisoners to the Clay County jail (in Henrietta) or to the Tarrant County jail (in Fort Worth) rather than to the Wichita County jail in Wichita Falls, but he was "persuaded against his better judgment" by Wichita County district judge George E. Miller to lodge the prisoners in the Wichita County jail.[18] This assertion seems patently absurd in light of what happened thereafter. As we shall see, later events proved that Judge Miller was the one person in Wichita County most concerned with the safety of the prisoners. McDonald himself admitted that he knew the situation was extremely volatile, and, as events later that same night demonstrated, the lives of the prisoners were in great danger.

McDonald and his Rangers initially dispersed a mob that had gathered at the Wichita County jail to demand possession of Lewis and Crawford. The mob retreated, and the Rangers spent the night at the jail. Still, lynch-mob fever was palpable—and rising. McDonald had to have realized this.[19] Sheriff Moses was still out of town, and deputy sheriff (and jailer) Frank Hardesty was left alone to guard the prisoners.

In answer to the plea from district judge George Miller that the Rangers remain to safeguard the prisoners, McDonald's biographer recorded the answer as follows:

> McDonald informed him [Judge Miller] that it was impossible for his force to remain in Wichita Falls; that other work was waiting for them; . . . that they had been away from their headquarters for two weeks. Besides being wet and cold and worn out from exposure and want of sleep . . . "I'm about used up, and likely to be sick . . . I'm going to get out of here tonight unless you get an order from Governor Culberson for me to stay."[20]

His response sounds a bit lame and whiney, especially when compared to the lionhearted bluster that was McDonald's usual coin. So that

Captain Bill McDonald, Sergeant W. J. L. Sullivan, and three other Texas Rangers captured Foster Crawford and Elmer "Kid" Lewis shortly after they robbed the City
National Bank in Wichita Falls. Pictured at the August 1897 Cowboy's Reunion in Seymour, Texas, are (*left to right*) Judge Jack Glasgow, famed Seymour trial lawyer; Quanah Parker's favorite wife, Too Nicey; Chief Quanah Parker; "Marshal of the Day"
Sergeant Sullivan; and ex–Baylor County sheriff Sam Suttlemeyer.
(From W. J. L. Sullivan, *Twelve Years in the Saddle for Law and Order*, 1907.)

afternoon, despite Judge Miller's protests, McDonald and his Rangers
boarded the Fort Worth and Denver train and headed home to Quanah.

The mob spirit smoldered throughout the next day (February 26), partly
fueled by the emotional funeral of Frank Dorsey. Dorsey, thirty-six
years old and well loved by the community, was married and the father
of three small children. The funeral was so large the church could not
accommodate the crowd, and the mourners all followed Dorsey's casket
to the cemetery to pay their last respects. School was dismissed that day
so that everyone, including children, could attend the funeral. The children were even afforded tours of the jail to observe the outlaws at close
range.[21]

Word had spread and armed men from throughout the area streamed
into Wichita Falls all day. Every incoming train brought droves more

into town "eager to join the hanging bee." Clusters of armed and determined men speaking in hushed, sullen voices were observed all over the
downtown area. Rage against the robbers was rampant for the wanton
murder of their beloved citizen. North Texans were incensed not only at
the outlaws but also at the federal government, which seemed to turn a
deaf ear to their pleas for effective law enforcement in the Oklahoma
and Indian territories. The Texans had long agitated for the federal government to open up these lands for settlement by homesteaders who,
they correctly believed, would bring law-abiding self-government to the
area, and thus solve the outlaw problem. In its account of the matter, the
Dallas Morning News explained the Texans' frustration:

> To understand . . . the feelings of the people . . . it must be remem-
> bered that for years, outlaws in the [Indian] Territory have been
> depredating upon them. Bands of marauders have been crossing Red
> River into Texas, seizing stock, robbing stores and committing other
> deviltry of an equally atrocious nature. The deed would be done and
> the guilty safely harbored in the territory before the luckless victim
> would learn [of it].[22]

Meanwhile, in Wichita Falls various speakers urged the mob to get
on with the business of vengeance. One speaker was Marion Potter, a
prominent rancher, who a year or so before had had a serious dispute
with Foster Crawford during which Crawford threatened to kill Potter.
Potter, fearing for his life and the lives of his family, had moved away.[23]
The mob also ignited a huge bonfire at the downtown corner of Seventh
and Ohio streets, just outside the City National Bank.

At 6:00 p.m. Dorsey was laid to rest. At approximately 8:45 p.m. the
city's fire bell rang and two shots were fired—a signal for action that
was a lighted match thrown into a powder keg.[24] The assembled mob
was three to five hundred angry members—strong as it marched on the
jail. As time went on, more and more people joined the mob. None of
them were disguised. Many were leading citizens of the town and surrounding counties.[25] Sheriff C. M. Moses was still absent, and the jail
was manned by only Deputy Hardesty. Ranger McDonald later claimed
that twenty-five citizens had been deputized to guard the prisoners
before he and the Rangers left town, but if that was the case, none of

them seemed to have been present at the jail when the mob arrived. Hardesty retreated inside the jail and locked the doors. Doubtless he recognized most of the mobsters.

Meanwhile, district judge George E. Miller, who had spent all day counseling moderation and pleading for restraint, appeared with R. E. Huff, president of the First National Bank of Wichita Falls, and county attorney C. D. Keys on the north steps of the courthouse-jail. Huff pleaded with the mob to desist as otherwise they "would have the murders on their conscience for the rest of their lives." Judge Miller, in stentorian tones, again argued with the mob to let the law take its course. A reporter described his appeal as "impassioned, eloquent, and logical."[26] He promised that if the mob would forbear from violence, he would see that Lewis and Crawford were brought to trial within eight weeks. He told them that he had talked with Frank Dorsey's widow and that it was her prayer that the law be allowed to take its course. But the mob was not about to be mollified; they were not in any mood to listen to that kind of talk. They jeered at Miller with taunts of justice delayed and justice denied. "Oh, yes. There will be a continuance, and then an appeal, and then a reversal, and then a bond, and finally liberty."[27] Someone else shouted, "Boys, did you see that good woman and her three orphan children kissing the dead lips of Frank Dorsey today?"[28]

And the talking was over. The mob grabbed a pole, bashed in the back door of the jail, overpowered Hardesty, and broke open the cell doors. Then they marched Lewis and Crawford several blocks east to the bonfire in front of the City National Bank. A telegraph pole at the site of the crime would serve as the hangman's gallows. Large boxes were placed at the foot of the pole, and the condemned men were made to stand on them with their hands shackled behind their backs.

About this time, Sheriff Moses finally arrived at the scene. But, as he later reported, he was promptly disarmed by the mob. No further account is given of his actions that evening. Burk Burnett and his son, Tom Burnett, also showed up. Burk had a short discussion with Foster Crawford, but accounts differ as to what was said. Probably Burk was seeking information about the cattle rustling that was depleting his herd. In any event, no account of the incident indicates that Burk Burnett encouraged the lynching. On the other hand, no account tells of him discouraging it.

An angry mob estimated to be about five hundred strong lynched outlaws Foster Crawford and Elmer "Kid" Lewis in downtown Wichita Falls, Texas, on February 26, 1896. A vast majority of area citizens applauded the mob's actions. (From the *Dallas Morning News*, February 27, 1896.)

When word of the lynching was telegraphed to nearby towns, spontaneous celebrations broke out. In downtown Seymour, some fifty miles to the west (where, less than a year before, the renegade sheriff, Joe Beckham, had murdered Sheriff Cook), a large group assembled and celebrated the lynching with an impromptu "anvil chorus": loose gunpowder was sprinkled on anvils and then set off by smashing the powder with sledge hammers. The *Wichita Daily Times* reported, "The anvils were booming all the time Crawford and Lewis were being lynched."[29]

Accounts differ as to exactly what was said before the bandits were hanged. Prior to his last moments, Lewis had refused to answer any questions, and no one even knew his name. Finally he said that his name was Elmer Lewis and that his folks lived in Neosho, Missouri. Lewis's only request was that his father be told that he died "nervy." He also taunted the jeering crowd with insults and curses. When asked if wanted to pray, Kid Lewis replied:

Pray? You ****, you, when you come to hell I will meet you at the gate with a Winchester. Go ahead and pull that rope you **** ****.[30]

Crawford, meanwhile, alternated between bravado and cowardice. He begged Burk Burnett for whiskey, which was furnished, and enjoyed it

Bank robbers, Foster Crawford (*left*) and Elmer "Kid" Lewis, on February 26, 1896,
shortly after they were lynch-mobbed and hanged in downtown Wichita Falls, Texas,
for robbing the City National Bank and killing cashier Frank Dorsey.
(From the *Wichita Falls Times Record News*, December 3, 2005.)

in great gulps.[31] One reporter commented on how "merciful" the mob
was for providing whiskey to the noosed outlaw before yanking him into
eternity. Crawford then claimed that he had about ten thousand dollars
in cash stashed at an Indian Territory hideout and promised to disclose
the location if the mob desisted. But the mob was in no mood for games.
Crawford was ultimately reduced to incoherent jabbering in English,
Spanish, and Comanche.[32]

When finally hanged, it was reported that Lewis "gave it up quickly
without a struggle," but that Crawford, with both curses and prayers on
his lips, fought against the noose and "died hard—awfully hard." Crawford, the reporter continued, "tried frantically to fight against the
inevitable, and his death writhings caused the mob to melt away like
snow before a tropical rain. He was fully ten minutes in quieting down,
and it looked at one time like he would never give up the ghost. His passing was the end of the chapter."[33]

The robbers were dead. The senseless and brutal murder of an innocent bank cashier at the hands of two crude, ignorant, and remorseless killers was avenged. And a warning signal was sent to other Oklahoma and Indian Territory desperadoes. Justice was served . . . or was it? It may have seemed to the *Wichita Times* reporter that it was the end of the chapter, but as we are about to discover, the chapter was far from over. And, in another and larger sense, it was just the beginning of a new chapter in the evolving story of frontier justice.

• • •

The next day's front-page *Ft. Worth Gazette* story[34] was a remarkable example of late-nineteenth-century journalism. The typical "news story" featured nearly equal helpings of news and editorializing liberally seasoned with a rich blend of hyperbole, unintended irony, and illogic.[35] "Cashier Dorsey Is Avenged," it exulted, while a subhead added, "Bodies Dangle Twixt Heaven and Earth." The article went on to congratulate the vigilantes who "meted out swift justice to the two lawless bandits [when] Judge Lynch . . . opened a special session of court." It further congratulated the mob members on the businesslike manner with which they conducted their activities. They were "a crowd of law-abiding citizens"; "orderly, sober and quiet." They conducted themselves as though "they were performing a sacred duty they owed to a loved friend, to the dignity of the city, and to their fellow men."

However, after complimenting the mob for its "sober" demeanor, the article noted that some members of the mob would undoubtedly "deplore" these acts "in their sober moments." And, having just applauded the mob for being "law-abiding," the article went on to observe that in view of the wanton slaying of Dorsey, "it is no wonder they forgot law in their desire for revenge." Although the members of the mob were roundly praised for their summary dispensation of justice, nary a one was identified. The closest the article came to doing so was to identify Burk Burnett and his son, Tom, as being present when the men were hung.

It is apparent that the overwhelming majority of the populace (including most of its leading citizens) supported this brand of frontier justice, although no one publicly stepped up to take credit for being a party to the lynching. In fact, *after* the lynching and despite considerable criticism from outsiders for taking the law into their own hands, a citizens' vigilante committee was formed at a public meeting for the purpose of vindicating the action of the mob and discouraging any future depredations from Indian Territory outlaws.[36] The citizens' committee also sought to energize other border states (Arkansas, Missouri, and Kansas) to pressure the federal government to open up the Indian Territory for settlement by homesteaders.[37]

The *Wichita Times* and the *Ft. Worth Gazette* lost no time in boarding that train, as well as endorsing the lynching itself. In its April 2, 1896, issue the *Ft. Worth Gazette* editorialized as follows:

> The *Gazette* declared the fate of Crawford and Lewis to have been a just one and suggested that it should serve as a warning to outlaws from the Indian Territory to abstain from murder and robbery in Texas. The people of Wichita Falls, in mass meeting assembled, appealed to Congress to establish a civilized government in the Indian Territory, and to exterminate the lawlessness prevailing there.

In that same issue the *Gazette* quoted a recent editorial appearing in the *Wichita Times,* which answered criticism of the lynching from its rival the *Dallas Morning News.* Obviously stung, the *Wichita Times* railed as follows:

> Some narrow-constructed, clay-brained newspapermen most emphatically condemn the action of lynching the robbers, who got their just dues at the end of a rope in this city lately. In our opinion, if some of these fellows were swung to the same telephone pole, the country would be in much better condition.

The *Dallas Morning News* returned the volley:

> The [Wichita] *Times* seems to be somewhat high-strung itself.[38]

If a majority of the north Texas populace supported the extra-legal dispensation of justice to Lewis and Crawford, there was a very vocal minority (in addition to Judge Miller) who voiced opposition. The day after the hanging, the *Dallas Morning News* weighed in on the matter:

> It must be regretted that their punishment was not meted out

according to law. It matters not how exasperating the offense . . .
every such example of collective tumultuous and irrepressible violence deprecates the dignity and repute of the state in proclaiming
its incapacity to cope with crime and to maintain an orderly admin-
istration of justice.

The editorial went on to decry the recent instances of injustice, which it
attributed to "loopholes" in Texas penal laws that permitted the guilty
to go free, and then the newspaper excoriated the legislature for not
passing remedial legislation as the paper had advocated. It then made
this point:

Civilization demands that mob violence be suppressed, but it
demands with just as much emphasis that the law punish the guilty,
and give to society the protection which government is supposed to
guarantee. Until something is done along this line it will devolve
upon officers to prevent lynches.[39]

The *Dallas Morning News* then proceeded to take a justifiable swipe
at "the officers who captured the victims" of the lynching for failing to
protect them from mob violence—a shot that must have stung McDonald considerably. If that were not enough, McDonald and Wichita
County sheriff C. M. Moses took another shot from George Jester, who
was then lieutenant governor of Texas (and father of future Texas governor Beauford Jester). Governor Culberson happened to be out of the
state when the lynching occurred, so Jester, as acting governor of Texas,
sent a scorching telegraph to Wichita County sheriff C. M. Moses.

Knowing that you were aided in the arrest by the state Rangers, I
supposed you were amply prepared to protect the prisoners . . . those
who participated in taking the law into their own hands committed an
act that is unjustifiable, indefensible and should be condemned by all
the law-abiding citizens, and constitutes a blot on the county and state.
The only [reason for a lynching] is that justice cannot be obtained
before the courts, which is a reflection on the laws of our state, or the
citizenship in not enforcing the law. I believe that the defect is more
in the latter than in the former. . . . [40]

A leading Wichita Falls citizen, Arch D. Anderson, replied to Acting Governor Jester, and his rebuttal appeared in the *Dallas Morning News.* Anderson took Jester to task for casting an adverse reflection of "the best citizens of the state and county . . . who administered justice to the murderers of that noblest of men, Frank Dorsey." Anderson went on to justify the mob action by saying that had the law been allowed to take its course, it would no doubt have resulted in considerable delay. Besides, there was always the chance that the murderers would escape justice altogether by a jailbreak or a pardon. Further, Anderson asserted that judges, because they have "very little practical experience dealing with the class continually committing these foul murders . . . are incapable of dictating to the common citizen his duty under such circumstances." Anderson concluded his commendation of the "gallant men" of the mob with these words:

A more becoming sight I never witnessed than when I saw their bodies dangling in the breeze in front of the bank where they committed the foul murder.[41]

Anderson did not see fit, however, to give individual credit to those "gallant men."

Sheriff Moses replied to Jester, explaining that he had been out of town searching for Crawford and Lewis when the robbery had taken place, and he returned only after his deputies had been "overpowered by a crowd of 500." He said that upon returning to town he himself was overpowered by a "detachment of citizens," disarmed and rendered "helpless as a child." Although Sheriff Moses was in the Oklahoma Territory at the time of the bank robbery and didn't return until after the jail had been stormed and Crawford and Lewis had been taken away, he, in the same telegram to Jester—in a claim that seems to defy logic—went on to state that he had "twenty-five men deputized to protect the prisoners," but to no avail. Moses further claimed that "a regiment of soldiers" could not have held the jail:

The community to almost a man seems to uphold the method employed in ridding the country of these two noted criminals.[42]

However, in closing, Sheriff Moses assured Jester that *he* certainly did not "approve or uphold such methods," and that he stood ever ready to "do his full duty in the premises."

The vigilantes also took a blast from a federal judge in the Indian Territory, Judge Constantine Buckley Kilgore, who weighed in with a response that was printed by the *Ft. Worth Gazette*. He compared the brutal killing of the bank cashier with the brutal lynching of the two robbers:

> The motive in one case was plunder; in the other revenge: and the spirit of outlawry was as conspicuous in one case as the other . . . [justifying this lynching upon the ground] that the courts of Texas could not be relied upon to enforce the law and punish the criminals . . . was dangerous ground upon which to seek to justify mob violence . . . and the people of Wichita Falls in their . . . malice undertook to shift the odium of these outrages and the responsibility of these crimes on another . . . the *Gazette* and the people of Wichita Falls insisted that the mob came out of that work whiter than snow . . .

Judge Kilgore continued his broadside as follows:

> On March 2, 1896, there was a called session of the Wichita Falls mob, the purpose of which was to unload on the people of the Indian Territory the responsibility for the wrongs perpetrated by that community, for the inefficient courts and officials of Texas and the uselessness of the "rangers."[43]

That Captain McDonald had called off his safeguard of the prisoners prematurely seems obvious. But McDonald was, as ever, simply incapable of admitting error. After the lynching, some citizens (including Judge Miller) complained to Governor Culberson that McDonald had abandoned his prisoners knowing full well that lynch fever was endemic. McDonald later attempted to avoid blame by explaining that once he had arrested Lewis and Crawford and locked them in the Wichita County jail, his duty was done and he had no further responsibility—an assertion that is just not true. Besides, if McDonald's duty ended the moment the Wichita County jail doors were slammed shut behind Lewis and Crawford, then why did he stay and disperse the mob the first night, and why did he spend the rest of that night at the Wichita County jail to ensure the prisoners' safety? Also, McDonald conveniently forgot to mention the fact that he had promised the outlaws protection from the mob if they would surrender. McDonald's biographer ended up by summarily dismissing the matter:

> Culberson wired to McDonald [seeking an explanation as to why the prisoners were not properly protected], and receiving the facts [from McDonald] in reply, commended him throughout.[44]

We have McDonald's word on that!

Vigorous protests continued to bombard the governor's office until finally, in 1896, the adjutant general demanded a full report from McDonald. In a letter of explanation to Texas adjutant general W. H. Mabry, McDonald, true to form, insisted that he was absolutely blameless and that he had done his "whole duty." After castigating Judge Miller, McDonald ended the letter on this self-pitying note:

> . . . there must always be some one to attach all the blame to and when they can not find any one else, the poorly paid Ranger, who dares open his mouth, gets all the blame and some of us can stand a reasonable amount of abuse at long range.[45]

At that point in time, it was apparent that almost all Wichitans would have preferred to see the controversy fade into history. Most, but not all. Wichita County district judge George E. Miller was still doggedly determined that the law should be satisfied. He refused to let the matter drop.[46]

Judge Miller brought the lynching incident to the attention of the Wichita County grand jury on April 28, 1896. In an unprecedented and innovative maneuver, he proceeded to lecture the grand jury on its duties. He bluntly told the grand jurors that the lynching of Crawford and Lewis was without legal justification and that the men who participated in it were guilty of murder. He ordered them to do their duty and not turn a blind eye to the law. (As we shall soon see, the defendants' lawyers used this lecture to their advantage.) Finally, without naming names (but read "McDonald"), Judge Miller sharply excoriated those peace officers who failed in their duty to protect their prisoners. "If they had done their duty," Judge Miller told the grand jury, "Wichita County would not have been disgraced by mob law."[47] After Judge Miller's tongue-lashing, the grand jury eventually returned five indictments against former Wichita County sheriff F. M. Davis, W. E. Cobb, Dick Quinn, Frank Smith, and Marion Potter.[48] However, there remained little doubt that prosecution of the mob members was not viewed favorably by most Wichitans, including the legal community, as evidenced by the clever bit of legal chicanery that followed.

Louise Kelly, a native Wichitan, compiled the best account of the whole affair. It appears in the Louise Kelly Collection in the Wichita County Archives in the limited edition *Wichita County Beginnings*. She describes the maneuver this way:

> When the five [murder defendants] came up for a preliminary hearing, Judge Miller was told his wife was in an accident in Graham. While he was away, the [Wichita County] lawyers selected a temporary [district] judge, C. M. Sherrod.[49]

Customarily, a "temporary" judge defers to the regular, duly elected judge and only considers routine matters and does not undertake to adjudicate serious, contested issues unless the matter results from an emergency situation requiring an immediate disposition. Nevertheless, temporary Judge Sherrod immediately conducted preliminary hearings in all five cases while, according to Kelly, Judge Miller was on a wild goose chase down at Graham. Since the defendants were indicted for capital murder, Judge Miller had denied them bonds. However, Temporary Judge Sherrod wasted no time in setting a five-thousand-dollar bond for each defendant and then, *on his own motion*, proceeded to change the venue. The cases against ex-sheriff F. M. Davis, W. E. Cobb, Dick Quinn, and Frank Smith were transferred to Vernon in Wilbarger County.[50] Later, Marion Potter's case was transferred to Gainesville in Cooke County.[51] A good guess, particularly in light of what had just happened and what was about to happen next, would be that Temporary

Judge Sherrod, in changing the venue, selected courts that were considerably more defendant-friendly.

The *Dallas Morning News* reported this highly unusual legal maneuvering on behalf of the defendants in its next edition. According to that account, "a majority of the best citizens of Wichita Falls went to the courthouse and offered to furnish a bond in any sum" for the defendants. In addition, upon their release on bond that day, each defendant was given a list of all the attorneys in town and instructed that each defendant could select two lawyers to represent himself, all of whom had agreed to represent the defendants "cheerfully without fee." The news story ended with this telling comment:

> . . . the expressions heard on the street would indicate that most people of [Wichita Falls] were very indignant at the grand jurymen and district judge for their action in the above matter. In fact, the feeling appeared to be about the same as it was the evening that Foster [*sic*] and Lewis were taken from jail and hanged. [52]

The four cases transferred to the Vernon court were called for trial on August 3, 1896. A jury was empanelled, but, before any witnesses were called, each defendant presented district judge G. A. Brown with a motion to set aside his indictment. Each motion alleged that the indictment was faulty since both district judge Miller and district attorney J. F. Carter were present when the grand jury was deliberating upon the proposed indictments. Presumably Judge Miller's stern pre-indictment tongue-lashing exhorting the grand jury to do their duty and indict those responsible for the lynching was alleged by the defendants to be tantamount to being present with the grand jury during its deliberations. Under Texas law, no one except the twelve grand jurors themselves is permitted in the grand jury room when the grand jury is deliberating. In any event, Judge Brown lost no time in granting all these motions and dismissing the indictments.[53] Since the defendants' trial had actually begun when Judge Brown dismissed the indictments, the defendants could not be re-indicted or ever again tried for the lynching of either Crawford or Lewis because of "double jeopardy" prohibitions in the Texas and U.S. constitutions. In short, the defendants were home free. Some three hundred witnesses and the four defendants were turned loose, and according to one observer, all returned to Wichita Falls very "happy, and I might say, hilarious."[54] The case of Marion Potter in Gainesville fared no better for the prosecution. It was dismissed by the Cooke County district judge on June 7, 1897, due to "insufficient evidence to convict." A disinterested newspaper reporter remarked that the dismissals of all the lynch mob indictments were a foregone conclusion: "Prosecutors and others were aware that no Texas jury would return a verdict of guilty."[55]

The Aftermath

Judge Miller paid a price for his unswerving dedication to the law and his courage in standing almost alone in his public condemnation of the vigilantes. Less than two years after these events, he chose not to run for re-election. Without doubt, the fact that he had bucked the overwhelming public sentiment that condoned the lynch mob cost him his office. Shortly after the election he moved to Kansas City and began practicing law there. However, in 1900 he was induced to return to Texas by a celebrated Fort Worth lawyer, A. L. Matlock, where he resumed his Texas law practice with the firm of Matlock, Miller, and Dycus. He continued to practice law in Texas (but never again in Wichita Falls) until his death on April 25, 1922.[56]

The members of the lynch mob who rejected Judge Miller's appeal to let the law take its course had one very valid point: Texas appellate courts were reversing substantial numbers of convictions of defendants who were obviously guilty. Against a backdrop of such infuriating malfunctions of the young Texas criminal justice system, it is not difficult to imagine why many ordinary citizens would succumb to the temptation of ignoring the law while striking a decisive blow for what they considered obvious justice. Shortly after the Wichita Falls lynching, an 1896 Dallas grand jury took the unusual step of venting its frustration in a public broadside aimed at the Texas Court of Criminal Appeals:

> We cannot refrain from calling attention to the peculiar action of the
> Court of Criminal Appeals in reversing cases. . . . That court seldom

or never looks at facts to see if the party is guilty, but seems to look at some farfetched matter that could not and did not affect the guilt or innocence of the man. Justice seems to be done in the trial court and undone in the Court of Criminal Appeals . . . it is certainly no part of the law that our highest criminal court continuously aid criminals to escape justice and something ought to be done to stop it. . . . Let the Court of Criminal Appeals be compelled to affirm all cases where there is no question about guilt.[57]

The 1896 editorial writer hit a nerve, and his sentiments were echoed across the state in a rising chorus that Texas lawmakers could not ignore. Therefore, the Texas legislature when it next met (in 1897) passed a remedial act that, at least partially, addressed these complaints. It amended the *Texas Code of Criminal Procedure* to reduce the number of appellate reversals of criminal convictions. Enacting a precursor of our present "harmless error" doctrine, the lawmakers decreed that certain technical trial court errors of procedure were thereafter to be "disregarded" on appeal "unless the error . . . [was] calculated to injure the rights of the defendant." Plus, to assert reversible error on appeal, the defendant must have objected to that error at the trial court level.[58] Only then was the Court of Criminal Appeals authorized to reverse a criminal conviction. However, it proved to be only a first step in reigning in the reverse-minded Court of Criminal Appeals.

In the same session the legislators also sought to strike a blow against mob justice. The solons enacted a brand new criminal statute entitled "Murder by Mob Violence," noting in its preamble that there existed "no adequate law for the suppression of mob violence." The new law provided that if two or more persons combined "for the purpose of mob violence" and in pursuance of such combination willfully took the life of "any reasonable creature" by such violence, then upon conviction the defendant would face the unpleasant alternative of either life imprisonment or death. The act also went on to provide that if any officer of the law permitted any person in his custody to be released to a mob, then that officer would be deemed guilty of "official misconduct" and, as a result, be removed from office.[59]

Off the Record

While it is true that one man's "legal technicality" is another man's "vital constitutional right," still it is not unfair to state that many of the 1890s reversals were supported by rather flimsy stalks of logic—tortured reasoning leading to hair-splitting distinctions invisible to ordinary mortals and to results that were sometimes absurd. It appears that appellate judges of that day, puffed up with self-importance, were bent upon demonstrating their intellectual superiority to the common, unwashed herd by discovering and expounding (at length) upon these minute distinctions. For example, in the year 1900 (even after the 1897 amendment), of all felony cases (excluding prohibition and liquor cases) reviewed on appeal by the Texas Court of Criminal Appeals, the court reversed an astounding 68.5 percent. About one-third of such reversals were attributed to technical errors in the wording of indictments or jury instructions. Also, as noted above, appellate courts did not painstakingly evaluate the seriousness of the trial court error as do modern courts. Today, even if the trial court erred in certain rulings, modern decisions posit that a reversal should not follow unless the error was such as to seriously undermine the fairness of the judicial process or very likely to have influenced the jury's decision.

Another factor that no doubt contributed to the eventual decline in reversal rates was the increased professionalism of the bar. As early as 1927 the tide had turned significantly. Instead of a 68.5 percent reversal rate, the percentage had fallen to 29.3.[60] By the year 2000 the reversal rate had dropped to less than 10 percent.[61] Modern defense attorneys, of course, vociferously contend that the pendulum has swung much too far in favor of the prosecutor and against the accused. For example, a recent article appearing in *Texas Monthly* magazine took the Texas Court of Criminal Appeals to task for having become a virtual rubber stamp for prosecutors as a result of its "tough-on-crime" philosophy.[62] Another commentator, however, made this insightful observation:

The position of the law has always been problematical in a republican democracy; the law has always seemed too weak in the eyes of some, while to others it has seemed in danger of becoming too strong, of subverting American liberties.[63]

The proper balance between ensuring that the guilty are convicted on the one hand and that the individual's rights under law are safe-guarded on the other has never been easy to attain. Clearly, however, at the 1890s stage of our law's development, the balance was tipped in favor of the criminal. Unfortunately, this occurred at a time when the tradition of vigilantism was still ingrained in—and very compelling to—a majority of Texans.

The Bloody Rampages of "Hell's Fringe" Outlaws

AN ALL-STAR CAST OF LAWMEN, OUTLAWS, AND LAWYERS

AFTER NEWS of the murder of their sheriff swept through the community, several folks came forward with important information. They all recalled seeing four strangers riding across the open prairie along the South Canadian River earlier that fateful day. Traveling westward, the four came from "Hell's Fringe," the wild and lawless Oklahoma Territory, headed toward the Texas Panhandle village of Canadian. Those who happened to cross their path paid particular attention to the strangers because they were all well armed and well mounted, because they weren't traveling on any existing road or trail, and because they all had grain sacks ("morrals") dangling from their saddle horns—long-riders for sure. Overcoats were buttoned against the bite of the High Plains autumn, overshoes lashed behind their saddles. And, instead of returning customary greetings, the riders just glared at folks.

Plus one other thing: one of the observers, by pure chance, happened to know, and thus recognize, one of the four horsemen—Will "Tulsa Jack" Blake, a lieutenant in Bill Doolin's notorious Oklahoma Territory outlaw gang.[1]

Later that day, two of the four were seen hanging out at Paul Hoefler's saloon in Canadian, a scant two hundred yards from the railroad depot.[2] Indeed, on that day, Friday, November 23, 1894, the Santa Fe depot seemed to be a magnet attracting the famous and the infamous—an unlikely assortment of heroes and villains . . . and losers. The depot also proved to be a lightning rod for an impending storm of events, both dramatic and tragic.

The previous day, however, at the Wells Fargo office in Kansas City, a mighty peculiar thing happened. A man whom nobody seemed to know (at least nobody in the law-abiding community) appeared claiming his five money packets contained more cash money than the Wells Fargo clerk had ever before handled. The stranger identified himself as George Isaacs and proceeded to make a most unusual request. He wanted Wells Fargo to ship his cash (via the Santa Fe Railroad) to himself at Canadian, Texas.

The next day George boarded the same Santa Fe train that was carrying his money packets. The train arrived that evening at about 8:00 at the Canadian depot. George disembarked, but, instead of going to the Wells Fargo office in the depot, he started walking toward downtown Canadian in search of a hotel room. Although George's three brothers lived in the Canadian area, he was unfamiliar with the town (or at least claimed to be), so he asked directions to the nearest hotel. Strangely enough, the man he chanced to ask was none other than the most famous lawman in all of the Panhandle and West Texas: Texas Ranger captain G. W. "Cap" Arrington.

The Canadian Wells Fargo agent, A. B. Harding, having learned of the huge money shipment to be delivered into his safekeeping, summoned Hemphill County sheriff Tom T. McGee to help guard the money. The stage was set, and the curtain about to rise on a drama of far-reaching consequences. Before the curtain rang down on this improbable and bizarre drama there would be two murders that, in turn, resulted in eight murder trials in Texas and Oklahoma Territory.

The Players

This frontier drama featured an all-star cast of Texas and Oklahoma Territory outlaws, lawmen, and trial lawyers. The headliners in the case included outlaw Bill Doolin and his gang; the junk-yard-dog mean A. J.

The depot and the fledgling town of Canadian shortly after the railroad arrived in 1887. Just seven years later it would be the site of Sheriff Tom T. McGee's murder.
(Courtesy of the Panhandle-Plains Historical Museum, Canyon, Texas.)

Fires, the eloquent and eccentric Temple Houston, W. B. Plemons, Lorenzo Dow Miller, and H. E. Hoover as flamboyant criminal trial lawyers; and law officers Texas Ranger captain G. W. "Cap" Arrington and U.S. Deputy Marshal Chris Madsen of Oklahoma Territory; plus a number of other famous men of the era. Ironically, George Isaacs, who started it all, was one of the few pygmies in this cast of giants.

Captain G. W. "Cap" Arrington was known as the "iron-handed" Texas Ranger and was acclaimed as "the first and greatest peace officer" in the Panhandle and West Texas. A battle-scarred Civil War veteran, Arrington joined the Texas Rangers in 1875. His combat and leadership skills were quickly recognized. He first gained fame as an Indian fighter on the West Texas frontier. Later, he teamed up with the venerable Colonel Charles Goodnight in an unrelenting war on cattle rustlers. Still later, he was drafted as sheriff of Wheeler County, Texas, when that county along with fourteen other attached, but still unorganized, counties covered about half of the Texas Panhandle.[3]

In Oklahoma Territory, where, because of widespread corruption, many U.S. marshals were viewed by the general populace as a curse worse than the outlaws they pursued, deputy U.S. Marshal Chris Mad-

Texas Ranger captain George W. Arrington gained fame first as an Indian fighter and later as a relentless foe of cattle rustlers and the outlaw element. Although he was not an official law enforcement officer in November 1894 when outlaws killed Hemphill County sheriff Tom T. McGee in Canadian, Texas, Arrington nevertheless organized a posse the next day, tracked the killers more than ninety miles into Oklahoma Territory, arrested one of the gang, and obtained incriminating statements from witnesses. (Courtesy of the Panhandle-Plains Historical Museum, Canyon, Texas.)

sen, together with deputy U.S. Marshals Heck Thomas and Bill Tilghman, were known in those lawless days as Oklahoma Territory's "Three-
Guardsmen"—the most feared and respected lawmen in the territory.[4]
Madsen's short stature and somewhat pudgy appearance caused a number of rank outlaws to underestimate him—a very serious mistake.
Another intrepid stalwart for law and order, an ex–U.S. calvary sergeant
named Fred Hoffman whose outspoken dedication cost him dearly,
would also represent the Oklahoma Territory.

By 1894 Bill Doolin had established himself as the undisputed king
of the Oklahoma Territory outlaws, but that dubious crown came with a
handsome price placed on the head of its bearer. Originally a member of
the famous Dalton gang, Doolin later formed his own gang, which was
even more successful. Trains and banks were their specialties. Intelligent, fearless, and cool-headed, Doolin was an expert horseman and a
deadly shot. Plus, in that wild and woolly country, where outlaws
abounded and where most inhabitants (outlaws and small nesters alike)
viewed banks and railroads (with considerable justification) as tools of
greedy, gouging robber barons, Doolin attained considerable support
among the common folks as a result of his Robin Hood–like generosity.[5]
Other outlaws in Doolin's gang included George "Bitter Creek" Newcomb (aka "the Slaughter Kid"), Bill Dalton (brother of Bob, Emmett,
and Grat), "Dynamite Dick" Clifton, Will "Tulsa Jack" Blake, Charlie
Pierce, George "Red Buck" Weightman, Roy Daugherty (aka "Arkansas
Tom" Jones), and Dick Yeager (aka "Zip Wyatt"). Young Alfred Son, a
Doolin gang associate, would also play an important role.

George Isaacs was a small, thirty-six-year-old man with only a third-
grade education who later listed his occupation as "laborer" and who
lived in the remote, outlaw-infested Indian Territory country located
near the present-day town of Chickasha, Oklahoma.[6] While most folks
had never heard of George Isaacs, the federal authorities in that sparsely
populated area were well acquainted with him. Shortly after the murder, deputy U.S. marshal H. E. Mocker of Purcell, Indian Territory,
stated that Isaacs had long been harboring the most notorious bands of
Oklahoma and Indian Territory desperadoes and thieves and "was
regarded as a member of them."[7] George, before throwing in with the
outlaws, worked for at least a short time as a straight-up cowboy for the
large T Anchor Ranch south and east of Amarillo in the Texas Panhan-

Bill Doolin was the king of outlaws in 1890s Oklahoma Territory. Although Doolin was apparently not present at the attempted Wells Fargo robbery and the killing of sheriff Tom T. McGee in Canadian, Texas, in November 1894, he had participated in planning the heist. Known members of his gang were present at the scene as well as at the later ambush and murder of U.S. commissioner Fred Hoffman in Oklahoma Territory.
(From *West of Hell's Fringe: Crime, Criminals, and the Federal Peace Officer in Oklahoma Territory, 1889–1907*, by Glenn Shirley, Oklahoma University Press, 1978.)

dle.[8] Although George Isaacs himself was a ne'er-do-well who hung out with disreputable pals in owl-hoot territory, he had three brothers, W. C. "Bill," Sam, and John Isaacs, who were prosperous pioneer ranchers in the eastern Texas Panhandle area around Canadian. Two of the three brothers, Bill and Sam, were players in the drama.

The Sheriff McGee Murder

As the marshals turned up the heat on the gang, Doolin took refuge in the Wichita Mountains area of Indian Territory, where, apparently, he ran into George Isaacs in the fall of 1894. It was there an ill-fated plan to defraud Wells Fargo was hatched. Isaacs later testified that Bill Doolin, a man Isaacs identified only as "Jim Stanley," and two other unidentified men came to his cabin near Chickasha and proposed the plan. Isaacs attempted to excuse his participation, saying that, after all, he was only a "poor man who had no money." He said that Doolin and Stanley proposed that he go to the Wells Fargo office in Kansas City and purport to send a large amount of cash (twenty-five-thousand dollars) in sealed Wells Fargo envelopes to himself in Canadian, Texas. Undoubtedly, Canadian was chosen as the delivery site in order to lend a patina of legitimacy to the nefarious enterprise, as George's three, more respectable, brothers had ranches in that area. In reality, George was to put a much smaller amount of cash in the envelopes. The Wild Bunch would then rob the train and confiscate the envelopes along with any other cash and valuables aboard, leaving George in a position—they reckoned—to recover the face amount from Wells Fargo. As other testimony later indicated, George was to put five thousand dollars cash in the envelopes, which would be the outlaws' share, leaving George (and perhaps other confederates) to pocket the difference. George testified that he suggested that it would appear more credible if he first shipped some cattle to Kansas City, sold them, and then pretended to send the cash proceeds of the cattle sale to himself in Canadian, Texas. The gang agreed.

George testified that "Jim Stanley" was in charge of putting a gang together to hijack the train near Canadian. Meanwhile, George would set about carrying out his end of the devil's bargain. On about November 20, 1894, George and the cattle were bound for Kansas City; he arrived there and presumably sold the cattle. Two days later he showed up at the Wells Fargo office in Kansas City, obtained five money packets, and departed. Later the same day he returned with the packets stuffed but not sealed. He then had the Wells Fargo clerk seal each packet, but the clerk did not count the money or verify the contents. The packets were sealed with hot wax. George signed each packet. Each packet contained only $100 in cash, for a total of $500. George then paid the clerk $31.50 in express charges and left. At George's trial the clerk identified George Isaacs as the man who shipped the packets. He also testified that another person was with George at the time, although he stayed in the background and the clerk could not identify him.[9]

Three questions come to mind:

1. Who was the mystery man in the background?
2. If, as George Isaacs testified, the notorious Bill Doolin was the man who devised the scheme, then why would he put someone else ("Jim Stanley") in charge of the gang and stay home?
3. Whose cattle did George ship to Kansas City and sell? Since

George testified that he was a "poor man who had no money," the cattle were undoubtedly not his. The Wild Bunch was in the business of robbing trains and banks, not raising cattle. Perhaps the cattle were stolen, but that would seem a bit risky considering they wanted to draw the cloak of legitimacy around this endeavor. Plus, it would have been foolhardy to move a fairly large number of stolen cattle all the way from southern Oklahoma Territory to the Kansas City market—a major cattle market where brand inspectors would likely spot stolen cattle. Whose cattle then? Were others involved in the conspiracy?

Zoe A. Tilghman, widow of famed deputy U.S. marshal Bill Tilghman, in an account of the incident written many years later, says George Isaacs sent a "large shipment" of cattle from Canadian, Texas, to Kansas City and that he went with the shipment. If the story is true, it would appear that the cattle were not stolen. Also, since all three of George's brothers were ranchers in the Canadian area, it seems at least possible that one or more of them was the source of the cattle. At any rate, after George got to Kansas City he sold the cattle and took the proceeds in cash.[10]

Wells Fargo officials may have become suspicious when, after having posted his money packets at the Wells Fargo office in Kansas City, George elected to ride the same train back to Canadian, Texas. His furtive actions may also have aroused suspicion, particularly in that day when train robberies were not uncommon. Plus, as the Kansas City Wells Fargo agent would testify, the twenty-five-thousand-dollar shipment was the largest amount of cash he had ever handled. In light of those details, the Wells Fargo folks were alert, and a messenger was dispatched to guard the express car.

Meanwhile, as noted earlier, the Canadian Wells Fargo agent, A. B. Harding, summoned sheriff Tom T. McGee to the depot. McGee was the first sheriff of the newly formed (1887) Hemphill County. Prior to that McGee had been foreman of the P O Ranch in unorganized Hemphill County since the ranch's establishment in 1884.[11] McGee was highly respected and was remembered as "honest, fearless, and of a kindly disposition."[12]

Tom T. McGee, shown here with his wife, was the first elected sheriff of Hemphill County, Texas. He was murdered by members of the Bill Doolin gang at the railroad depot in Canadian, Texas, on November 23, 1894, during an attempted robbery of the Wells Fargo office.
(Courtesy of the Panhandle-Plains Historical Museum, Canyon, Texas, and the family of Sallie B. Harris, author of *Cowmen and Ladies: A History of Hemphill County*.)

George Isaacs testified that the plan was for the Wild Bunch to hijack and rob the train between Higgins and Canadian, but that didn't happen. George, therefore, must have been somewhere on the high side of panic when the train, unrobbed, pulled into the station at Canadian that evening. Undoubtedly he figured that the gang had aborted the plan for some reason.

But not so—they were waiting at the train station.

When the train arrived, George Isaacs detrained and, as mentioned previously, he happened to encounter Cap Arrington. Isaacs then walked about three hundred yards to the Sutherland Hotel where he registered as a guest for the night. Arrington, meanwhile, boarded the westbound Santa Fe train. Shooting broke out shortly after the train departed.

Wells Fargo agent A. B. Harding testified that when the train arrived, he went to the express car and retrieved the Wells Fargo packages, including the five money packets belonging to George Isaacs. When he came out of the express car he came face-to-face, in good light, with a man he positively identified at subsequent trials as Jim Harbolt. He also testified that he saw one or two other men standing nearby. He tentatively identified one of them as Joe Blake. Joe Blake, as it turned out, was a brother of Will "Tulsa Jack" Blake, one of the regulars in Doolin's gang. For some reason, the gang did not accost the depot agent carrying the Wells Fargo packets.[13] We might guess that they decided to wait until the train pulled out of the station, wait for everyone to clear out, and then go into the depot and rob the lone Wells Fargo agent.

After Harding had taken the packets into the depot, Sheriff McGee arrived and went out onto the depot platform to scout the premises. He encountered a stranger on the platform, and McGee hailed him and asked him to state his business. According to the sheriff's dying statement, the stranger immediately whirled, jerked out his pistol, and began firing. Apparently the other gang members joined in because, according to both the sheriff's and the station agent's account twelve to fifteen shots rang out. The sheriff said he tried to draw his gun, but it hung up on his holster. The sheriff was hit only once—but fatally. According to Dr. A. M. Newman, the attending physician, Sheriff McGee was shot just above the right hip bone. The bullet's trajectory went upward and forward until it finally lodged near the sheriff's navel. The sheriff lingered throughout the night but died the next morning—not, however, before giving the doctor a full account of what happened and a description of the shooter he originally challenged.[14]

Strangely enough, even though the gang had incapacitated the sheriff, they did not enter the practically undefended depot to complete their mission. Instead, they mounted their horses and fled back east to Oklahoma Territory. Their action begs another query: if Bill Doolin had been running the show, would he have aborted the plan and run off empty-handed?

With the new sheriff disabled and dying, no one was available to pursue the bandits except the aging warhorse, Captain G. W. Arrington. However, Arrington was already aboard the westbound train that had just departed the Canadian depot. Harding had a telegraph waiting for Arrington at the next station; the old trooper quickly commandeered a Santa Fe locomotive and was back on the scene in no time. He immediately took charge, and by daylight Arrington was conducting his investigation. He found the footprints of four desperadoes leading to the hoofprints of their four horses. Shortly thereafter he assembled a posse and was hard on the outlaws' trail, heading eastward along the Canadian River into Oklahoma Territory. He performed the Herculean task of trailing the four criminals for about sixty miles to a point not far from the town of Taloga, Oklahoma Territory. Darkness overtook them near Dan McKenzie's farm. Pressing on in the dark, they arrived at the McKenzie homestead where Arrington and his posse found McKenzie, his wife, his daughter, and Joe Blake. Blake had been living with the McKenzies, but a lathered sorrel horse was resting in the corral. Several witnesses testified that the horse belonged to Joe Blake. Moreover, the horse's hooves matched one of the four hoofprints Arrington had followed from the scene of the killing. The other outlaws, it turned out, had departed shortly before Arrington's arrival. The next morning, after arresting Joe Blake, Arrington took his men back up the trail to the point where darkness had overtaken them the night before. They were then able to track the four horsemen straight back to McKenzie's cabin. But, just before they got there, Arrington noted that a *fifth* horseman had joined the group and ridden with them to McKenzie's farm. Tracks were found showing that four horsemen had left the McKenzie place sometime before Arrington and his posse had arrived the night before. Arrington and his posse did not pursue these four farther but instead returned to Canadian with Joe Blake in captivity.[15]

Meanwhile, back at Canadian, some very interesting events had occurred. On the morning following the shootout George Isaacs, together with his long-lost brother, Canadian rancher Sam Isaacs, showed up at the Wells Fargo office in the Canadian depot to claim his five money packets, and they were duly delivered to him. George, of course, signed a receipt. Then George and Sam left with the packets still unopened.[16] What George did next seems incredible. Instead of retrieving the five hundred dollars and then destroying the packets, he and brother Sam took the unopened packets to local merchant J. A. Chambers. The merchant had a safe, so Sam gave the packets to Chambers and asked him to secure them. Locking up the money packets in Chambers's safe must have been intended to *shield* the incriminating evidence from public discovery, but it had the exact opposite effect—it secured and preserved incriminating evidence for official discovery, evidence that would prove crucial to the state's case against George.

By morning every citizen of Hemphill and the surrounding counties was lynch-fever outraged at the killing of the popular sheriff. When word got out that this outsider, George Isaacs, had placed packages on the train supposedly containing twenty-five thousand dollars and all of a sudden murderous thugs showed up at the depot in an apparent attempt to rob the train . . . well, it just started to stink. Real bad. A "citizens' committee" was formed, headed by D. J. Young, a cashier of the Canadian Valley Bank, and they soon discovered that George and Sam Isaacs had retrieved the packets and stored them in Chambers's safe. The committee converged on Chambers's store that Sunday. Chambers testified that Young and his committee, with poor old George Isaacs in tow, confronted him and demanded he open his safe. In a classic understatement, Chambers testified, "Some parties came to me and asked me to keep out of the way as they wanted to examine the packages."[17]

When he was shown the packages, George had to admit that they were his, that his signature was on all five, that the sealing wax had not been broken, and that the packages had not otherwise been tampered with. If George had been nervous the night before, when his partners in crime failed to rob the train before it pulled into Canadian, he must have been damn near panicked waiting for the committee to open the packages and make the inevitable discovery—which, of course they did. Each package contained only one hundred dollars in one- and two-dollar bills plus a lot of paper scraps. George admitted his part in the scheme to defraud Wells Fargo, but he denied having anything to do with the murder of Sheriff McGee. That was definitely not part of the plan, he explained. *And* he was asleep in the Sutherland Hotel when all the shooting took place. D. J. Young, leader of the committee, testified that after this mind-boggling discovery, he gave the five hundred dollars cash to Sam and turned the other incriminating documents over to the authorities.

These events lead to more queries, some of which have never been fully answered. If George had been the long-lost Isaacs brother—gone for more than a decade—why would brother Sam show up with George

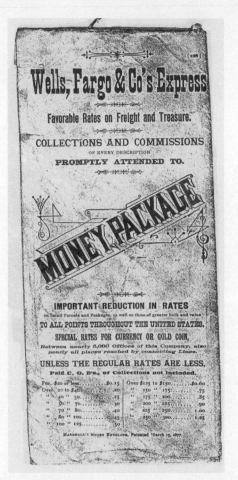

Pictured are the front and back of one of the five Wells Fargo money packets George Isaacs sent from Kansas City to himself in Canadian, Texas. He claimed each packet contained $5,000 cash, but actually each held only $100 in small bills.

(Original money packets in official court records, *State v. Jim Harbolt*, Cause No. 647, Donley County District Court in Clarendon, Texas.)

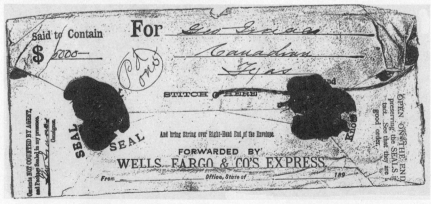

Deputy U. S. marshal Chris Madsen (*pictured*) and fellow Marshal William Banks captured two gang members, Joe Blake and Dan McKenzie, involved in the killing of Hemphill County sheriff Tom T. McGee in 1894. Masden later arrested Alfred Son, another Doolin gang associate, for the murder of U.S. commissioner Fred Hoffman, who was investigating the McGee murder.

(From *West of Hell's Fringe: Crime, Criminals, and the Federal Peace Officer in Oklahoma Territory, 1889–1907*, by Glenn Shirley, Oklahoma University Press, 1978.)

first thing next morning to claim the packets? Who were the four men actually present at the scene of the shooting? Who was "Jim Stanley?" Who aided the conspirators either before or after the attempted robbery and murder? And again, whose cattle did George Isaacs sell in Kansas City? How, and to what extent, was the attempted Wells Fargo robbery and the resultant McGee murder in Canadian, Texas, connected with subsequent crimes? Even more questions would arise as the events unfolded.

George Isaacs and Joe Blake were arrested. Then deputy U.S. marshals William Banks and Chris Madsen rounded up Jim Harbolt and Dan McKenzie from Oklahoma Territory and brought them back to Canadian, Texas. Isaacs, Blake, and Harbolt were all indicted (separately) by a Hemphill County grand jury for the murder of Sheriff Tom T. McGee. These three, plus Dan McKenzie, Will "Tulsa Jack" Blake, Sam Blake, and George "Bitter Creek" Newcomb were also jointly indicted for conspiracy to commit robbery.[18] Conspicuous in his absence from the indictments was the mysterious "Jim Stanley."

Meanwhile, lawmen and the Wells Fargo detectives continued their investigations.

The Texas Trials

Because of the notoriety of the case and sheriff Tom McGee's popularity in Canadian, the district judge changed the venue of all three murder trials to other Texas counties: George Isaacs to Quanah, county seat of Hardeman County;[19] Joe Blake to Vernon, county seat of Wilbarger County;[20] and Jim Harbolt to Clarendon, county seat of Donley County.[21] The conspiracy to rob Wells Fargo case against the three Blake brothers, Newcomb, Isaacs, Harbolt, and McKenzie was also transferred to Hardeman County.[22] Even though it was never contended that Isaacs was the actual shooter or that he was even present when the sheriff was killed, he was nevertheless tried first for McGee's murder, then Harbolt (who officers believed was the actual triggerman), and then Joe Blake.

Harry Koch, owner and editor of the *Quanah Tribune-Chief* weekly newspaper, later recalled the celebrated George Isaacs trial and his coverage of it. He wrote:

> The defendant, Isaacs, was the black sheep of a good family, and had thrown in with a bunch of outlaws of the Indian Territory, and conspired to rob the Wells Fargo Express Company. . . . The defendant had two rich brothers, who spared no money in getting him clear, and a battle royal was the result.[23]

At his trial in Quanah George Isaacs was represented by no less than seven lawyers. The heavyweights were the famous A. J. Fires of Childress and W. B. Plemons of Amarillo. Plemons and his partner, John Veale, were then the foremost criminal defense attorneys in Amarillo. Plemons had served the entire Civil War in General Stonewall Jackson's famous corps and was wounded three times. He was with General Robert E. Lee at Appomattox when Lee surrendered. Later in his career he served as the first county judge of Potter County in Amarillo and still later was elected district judge of the 47th Judicial District Court. He was elected to the Texas legislature in 1894 and served one term. Yet he was best known as an almost unbeatable criminal defense lawyer. A fellow attorney once remarked that Plemons "glorified in agitation and dispute" and "was never excelled in repartee." The pugnacious Plemons

W. B. Plemons of Amarillo
defended George Isaacs and Jim
Harbolt in separate trials for the
murder of sheriff Tom T. McGee.
A thrice wounded Confederate
veteran, Plemons also served in
the Texas legislature and was later
elected judge of the 47th Judicial
District in Amarillo.
(Courtesy of the Panhandle-Plains
Historical Museum, Canyon, Texas.)

believed there were two sides to every question—his side and the wrong side.[24] Interestingly, Plemons and Veale were later hired to defend Jim Harbolt.

Representing Joe Blake during his murder trial in Vernon were four attorneys headlined by the colorful Lorenzo Dow Miller of Amarillo, a former district attorney. As it happened, one of the attorneys assisting the prosecution in Joe Blake's case was H. E. Hoover, a prominent Panhandle lawyer known as "the Father of Canadian," Texas. These two frontier lawyers had tangled before in clashes of legendary proportions. Lorenzo Dow Miller was also the author of a withering judicial remark that became a classic. He became infuriated when an adverse witness skipped glibly from one lie to another with effortless ease. "Gentlemen of the jury," he fumed, "I could take that witness and prove that Jesus Christ runs a hog ranch on the North Fork—yes sir, a hog ranch on the North Fork."[25]

George Isaacs's murder trial in Quanah began on October 20, 1895. In that time, before radio or television, a murder trial was always more than just a murder trial, it was an exciting, even festive, social event. This murder trial was, without a doubt, a bigger draw than any circus, revival, political debate, or rodeo in the history of Hardeman County.

H. E. Hoover, prominent pioneer lawyer of Canadian, Texas, assisted Jim Cowan of Fort Worth in the prosecution of George Isaacs, Joe Blake, and Jim Harbolt for the murder of Hemphill County sheriff Tom T. McGee. Hoover, who was involved in every phase of the development of the region, became known as "the Father of Canadian." (Courtesy of the Panhandle-Plains Historical Museum, Canyon, Texas.)

Not a hotel room was left vacant. Concerned, law-abiding citizens from Canadian, as well as friends and family of the popular Sheriff McGee descended from the Panhandle. Adding to the crowd, the prosecution subpoenaed scores of witnesses, including the Wells Fargo clerks and investigators from Kansas City and the indomitable old Ranger G. W. Arrington. But the defense, bankrolled by the Isaacs brothers, was not to be outdone. According to the Quanah weekly newspaper, the defense subpoenaed more than two hundred "character" witnesses from "D" County, Oklahoma Territory, the stronghold of the outlaws.

The October 24, 1895, edition of the *Quanah Chief* reported, "A number of the Wells Fargo boys, assisted by a portion of the Quanah orchestra, made some good music the other evening." Moreover, time hung heavily on the hands of all those witnesses while waiting for their turn to testify. They proceeded to solve that problem in a most innovative and entertaining fashion. The opposing witnesses—the laws and the outlaws—chose up sides and challenged each other to a series of baseball games on the courthouse lawn. The Quanah weekly duly noted that the two teams "gave good account of themselves" but, unfortunately, failed to give any scores.

The *Quanah Chief's* pretrial story continued:

[Isaacs] admitted that he had sent only $500 and had marked the envelope to contain $25,000. Isaacs also confessed to different parties that before going to Kansas City, he entered into a conspiracy with Jim Harbolt, Joe Blake, [Jim] Stanley and one Bitter Creek [Newcomb], that he would go to Kansas City and ship the money to Canadian and that the other four would be on hand upon its arrival, and rob the express and that Isaacs would collect the $25,000 from the Express Company and divide the spoils.

Two of Isaacs's pals have since been killed by officers while resisting arrest and one of the remaining, Jim Harbolt, has been shot in a row and his bond forfeited, the Isaacs brothers [Bill and Sam] being on the bond.[26]

It was, in fact, true that "two of Isaacs's pals" had been killed before the Isaacs, Harbolt, or Blake cases were called for trial. Both were members of the Bill Doolin gang. Joe Blake's brother, Will "Tulsa Jack" Blake, and George "Bitter Creek" Newcomb had both come to violent ends as pressure on the Doolin gang mounted. Tulsa Jack was killed on April 4, 1895, by a Chris Madsen–led posse that overtook the Doolin gang, which was fleeing from the scene of yet another train robbery (a Rock Island train near Dover, O.T.), and Bitter Creek Newcomb was ambushed in his sleep and killed on May 1, 1895, by a former friend turned bounty hunter. The same turncoat, Bee Dunn, later collected the munificent sum of thirty-six dollars for helping U.S. marshal Heck Thomas ambush and kill his former compadre Bill Doolin on August 25, 1896.

In reporting the events of the trial itself, *Quanah Tribune-Chief* editor Harry Koch took a rather dim view of the defense's two hundred plus witnesses from Oklahoma Territory:

There was a great deal of perjury among the witnesses of the defense, which caused Prosecuting Attorney Jim Cowan to exclaim in his argument that for rottenness and general viciousness, these witnesses were the vilest scum he had ever met, which was received with snickers by the men thus alluded to.[27]

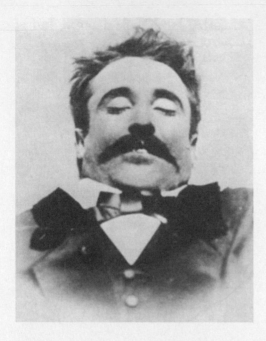

A Bill Doolin regular with a price on his head, Will "Tulsa Jack" Blake was indicted as a co-conspirator in the November 1894 attempted robbery of the Wells Fargo Express at Canadian, Texas, when Sheriff McGee was killed. His brother, Joe Blake, was also indicted as a conspirator and was further indicted for the murder of Sheriff McGee.
(From *West of Hell's Fringe: Crime, Criminals, and the Federal Peace Officer in Oklahoma Territory, 1889–1907,* by Glenn Shirley, Oklahoma University Press, 1978.)

Some two decades after the trial, editor Koch would reflect that the army of defense witnesses constituted "the finest collection of horse thieves and perjurers that ever congregated in any small town."[28] The district attorney and the Hardeman County grand jury must have also shared the editor's belief that there was a "great deal of perjury" going on during the George Isaacs trial because the grand jury returned several perjury-related indictments. Grant Pettyjohn was indicted for suborning perjury because he was alleged to have bribed defense witnesses A. G. Wooley, Bert Sexton, and John Shumate into committing perjury while they were on the stand.[29] Shumate and Sexton were indicted for actually committing perjury during the Isaacs trial.[30] All four were residents of the Taloga area. Grant Pettyjohn, a practicing lawyer, was also the editor of the *Taloga Tomahawk* weekly newspaper.[31] The going price for perjury, according to the indictments, appears to have been one hundred dollars per witness. All indictments, however, were later dismissed for "insufficient evidence." It should be noted, however, that the indictments were dismissed only *after* George Isaacs's conviction was affirmed on appeal, and *after* Joe Blake and Jim Harbolt had been tried.

One of the "vile scum," Dan McKenzie, turned state's evidence in an obvious attempt to save his own hide and avoid prosecution for conspiracy to commit robbery. McKenzie testified that after the attempted robbery and murder he had had a conversation with Tulsa Jack Blake, who, he said, admitted that he and his brother Joe Blake were participants. McKenzie testified that Tulsa also told him this:

> There were only four of us. Three went up to the depot, and Joe Blake stayed back with the horses . . . that son of a bitch, George Isaacs, tried to swindle [us] and the railroad company, too; he promised to ship $5,000 and sent only $500.[32]

McKenzie's testimony was later corroborated by Zoe A. Tilghman's account of the incident. She writes that George Isaacs told the outlaws that he was shipping $5,000 cash in the envelopes. "It was his intention to double-cross them as well as the express company."[33] Apparently, it never occurred to our hero that it might not be a bright idea to stiff Bill Doolin and company to the tune of $4,500. Turns out George was not even as clever by half as he thought, for his crackpot scheme was fatally flawed from the start. Wells Fargo accepted shipments of cash in two quite different ways. If the shipper wanted to insure the cash shipment, he had to let the station agent count the cash and thus verify contents of the packet and then pay an insurance fee in addition to the ordinary shipping fee. At that point the Wells Fargo agent would seal it with hot wax and impress a "Wells Fargo" stamp on the hot wax. However, if the shipper did *not* let the agent count and verify the cash contents and did not pay an insurance charge, then a "For Public Use" seal was imprinted on the wax. According to the clear Wells Fargo rules, if the uninsured packets were lost or stolen, Wells Fargo would not be liable for any loss of the contents. Predictably, George Isaacs chose the latter method and paid the nominal $31.50 shipping fee, and his packets were clearly marked "For Public Use." Genius George would have, even had the heist gone down without a hitch, been entitled to recover from Wells Fargo only his $31.50 shipping fee. His effort would have resulted in a net loss of $468.50, not to mention the wrath of his cutthroat pals.[34]

• • •

George Isaacs had the right, under the Fifth Amendment, not to testify. Moreover, the undisputed facts were these: George Isaacs was in his room in a hotel in Canadian at the time Sheriff McGee was murdered. The state conceded this point. Ranger Arrington himself testified that shortly before the murder, he encountered George coming from the railroad depot, and that George had inquired where a nearby hotel was located. Arrington noted that George was walking at a brisk pace. However, when he met George, Arrington was walking north along Main Street toward the depot while George was proceeding southward on Main Street away from the depot. When George asked where a hotel could be found, Arrington pointed back north across the railroad tracks to the nearest hotel, the Fay Hotel. To get there, George would have had to turn around, walk back toward the depot, and cross the railroad tracks to the Fay Hotel. Oddly, even though he claimed not to know the location of any other hotel, George ignored Arrington's directions and kept striding south, away from the depot and the Fay Hotel, finally ending up at the Sutherland Hotel.

Even though the prosecution conceded that George was not present when McGee was murdered, George was not home free—not by a long shot. Two laws applied in this case. First, any murder committed during the course of a robbery or an attempted robbery is a first degree murder. Second, any person who participates in the robbery in any way, including aiding, assisting, or conspiring with the actual robbers to commit a robbery, is also guilty of any murder that occurs during the course of the robbery. If one of the conspirators is not actually present at the crime scene, the rule still applies. Even if none of those involved contemplated a killing it's immaterial.

In view of the state's evidence (including George's own confession that he was a part of the Wells Fargo heist conspiracy), what did that leave George? Not much wiggle room, for sure. George's lawyers had to waive his Fifth Amendment right to avoid the stand; he had to testify. But when he did, he would have to acknowledge the malodorous truth that he had conspired with some of Oklahoma Territory's sorriest and most violent outlaws to defraud Wells Fargo, an admission that most certainly would not endear him to the jury. What was George's defense? Two-pronged, both technical. George's first line of defense was that the state failed to prove that any person with whom he had conspired to defraud Wells Fargo was actually present at the depot that night. George's second technical defense had logical if not "gut-justice" appeal. George could be found guilty of being an accomplice to the crime of murder (as an admitted co-conspirator to the crime of robbery) if, and only if, the murder had occurred *during the course of the robbery*. But, the defense argued, the shooting had occurred *before* the contemplated robbery commenced. And, in fact, the outlaws had abandoned the plan, and no robbery ever occurred or was even attempted.

George once again pointed out that he was not present when the shootout occurred, that he had no part in it, and that he never contemplated or even condoned any killing in furtherance of the scheme. Although George admitted during his testimony that he, together with Bill Doolin, Jim Stanley, and two other unnamed gang members, had previously plotted the Wells Fargo fraud, he testified that he didn't know who, if any, of his co-conspiritors were present at the Canadian depot shootout, "except Stanley." The groans of George's distinguished defense team must have been almost audible when he favored the prosecution with that helpful tidbit. It seems curious indeed that George, during his testimony, readily gave up "Jim Stanley," but no other, as present at the shootout. (Dan McKenzie also gave up that name, although he also named other known members of the Doolin gang including Tulsa Jack Blake and Bitter Creek Newcomb.) The testimonies are curious, indeed, because "Jim Stanley" was not a known member of the Doolin gang. There is no record that a "Jim Stanley" was ever arrested or even pursued by investigating officers. He was not named in the murder or conspiracy indictments. In fact, no record of the existence of such a person has ever been discovered. Obviously, "Jim Stanley" was a fictitious name. Perhaps George, never once accused of posessing excessive brilliance, may have reckoned that, by admitting only a fictitious name as a co-conspirator present at the shootout, it wouldn't count against him. In any event, the jury was not impressed by George's testimony or that of his army of Oklahoma Territory outlaw sympathizers. It did not take the jurors very long to come back with a guilty verdict and a life sentence. At least George had escaped the noose.

On appeal it did not take the Texas Court of Criminal Appeals very long to dispose of George's two principal points of error. It made short shrift of George's first argument that the state had failed to prove that any member of the gang who murdered Sheriff McGee was a person with whom George had conspired to defraud Wells Fargo. In so concluding, the appellate court cited George's own testimony when he let it slip that he knew his co-conspirator "Stanley" was among the shooters. Neither did the appellate court buy into the defense lawyers' argument that, at worst, the events amounted to only a "pre-robbery" murder, not a murder committed *during* an attempted robbery. The court countered, with undisputed evidence that established the following facts:

Four men had ridden 80 to 100 miles, armed to the teeth, well prepared for traveling; surrounded the depot for no other purpose on earth than to rob the agent of the money shipped by appellant [George Isaacs] to Canadian. When the deceased [Sheriff McGee] stepped to the door, and asked one of them to stop . . . he was fired upon from different directions, and killed.

The appellate court thus found that defendant's interpretation of the events was a bit too strained for its taste. The conviction was affirmed, and poor George would spend his life in jail.[35]

Jim Harbolt was the next to be tried. The Harbolt family, never known for strong ties to law enforcement, had squatted years earlier in Indian Territory not far from George Isaacs's cabin near Chickasha. As neighbors, it's very probable that George was well acquainted with the Harbolts long before the events of this story occurred. In 1888 Jim Harbolt shot and killed Giles Flippin at the Duncan Store in the Chickasha Nation. However, Harbolt was never convicted for the killing. In early 1894 he migrated westward to Oklahoma Territory, where he staked a claim in the southeast quadrant of "D" County.

The state's star witnesses in George's (and later Joe Blake's) trial were Depot Agent Harding, Cap Arrington, and Dan McKenzie, the defendant's erstwhile accomplice turned state's witness. McKenzie's testimony was introduced to shoot down Jim Harbolt's and Joe Blake's alibi defense.

McKenzie, his wife, and his daughter all testified that Joe Blake was living with them when these events occurred; that Blake left their home on the Monday before the attempted robbery and the killing of Sheriff McGee (the following Saturday night), and that Blake did not return to their cabin until Sunday night. When he returned, Joe Blake was accompanied by Jim Harbolt, Will "Tulsa Jack" Blake, George "Bitter Creek" Newcomb, and the mysterious "Jim Stanley." At about 9:00 that night, while everyone was gathered in McKenzie's home, yet another Blake brother, Sam, arrived with galvanizing news, "The Canadian Sheriff has died." Upon hearing that, all of McKenzie's guests leaped to their feet, went outside, and held a pow-wow. After that, everyone except Joe Blake saddled up and fled. However, McKenzie testified, before they departed, Tulsa Jack and "Jim Stanley" called him to the door, pointed their pistols at him, and said, "If anyone comes here inquiring for us and you tell that we were here, we will kill you!" McKenzie also testified that the jaded sorrel horse that Arrington found in his lot later that night belonged to Joe Blake.[36] The sorrel horse was taken back to Canadian by Arrington, where it was identified by three witnesses who testified that the sorrel was one of the four horses they had seen the outlaws riding while en route to Canadian on the day of the murder.

The state called a number of other witnesses from the Canadian area who definitely identified Joe Blake and Harbolt as two of the four heavily armed gunmen seen riding over from Oklahoma Territory early the day of the murder. Later the same day they were observed in Paul Hoefler's saloon, just a stone's throw from the Canadian depot. The depot agent definitely identified Harbolt as one of the men on the scene just before the shooting and testified that he believed Joe Blake was the man he saw with Harbolt. Moreover, the dying sheriff had given a detailed description of the man who drew his pistol and precipitated the fatal shootout. That description fit Jim Harbolt head to heel.

Both Harbolt and Blake, in their respective trials, claimed mistaken identity. They both testified that they were in the territory at the time Sheriff McGee was gunned down. And they even used the same army of Oklahoma Territory witnesses that had testified for George Isaacs to substantiate their alibis.

In Joe Blake's trial, the prosecution introduced several letters Blake

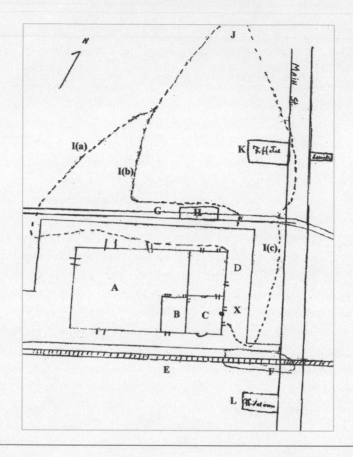

The above sketch was introduced into evidence at the trial of Jim Harbolt for killing
Hemphill County sheriff Tom T. McGee at the Santa Fe depot in Canadian, Texas. **X**
marks the location on the depot platform where Sheriff McGee was fatally wounded; **A**
is the depot itself; **B** is the Wells Fargo office inside the depot; **C** is the depot waiting
room; and **D** is the depot platform. **E** indicates the main Santa Fe track, and **F** marks the
location of the Wells Fargo Express car when it first arrived; **G** is the "house track"
coming off the main Santa Fe track, and **H** is where the Wells Fargo Express car was
parked after being uncoupled from the train. **I(a)**, **I(b)**, and **I(c)** trace the paths taken by
three of the four outlaws as they fled the scene of the murder and headed north to rendezvous with the fourth outlaw who was holding their horses in the stockyards, **J**, north
of the depot. From there, Ranger Arrington and his posse picked up the outlaws' trail.
K is the Fay Hotel, and **L** is Paul Hoefler's saloon where witnesses testified they saw
Blake and Harbolt drinking late in the afternoon before McGee was murdered. Letters
A–L and **X** were added by the author based on evidence presented during the trial.

(*State of Texas v. Jim Harbolt,* Cause No. 647, Donley County District Court.)

had written from jail to Dan McKenzie shortly after his arrest but before he learned that McKenzie had turned state's witness. The letters were certainly incriminating. Blake was not at all subtle in trying to conjure up and coordinate perjurous and consistent alibi testimony to exonerate himself and McKenzie.

It didn't work—at least not initially. Both Blake and Harbolt were found guilty (Harbolt on February 12, 1897; Blake on March 6, 1897), and both were sentenced to life imprisonment. Both appealed, and both convictions were reversed by the appellate court.[37]

In Harbolt's first trial, the jury was instructed in writing by the district judge on the punishments for both first degree murder (life imprisonment or death) and second degree murder (imprisonment for any number of years, not less than five). The jury had the choice of finding Harbolt guilty of first degree murder or second degree murder. When the jury returned, they found "the defendant guilty as charged in the indictment, and assess his punishment at confinement in the penitentiary for life."

The case sounds simple and straightforward. But it wasn't good enough to suit the Texas Court of Criminal Appeals. The jury's fatal mistake was not stating specifically in the verdict whether it found Harbolt guilty of first degree murder or second degree murder. It would seem obvious to anyone not afflicted with a case of terminal legalitis that the jury must have found Harbolt guilty of first degree murder since it fixed the punishment at life imprisonment instead of a term of years in prison. Nevertheless, on that hypertechnical point (typifying the legal hair-splitting common to appellate courts in criminal cases at that time), the higher court overturned Harbolt's conviction and ordered a retrial.

What was the fatal flaw in Blake's conviction? In furtherance of Blake's alibi defense, he called a number of live witnesses from Oklahoma Territory to testify that he was elsewhere at the time of the shooting. In addition, he had taken pretrial depositions (via written interrogations) of three of his buddies to be introduced into evidence at the trial. The three defense witnesses included "D" County attorney George Sexton, Lenora rancher Jim Riley, and Taloga saloon keeper M. K. McFadden. However, during the trial, the prosecution objected to the admission of these depositions into evidence because the state contended that there was a technical defect in the taking of the depositions. The trial court ruled for the state and excluded the defense depositions.

The appellate court agreed with the prosecution that there was a defect in the taking of these depositions, but it held that the trial court erred in granting the prosecution's motion to exclude the defense's depositions because the state had not raised its objections in a *timely* manner. The appellate court held, in effect, that the state had unfairly "laid behind the log" and thus ambushed the defense by waiting until the day of trial to make its objection. Therefore the case was reversed and a retrial ordered.

Both cases were retried and achieved identical results: not guilty. Harbolt was acquitted August 14, 1897; Joe Blake, February 25, 1898. Why? By what strange alchemy did the defense transform the dross of defeat into the gold of victory? How did the prosecution manage to lose what appeared to be two easy convictions? How could any jury fail to give due credence to the eyewitness testimony of a host of disinterested witnesses who saw the defendants riding into town, drinking at Paul Hoefler's saloon, and then arriving at the depot moments before the shootout? How could they ignore identifications made by the depot agent? Ignore the dying sheriff's statement? Ignore Cap Arrington's testimony? Ignore the corroborated testimony of Dan McKenzie and his wife? Ignore the damning incrimination in Joe Blake's own handwritten letters?

The defense had obviously beefed up its "alibi" defense considerably. The written interrogatories that the defense submitted to several key Oklahoma Territory alibi witnesses give us a clue.

In modern practice, if testimony is needed from a witness who, for whatever reason, cannot be present in person at the trial, it is customary for the two opposing attorneys to meet with the witness and take an oral deposition. Through this practice, both lawyers have the opportunity to examine and cross-examine the witness at length. However, in the 1890s, when transportation was primitive, expensive, and slow, the testimony of out-of-state witnesses in criminal cases was frequently introduced as answers to written interrogatories. The party proposing to take the out-of-state deposition would submit a written list of proposed questions for the witness. Then the opposing attorney would add his list of "cross-interrogatories." At that point, both sets of questions were forwarded to an official such as a notary public in the witness's hometown. The witness's answers would be recorded under oath, and the complete written deposition would be returned to the trial court and read to the jury.

This procedure tilted the scales heavily in favor of the party seeking to take the witness's testimony. Ordinarily, the witness was favorable to the party initiating the procedure and would attempt to be as helpful as possible. Then, the opposing party's cross-interrogatories could be fairly easily dodged or evaded. Incomplete answers and flat-out lies were common—and the witness could get away with it. The opposing attorney was not present when the answers were taken, and even if he was present he could not pursue the point and pin the witness down through further examination of the witness's information, opinions, motives, or past relation with the defendant because he was limited to the prior *written* questions he had propounded to the witness. The lawyer could not clarify vague, incomplete, or evasive answers. Not to mention it was almost impossible to check the witness's past, including his criminal history, so he could portray himself just about any way he wished.

W. B. Plemons, representing Jim Harbolt, and Lorenzo Dow Miller, representing Joe Blake, took full advantage of this written interrogatory device. Obviously, neither was anxious to dwell on the background of their Oklahoma Territory alibi witnesses, on the potentially embarrassing details of the proffered alibi, or on why their memories were extremely selective in certain points of the testimony. Some of the prosecution's cross-interrogatories speak volumes, as the questions themselves were often more likely to shed light on a witness's true character or past history than the answers (since, after all, the witness could answer however he wanted). For example, the prosecution inquired about the witnesses's prior criminal history, where the witness resided before coming to Oklahoma Territory, what name the witness used in his prior residence, why he left that state, and whether law enforcement officials there were aware of the witness's present name and location? Was the witness a member of the Oklahoma Territory "Horse Thief Association?" Not surprisingly, the defense witnesses managed, without much effort, to either flatly deny prosecution assertions or to dance around any embarrassing questions. We can assume with reasonable assurance that the defense had a helpful representative present when their witnesses were answering these questions. One of the key defense witnesses, however, did make a refreshingly candid remark. When asked on cross-examination to recite all of the crimes with which he had been charged, George Sexton, himself an Oklahoma Territory attorney, admitted he had been tried and acquitted for murder back in Missouri, and "As to misdemeaners [sic], I can't give a fourth of them. Have been tried for gambling. I have been tried for contempt of court and plain drunks [sic]." However, Sexton continued, even though he had "been repeatedly charged with misdemeaners [sic]," he had contested them all "and beat every case." All of the defense witnesses, however, denied any serious wrongdoing or membership in, or knowledge of, any Horse Thief Association. Each went on to proclaim themselves to be 100 percent in favor of "law and order."

Both Plemons and Miller journeyed to the Taloga community and, in preparation for the retrial of Jim Harbolt and Joe Blake, cultivated more impressive alibi witnesses. In addition to the usual platoon of ordinary Oklahoma Territory witnesses, they enlisted John Shumate, a former deputy U.S. Marshal, as a member of the alibi team. Three other high-profile alibi witnesses included "D" County, Oklahoma Territory, officials Bert Sexton (deputy sheriff), his father, George Sexton (county attorney and witness who couldn't remember "a fourth" of the "misdemeaner" criminal charges lodged against him), and O. L. McClung (probate judge). Recall that John Shumate and Bert Sexton had been indicted by the Hardeman County, Texas, district court for committing perjury in the George Isaacs trial. Years later, Charles Cary, a pioneer Dewey County homesteader, teacher, and eventual Taloga attorney, recalled that the Sextons (George and Bert) and the Shumates (brothers Will and John) "were hand in glove with the outlaws."[38] In any event, deputy Bert Sexton, county attorney George Sexton, and Judge McClung all testified they saw Jim Harbolt, Joe Blake, and Dan McKenzie (contrary to the latter's testimony) in Taloga on November 22, 1894, the day before Sheriff McGee was murdered. If that was true, then it would have been impossible for them to have ridden horseback ninety miles or more to Canadian, Texas, in time to murder Sheriff McGee.

They all clearly remembered this date, they testified, because it was the day that a theft case was being tried in the "D" County Probate Court, presided over by Judge McClung. And, they claimed, county attorney George Sexton prosecuted the case while George Sexton's son, deputy sheriff Bert Sexton, was acting as the bailiff. They referred to (although did not produce) "D" County Probate Court records to verify their claims.

The probate court docket entries do purport to show that Lew Herring and William Kopp were tried on November 22, 1894, in Taloga for the theft of barbed wire and timbers valued at ten dollars.[39] However, these same court records, so heavily relied upon by the defense, made a liar out of county attorney George Sexton. He testified in both the Blake and Harbolt murder trials that *he* prosecuted the wire theft case. But the docket entries plainly state that George Sexton did *not* prosecute the case, that in his absence the court appointed a substitute counsel to prosecute the case. The substitute lawyer was none other than editor/lawyer and outlaw-friendly Grant Pettyjohn—the same Grant Pettyjohn who had been indicted for suborning perjury during the George Isaacs trial. The records caught George Sexton in yet another lie. He testified in the Jim Harbolt murder trial that Harbolt appeared as a witness in the wire theft case in Taloga. The docket book lists all witnesses appearing for both the Territory and the defense, and Jim Harbolt's name does not appear on either list. Neither do Joe Blake or Dan McKenzie.

Furthermore, the prosecution contended that these official records had been altered, that the trial actually occurred on December 22, 1894. Of course, all three alibi witnesses stoutly denied that the books were cooked. Even if the records were correct, had the prosecution produced them they would have clearly discredited George Sexton's testimony and cast serious doubt on the testimony of the other alibi witnesses. Unfortunately, the prosecutors, apparently overconfident as a result of their initial victories, failed to send anyone up to Taloga to actually review the probate court records. Since the key alibi witnesses escaped impeachment, the jury must have believed this array of "D" County officialdom, or, at least, the added weight of these "official" alibi witnesses caused the jury to have a "reasonable doubt" as to the guilt of the defendants. Joe Blake and Jim Harbolt walked.

Perjury was common, and liars came cheap in the Oklahoma Territory. U.S. marshal E. D. Nix was fired by the U.S. attorney general when, in 1896, it was discovered that he was more than one hundred thousand dollars short in his accounts. A federal inspector was sent to investigate, and his report asserted that Nix had indeed defrauded the government out of large sums of money, had committed perjury during the investigation, had offered bribes to investigators, had solicited illegal kickbacks from government contractors, had overcharged the government by filing fictitious deputy vouchers, and had set up false bank accounts to hide his chicanery. Nix was removed from his post in Oklahoma Territory as a result of the investigation, but the federal investigator recommended that criminal charges not be pursued even though overwhelming proof of guilt was available. It would not be practical to do so, he concluded, explaining, "testimony in Oklahoma is cheap, many of the witnesses likely to be of service to the government are tainted or have already been impeached in prosecutions for perjury involving almost every land claim in the Territory . . . conditions existing in Oklahoma are different and more extreme than those existing in any other district of the United States."[40]

Before turning to the next episode, we should pause to look at the roles of George Isaacs's brothers Sam and Bill. Although brother John apparently took no active interest in George's plight, Sam and Bill were active in the defense of not only George but also Joe Blake and Jim Harbolt. The newspaper reports and the trial records pertaining to Bill and Sam Isaacs reveal four important facts:

1. Bill Isaacs testified for the defense in both the Jim Harbolt and Joe Blake murder trials. He testified that his brother George lived near Chickasha, Indian Territory, at the time of the trials and that he hadn't seen him for eleven years before the crime. Yet, upon cross-examination Bill admitted that he was in Kansas City the same day that George deposited the five bogus money packages with Wells Fargo in that city. The Kansas City Wells Fargo clerk testified that while George was going through the process of sending the bogus money packets someone else lurked in the background, but the clerk could not identify him. Bill Isaacs denied on cross-examination that it was he. Bill also testified that he didn't return to Canadian from Kansas City until three or four days after the murder.[41]

2. The Canadian, Texas, depot agent, A. B. Harding, testified that on the morning after Sheriff McGee was killed in the failed robbery attempt, George and Sam Isaacs showed up at the Wells Fargo office and claimed the five bogus money packets, which were released to them unopened.[42] Sam and George then took them to J. A. Chambers's store and put them in his safe.

3. Bill and Sam Isaacs made bond for George's co-conspirator, Jim Harbolt (who the prosecution believed actually killed Sheriff McGee). Undoubtedly, Bill and Sam Isaacs soon regretted this move—Harbolt promptly skipped bail, and the state obtained a forfeiture judgment against Bill and Sam Isaacs on Harbolt's bond. The brothers appealed and, with the help of W. B. Plemons, were ultimately successful in getting the bond forfeiture judgment overturned on a technicality.[43] Some months later Harbolt was recaptured and forced to stand trial.

4. When George Isaacs and his erstwhile pals Joe Blake and Jim Harbolt were finally put to trial (separately), they each were defended by a platoon of defense attorneys including the foremost criminal defense attorneys of the day. Certainly "poor man" George could not have afforded all of those lawyers. And it is reasonable to assume that neither Blake nor Harbolt, both penny-ante outlaws, had any significant fortune with which to bankroll such an impressive array of legal talent. Given that, plus the fact that Bill and Sam Isaacs went on Blake's and Harbolt's surety bonds, it seems probable that Sam and Bill financed not only George's defense but also the defenses of Joe Blake and Jim Harbolt. Also, the Amarillo law firm of Plemons and Veale defended both George Isaacs and Jim Harbolt. As the Quanah newspaper observed, George "had two rich brothers who spared no money in getting him clear."

While family bonds may have accounted for the generosity of Bill and Sam Isaacs in mounting an expensive defense for George, it begs the question: why were they so supportive of Joe Blake and Jim Harbolt? Also, why did Bill appear as a witness for both Blake and Harbolt—*after* George had already been tried and convicted? Three final questions arise: If, as it appears, Bill Doolin (contrary to George Isaacs's testimony) was *not* the leader of the gang of four who attempted to carry out the robbery; and if, as it appears, the gang of four consisted of Jim Harbolt, Joe Blake, Will "Tulsa Jack" Blake, and Jim Stanley (with Dan McKenzie and Bitter Creek Newcomb as accessories); and if, as it appears without much doubt, "Jim Stanley" was a fictitious name—then who was the mastermind of the whole scheme? And who led the gang of four who killed Sheriff McGee in the robbery attempt? And who *was* the fourth member of that gang, the mysterious "Jim Stanley?"

Some, at least tentative, answers may be found by examining what had been happening at the same time in Oklahoma Territory.

The Fred Hoffman Murder

While the attempted robbery, the murder, and the trials were playing out in Texas, a related series of events unreeled in Oklahoma Territory. Canadian, Texas, where Sheriff McGee was murdered, is located on the south bank of the South Canadian River. Approximately ninety miles east of Canadian, and also perched on the south bank of the same river, is the village of Taloga. In 1894 Taloga was located in what was formerly the Cheyenne-Arapaho Indian Reservation in Oklahoma Territory. The area had been opened to settlement on April 19, 1892, and "D" County was established with Taloga as the county seat.[44] Oklahoma was granted statehood in 1907, and "D" County became Dewey County. Years later, George E. Black, the "D" County attorney from 1897 to 1898, would look back on this era and recall, "Outlawry was rampant. . . . About all of [the outlaws] operating during the period from 1885 to 1901 came through Dewey County or lived here."[45]

During that time frame, "D" County was the perfect sanctuary for outlaws: sparsely populated, no law enforcement to speak of, remote, miles of rivers, deep canyons, and dense blackjack forests. These features concealed plenty of characters in dire need of concealment—characters who tended to change their names with each phase of the moon. The outlaws had yet another valuable concealment resource, as explained by western history author Homer Croy in an article entitled, "Where the Outlaws Hid":

> One reason the Oklahoma outlaws were so hard to bring to their knees was the multitude of hiding places in which they could tuck themselves away for weeks at a time. . . . The owners of many ranches welcomed the saddle boys. In fact, some of the owners were

just a step above being outlaws themselves. . . . There [also] the outlaws got fresh horses and supplies. Sometimes the owners shared in
the loot; mostly they didn't share, but were afraid to openly oppose
their "visitors." . . . On occasion as many as five outlaws would be living at a harboring place. They would sleep in the house when they
thought it was safe; when they thought it was dangerous . . . they
would hide [nearby] where they had fortified huts . . . most of the
dugouts were well concealed and well equipped. . . . They not only
posted their own lookouts but also had friends who would rush word
that officers were in the neighborhood.[46]

All of the Dalton gang, and later the Bill Doolin gang, as well as a mul-
titude of lesser miscreants, called "D" County home or a temporary
refuge.

When the Cheyenne-Arapaho Reservation was opened for settlement
in 1892, honest and law-respecting citizens began to move into the
county and stake their claims in this productive land. Although most of
the newcomers did not support the outlaws, their dark and menacing
presence was both pervasive and intimidating. Few settlers dared to
speak up too forcefully for law and order or to point fingers at surly and
well-armed neighbors who made their living outside of the law.

One citizen who did openly stand up for the law was Fred Hoffman.
A German immigrant, young Hoffman volunteered to serve in the U.S.
calvary and was soon promoted to the rank of sergeant. He was stationed
in Oklahoma Territory at Camp Supply and Fort Reno, where he met
and fell in love with a beautiful Cheyenne named Crooked Woman Redeye. She first attended school at the Darlington Agency and later at
Carlisle Institute in Pennsylvania. When Hoffman met her she was
serving as an interpreter for U.S. officials at the Darlington Agency.[47]
The couple married on March 27, 1890, and she became known as Florence Redeye Hoffman. Soon thereafter, Florence obtained a 160-acre
allotment of land on the Cheyenne-Arapaho Reservation about four
miles west of Taloga, and when Fred's enlistment was up, he and Florence moved there and settled in—settled, as it turned out, in a neighborhood where support for law and order was considerably less than
robust.

Fred Hoffman, a U.S. commissioner and county treasurer of "D" County, Oklahoma Territory, was ambushed and murdered near Taloga on January 22, 1895. The murder was intended to stifle his investigation of a Wells Fargo heist of a U.S. Army payroll in March 1894 at Woodward, Oklahoma Territory, and the attempted Wells Fargo robbery and murder of sheriff Tom T. McGee in Canadian, Texas, on November 23, 1894. The picture is from about 1887 during Hoffman's time as a U.S. Army cavalry sergeant stationed at Camp Supply and Fort Reno. (Courtesy of Robert E. King, Seiling, Oklahoma.)

Crooked Woman Redeye, a full-blooded Cheyenne, became known as Florence Redeye Hoffman after she married Fred Hoffman in 1890. A graduate of Carlisle Institute in Pennsylvania, she was an interpreter for U.S. government officials at the Darlington Agency in the Oklahoma Territory when she met her future husband. (Courtesy of Robert E. King, Seiling, Oklahoma.)

"Little Bill" Raidler was one of Bill Doolin's regular gang members in the early 1890s and was a next-door neighbor of Fred and Florence Hoffman. Raidler's claim was located about a mile west of the Hoffman homestead near Lenora in "D" County, Oklahoma Territory.
(From *West of Hell's Fringe: Crime, Criminals, and the Federal Peace Officer in Oklahoma Territory, 1889–1907*, by Glenn Shirley, Oklahoma University Press, 1978.)

Known outlaws and outlaw sympathizers living within a stone's throw of the Hoffman claim in "D" County[48] included Dan McKenzie; the infamous Blake brothers, including known Doolin outlaws Will "Tulsa Jack" Blake, his half brother Charlie Pierce, Sam Blake, and Joe Blake; Doolinite William F. "Little Bill" Raidler; Jim Harbolt; Nannie Wray, who extended hospitality to her son-in-law, the renegade Texas sheriff Joe Beckham; Levi Moors Smith, who harbored the boyfriend of his daughter and notorious Doolin rider, George "Red Buck" Weightman; E. C. Kinney, who was married to Bill Doolin's sister; Jim Riley, who employed Joe Blake and Doolin rider Roy Daugherty (aka "Arkansas Tom" Jones) and who harbored and horsed other Doolin members from time to time; and Alfred Son, who was either a fringe member or an associate of the Doolin gang. Alfred Son's older brother, who went under the alias of "Lee Moore," was foreman of the Amos Chapman ranch, and he, like his friend Jim Riley, often harbored Doolin members. According to county attorney George Black, other known outlaw sympathizers living in "D" County at the time included Dutch

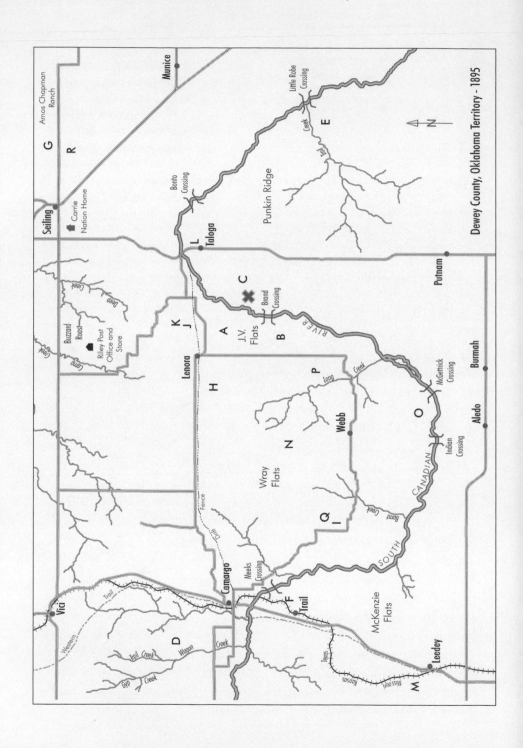

Dewey County, Oklahoma Territory - 1895

On the morning of January 22, 1895, Fred Hoffman mounted his horse and left home just southeast of Lenora **(A)** en route to his office at Taloga. He rode south for a short distance and then crossed the South Canadian River at the Brand Crossing **(B)** and turned north on the river road heading for Taloga. He was ambushed and killed shortly thereafter at **X**, which was only a short distance from a well-known hideout of the Dalton and Doolin gangs **(C)**. Dewey County's rough terrain, remoteness, and lack of law enforcement made it a favorite haven for outlaws in the late 1800s. Many of Hoffman's neighbors were known outlaws and outlaw sympathizers. Their homes and hideouts are indicated here and in the map with corresponding letters. Blake brothers Will "Tulsa Jack", Joe, Sam, and half-brother Charlie Pierce **(D)**; Jim Harbolt **(E)**; Dan McKenzie **(F)**; Alfred Son **(G)**; William F. "Little Bill" Raidler **(H)**; Joe Beckham **(I)**; Roy Daughtery, aka "Arkansas Tom" Jones **(J)**; and Big Jim Riley **(K)**; Brothers Bill, John, and Charlie Edwards **(M)**; Dutch Anderson **(N)**; Levi Moors Smith **(O)**; E. C. Kinney, married to Bill Doolin's sister **(P)**; Nannie Wray, Joe Beckham's mother-in-law **(Q)**; and Lee Son, aka Lee Moore, brother of Alfred Son, cousin of Bailey Son, and son-in-law of Amos Chapman **(R)**. Taloga residents or regular visitors of the town included newspaper editor and lawyer Grant Pettyjohn, Probate Court Judge O. L. McClung, County attorney George Sexton, deputy sheriff Bert Sexton, saloon owner M. K. McFadden, Charlie Smith, George "Red Buck" Weightman, brothers Will and John Shumate, and Bailey Son, cousin of Alfred Son and Lee Moore. Note the routes of the Western (Texas) Cattle Trail and the M-K-T Railroad (formerly the W.F. & N.W. Railroad) traversing the county from north to south along the western edge. Although a number of "D" County towns are depicted on the map, the only established towns in 1895 were Taloga, Lenora, (old) Camargo, and the Riley post office and store. The north boundary line of "D" County prior to 1892 was the south boundary of the Cherokee Strip and the north boundary of the Cheyenne-Arapaho Indian Reservation.

(The above map and data were compiled by the author from maps, location designations, and historical information provided by the Dewey County Historical Society and Dewey County historians Robert E. King and Patsy Smart.)

Anderson, John Brooks, and the Edwards brothers—Bill, John and Charlie.[49] In the town of Taloga, known outlaws with sizeable bounties on their heads casually strolled the streets and frequented the McFadden Saloon, a favorite outlaw watering hole owned by M. K. McFadden. Taloga was the home of outlaw sympathizers Grant Pettyjohn, editor of the *Taloga Tomahawk*; County probate judge O. L. McClung; county attorney George Sexton; deputy sheriff Bert Sexton, and brothers Will and John Shumate. Many of these outlaws, sympathizers, and town leaders were involved in the McGee murder trials—either on trial themselves or as alibi witnesses for the defendants.

Historian Croy listed three outlaw-friendly sites that figure prominently in this tale:

1. Jim Riley's Ranch . . . Riley was a water-carrier; he tried to keep on good terms with both law and outlaw, a difficult balancing feat.
2. Amos Chapman's, where the town of Seiling is now located. Chapman had a wooden leg and was a squaw man. Sometimes he was a deputy upholding the law; sometimes he wasn't. Anyway, he was one of Oklahoma's early picturesque characters.
3. George Isaacs's on the north side of the Washita River, four miles from Chickasha, Indian Territory. Timber came close to the ranch house; if the outlaws were disturbed they would rush into the timber, where no officer would be foolhardy enough to follow.

Fred Hoffman, however, was not intimidated by the outlaw ambience. As industrious as he was honest, Hoffman managed to get himself elected as the first treasurer of the newly formed "D" County, and he also wrangled an appointment as a U.S. commissioner. Plus, he managed a hardware store in Taloga. As time passed, anti-Hoffman sentiment among the outlaw faction spread and grew more vindictive. Grant Pettyjohn regularly peppered him with snide remarks in the *Tomahawk*.[50]

Undeterred, Hoffman took on yet another task. Wells Fargo secretly hired him to investigate two unsolved Wells Fargo heists: the botched Canadian, Texas, attempt and an earlier, successful robbery of the Wells Fargo office at Woodward, Oklahoma Territory. At about 1:00 in the morning of March 13, 1894, two bandits had awakened George W. Rouke, the Woodward Wells Fargo agent, and marched him from his hotel room to the express office where they forced him to unlock the safe and surrender its contents, which included between six and nine thousand dollars in army payroll cash destined for Fort Supply. Nearby hoofprints indicated that six additional riders joined the pair a short distance from the robbery site. Two posses were soon afield, but the trail was lost in the rough canyons and gulches.[51] The modus operandi in both cases was similar: the outlaws waited until the loot had been delivered to a Wells Fargo office before making an appearance, and they obviously had advance notice of sizeable cash shipments. The Bill Doolin gang—or at least some members thereof—topped the list of suspects in both cases.

Fred Hoffman's investigation quickly led to results. Sometime in mid-January 1895, Hoffman told Wells Fargo officials T. M. Cook and Thomas Smith that he was directing his efforts toward eighteen-year-old Alfred Son and his "near relatives." Alfred Son (also referred to as "Al Sohn" and "Alford" Son) had only two "near relatives" in the area at that time: his cousin Bailey Son, who hung out with hardcases around Taloga, and his older brother, Lee Moore, who, for reasons of his own, had unofficially changed his name before showing up in "D" County.[52] Lee Moore, ranch foreman for the famed army Indian scout Amos Chapman, was not, by any stretch, a supporter of law enforcement. He was one of the Oklahoma Territory witnesses who testified for the defendants in the McGee murder trials, and the Chapman Ranch was one of the Doolin gang's favorite retreats. In fact, Moore even had a cabin (still standing to this day) moved onto a remote part of the Chapman Ranch on the North Canadian River about three miles east of Seiling for the sole purpose of hosting outlaws on the dodge.[53] Young Alfred Son worked as a cowboy on the Chapman Ranch for his older brother, and he also took up with the outlaw element.[54]

Hoffman might have zeroed in on Alfred Son, believing that if the naive young cowboy was not directly involved in either robbery, he more than likely knew who the guilty parties were. Hoffman figured that if Alfred was pressured, he might confess his role, if any, or at least implicate the guilty parties. As further events demonstrated, however, his was an ill-conceived strategy—young Alfred Son was much more afraid of the outlaws than the law.

On the morning of January 22, 1895 (just two months after the attempted Canadian heist and the murder of Sheriff McGee), Hoffman mounted his horse at his homestead about a mile southeast of Lenora and headed for his office at Taloga. He rode a short distance south, crossed the Canadian River at the Brand Crossing, and turned north

A celebrated Indian scout for the U.S. Army during the late 1800s, Amos Chapman acquired a sizeable ranch in northeast "D" County, Oklahoma Territory, near the town of Seiling. His ranch foreman and later son-in-law went under the alias "Lee Moore." His real name was Lee Son, and he was a brother of Alfred Son and cousin of Bailey Son. Lee Moore reportedly paid Doolin gang member George "Red Buck" Weightman $500 to assassinate Fred Hoffman. (Courtesy of the Dewey County Historical Society.)

along the river road leading to Taloga. Shortly thereafter he was ambushed. The outlaws first shot him through the heart, and then they shot him again in the mouth. The latter shot was fired at such close range it left powder burns. For good measure, they also shot and killed Fred's horse. Both bodies were discovered several days later in a sandy "blowhole" near the river bank. The killing site was only a few hundred yards from a well-known Dalton-Doolin outlaw hideout—a dugout in the rugged hills a short distance east of the river and about four miles southwest of Taloga.

On April 23, 1895, the "D" County grand jury jointly indicted Alfred Son, Bailey Son, Dick Yeager (alias Zip Wyatt), Dan McKenzie, and Grant Pettyjohn for the murder of Fred Hoffman.[55] Because the evidence against Alfred Son was the most damning, his case was severed from the others and transferred to the Oklahoma Territory District Court in El Reno.[56]

According to trial testimony,[57] officers at the crime scene observed the tracks of a team and buggy leaving the river road and stopping at

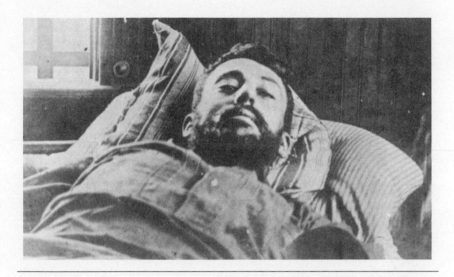

Zip Wyatt's real name was Nelson Elsworth Wyatt, but this Bill Doolin gang member went under several aliases including "Dick Yeager," and "Wild Charlie." He was indicted for the assassination of Fred Hoffman, but shortly thereafter he himself was killed. This photo was taken as Zip lay dying in the Enid jail.
(From *West of Hell's Fringe: Crime, Criminals, and the Federal Peace Officer in Oklahoma Territory, 1889–1907,* by Glenn Shirley, Oklahoma University Press, 1978.)

the rim of the sandy blowhole where the bodies of Hoffman and his horse were found. Footprints indicated that two people had gotten out of the buggy and walked over to Hoffman's body and then returned to the buggy, which they drove back to the roadway. One of the sets of footprints leading up to the body was particularly distinct: the footprints were very small and made by a peculiar, sharp-heeled pair of boots. Also, about one hundred feet south of where the buggy stood, the officers discovered the tracks of two more persons leading into and then out of a blowhole created by wind and erosion along the shoreline.

By fortuitous happenstance, R. Burkhart, a homesteader, and his wife were repairing a fence approximately half a mile away at the time of the shooting. They testified that just before the shooting, they had seen Hoffman ford the South Canadian River on his horse at the Brand Crossing and then turn north toward Taloga. They also saw a buggy come down the road from the opposite direction. About the time the parties met, they heard shots. Although they did not see the buggy again, they did see "a party on a gray horse" riding away from the shooting scene and going toward the river crossing that Hoffman had just forded. They were not close enough to identify the rider, however.

Other circumstantial evidence presented at the trial linked Son to the shooting. A few hours before Hoffman was killed, Alfred Son and "Bert Collins" were seen together in a Taloga saloon. Son became very drunk and shot his revolver into the air. He later bought a box of cartridges for his pistol. Afterward he and Bert Collins went to a livery stable where Son rented two horses and a single-seated buggy. He was so drunk, however, that the stable man attempted to take the buggy and horses back, and he would have done so if Bert Collins had not intervened and assured him that he would make sure the team and buggy were properly cared for. Bert Collins was armed with a revolver and a Winchester rifle. The pair got in the buggy and left, leading a gray horse. They were observed heading southwest along the same river road that Hoffman was traveling toward Taloga. Hoffman was killed at about the time he would have encountered Son and Bert Collins on the same road, assuming that the two groups traveled at a normal pace. Moreover, the homesteader and his wife both identified the buggy that they saw on the day of the murder as the same buggy the livery stable owner testified he had rented to Alfred Son and Bert Collins. Still worse, when deputy U.S. marshal Chris Madsen arrested Alfred Son he was wearing extra-small, sharp-heeled boots that perfectly matched the tracks observed near Hoffman's body. After the killing, Bert Collins disappeared.

Given the formidable evidence against Son, it was obvious he needed the services of a good trial lawyer. Actually, he needed a *great* trial lawyer to extricate himself from the bull-stout strands of circumstantial evidence binding him to the murder. The community outrage was palpable; after all, the victim was not a Texas sheriff but one of their own.

Alfred Son succeeded in getting a great lawyer. He got the best and the most eloquent, the most overpowering, and the most brilliant criminal defense attorney in the whole southwest: Temple Houston, youngest son of Texas hero Sam Houston. Temple Houston was a rounder, and a rake to boot. But no one could deny that, in addition to his glib tongue,

Temple Lea Houston, the gun-totin', Bible-quotin' premier defense attorney in the turn-of-the-century Texas Panhandle and western Oklahoma Territory. Sam Houston's youngest son was as eloquent as he was eccentric—and always innovative. This picture was taken when he was a senator in the Texas State Legislature, 1884–1888. He successfully defended Alfred Son, accused of the murder of U.S. commissioner Fred Hoffman.
(From *Temple Houston: Lawyer With a Gun,* by Glenn Shirley, Oklahoma University Press, 1980.)

Temple Houston had quite an eccentric side. Before a jury he was a spellbinder without equal, liberally seasoning his arguments with quotations from classical literature and the Bible. He cut a dashing figure in court. Standing six feet plus two inches tall, he was slender and had gray eyes and auburn hair that flowed in curling locks down to his shoulders, all of which was accentuated by his flamboyant attire. Typically he would appear in an extra long ("Prince Albert") frock coat, black cravat, yellow-beaded vest, Spanish-style, satin-striped trousers cut with a bell flare at the bottom, and boots of the finest leather. Plus, both in and out of court, he was never without "Old Betsy," his pearl-handled .45 pistol. "Old Betsy" was not just for show. Houston gained considerable renown as a crack pistol and rifle marksman.

With his famous Houston name and native brilliance, charisma, and eloquence . . . well, politically speaking, the sky would have been the limit in Austin or Washington. But Temple Houston was not about to languish in the afterglow of Sam Houston's glory.

A man is only what he makes of himself. If a lion, he can fight his own battles; if a weakling, no rumor of distinguished lineage can make him strong. . . . I care not to stand in the light of reflected glory. Every tub must stand on its own bottom.[58]

Moreover, Washington and Austin were way too civilized to suit Temple Houston; he craved the freedom, excitement, and adventure of the untamed wilderness. And frontier folks took to Temple as much as Temple took to the frontier. When folks heard that "Old Sam's boy" was trying a case, they congregated from miles around to witness the show. The ever-inventive Temple Houston, in addition to his much-celebrated eloquence, usually had a dramatic trick or two up his sleeve.[59]

How did a lowly young cow puncher manage to acquire the services of such a high-powered legal talent? Perhaps his brother, Lee Moore? Amos Chapman? Jim Riley? Bill or Sam Isaacs? Or maybe this was not the case at all. Houston marched to the beat of a different drummer, and he often took cases for reasons other than financial. In a eulogy for Temple upon his untimely passing at age forty-five in 1905, fellow lawyer H. E. Hoover made these remarks:

He was a friend to and admirer of children, horses, dogs, the outcast, the unfortunate, the underdog, the one in trouble who had need of his sympathy and support. . . . His rough, sympathetic nature naturally inclined him to the defense rather than the prosecution. . . . He often had to reject a good fee to devote his time and his efforts in defense of some unfortunate outcast from whom he expected and received no compensation.[60]

Perhaps the terrible plight of young Alfred Son caught Temple Houston's fancy; perhaps he was lured by the challenge of a near hopeless case, enhanced by its inevitable hoopla and publicity.

The Alfred Son Trial

For whatever reason, Houston undertook the defense of Alfred Son. His defense was based on "coincidence" and "lack of motive." It was just a

The McFadden Saloon in Taloga, Oklahoma Territory, was a favorite hangout of outlaws in the 1890s. In this photo Temple Houston (*third from left*) is accompanied by
unidentified associates in front of the infamous watering hole.
(Courtesy of the Western History Collections, University of Oklahoma.)

coincidence that Alfred Son happened to be in the vicinity of the killing
when Hoffman was murdered by an unknown party—a murder with no
eyewitnesses. Actually, Houston contended, Alfred Son was on a completely innocent errand at the time; he was traveling from Taloga to
Lenora to retrieve his girlfriend, Minnie Shanholster, and return her to
her home in Taloga. Houston produced a note from the young lady
addressed to Son requesting that he come to Lenora and take her home,
and so, according to Houston, he had rented the buggy on that fateful
day to comply with her request. Besides, Houston pointed out, Alfred
Son had no motive to kill Hoffman. The state's case relied heavily on the
small, sharp-heeled bootprints observed at the scene of the killing that
perfectly matched the boots Alfred Son was wearing when he was
arrested.

This was the gist of the first Alfred Son trial. Son barely dodged the
bullet when the jury hung up at eleven to one for conviction.[61] The juror
who held out for acquittal the required seventy-two hours, which led to

a mistrial, left the courthouse bruised and bandaged, having apparently endured considerable punishment at the hands of his fellow jurors. Straightaway after the trial, he mounted up and departed, never to be heard from again in those parts.[62] A question was thus left a-dangling: did the holdout endure such punishment because of his extraordinarily steadfast conviction of conscience, or was he bought and paid for by the outlaws and knew beyond the shadow of a doubt that a much worse fate awaited him if he reneged on his Faustian bargain?

Meanwhile, Son confided to Houston that "Bert Collins" was the actual killer and that "Collins" was really Red Buck Weightman, but for him to publicly finger Weightman, a notorious killer, would be a serious error in judgment. As Son put it to Houston, he would rather "take the rap than be six feet under."[63] county attorney Black recalled Red Buck as "the basest and most cruel outlaw to infest that area,"[64] and his rate as a killer-for-hire was well known: fifty dollars per man, cash up front, and no questions asked.[65] The event that followed lends credence to Alfred Son's remark. According to Houston, a message from the infamous outlaw himself directed Houston to meet Red Buck alone and unarmed at night at a designated spot near Seiling, Oklahoma Territory. Houston kept that appointment, and sure enough, standing in the moonlight with a Winchester leveled at Houston, was Red Buck Weightman, the auburn-haired, mustached, cold-eyed, gray-horse bandit. He told Houston that he had killed Hoffman and that he "didn't want another man taking credit for my crime."[66]

However noble that sentiment might have sounded, though belatedly expressed, his conviction was apparently not rooted deeply enough for Red Buck to come forward publicly and take the blame and save Alfred Son. Still, was Red Buck's message really about him taking credit for the kill, or was it, more believably, a threat: "Don't implicate me—or else!" Houston assured him that this business was only to defend the innocent boy and not to point the finger of guilt at any other identified suspect, and Red Buck simply faded back into the darkness.

Houston kept the outlaw's confidence. He did not mention the rendezvous with Weightman until after Red Buck was killed in a March 1896 shootout at his hideout near Canute in Custer County, Oklahoma Territory, by a posse led by deputy U.S. marshal Joe Ventioner.[67] In fact,

George "Red Buck" Weightman, shortly after having been killed in a shootout with Oklahoma Territory officers in March 1896. The worst of Bill Doolin's gang and a "stone killer," Red Buck confessed to Temple Houston that he killed district U.S. commissioner Fred Hoffman when Hoffman's investigation of the Wells Fargo debacle in Canadian, Texas, began to focus on himself and his accomplice, Alfred Son. (From *West of Hell's Fringe: Crime, Criminals, and the Federal Peace Officer in Oklahoma Territory, 1889–1907*, by Glenn Shirley, Oklahoma University Press, 1978.)

before Alfred Son's second trial began in December 1896, the entire Bill Doolin gang had been decimated, the climax of which was the ambush killing of Bill Doolin himself near Ingalls, Oklahoma Territory, on August 25, 1896.

In December 1896 Judge John C. Tarsney presided over Alfred Son's second murder trial at El Reno. The circumstantial evidence case against Son was even more damning this time. In addition to the evidence revealed during the first trial, the prosecution, over Houston's strenuous objections, was permitted to put the two Wells Fargo officials, T. M. Cook and Thomas Smith, on the stand, and let them testify that just prior to Hoffman's murder, Hoffman had been employed by Wells Fargo to investigate the attempted robberies at Canadian and Woodward. And again, over Houston's objection, Cook and Smith were allowed to tell the jury that Hoffman had told them his investigation was focusing on the defendant, Alfred Son, and his "near relatives." The Wells Fargo witnesses admitted on cross-examination by Houston that few knew that Hoffman was engaged in this investigation, and that Hoffman's investigation and its focus had *never*, to their knowledge, been communicated to Alfred Son. The prosecution's purpose in introducing this hearsay evidence (about Hoffman focusing his investigation on the defendant Son or his relatives) was to demonstrate a motive for Son to kill Hoffman.

The impact of this evidence (when combined with all the other circumstantial evidence tying Son to the crime) was devastating, and the second jury had little difficulty finding young Alfred Son guilty. His punishment was fixed at life imprisonment, and he was sent to the nearest prison, in Kansas. Houston appealed to the Oklahoma Territory Supreme Court, and his primary point of appeal was that the trial court had erred in admitting Cook's and Smith's testimony. Houston contended that before the prosecution could attempt to prove that Son had a motive to kill Hoffman, they must first show that, prior to the killing, Son had knowledge of Hoffman's pending accusation. Otherwise, if Son didn't know of the investigation, how could it be argued that Son had a motive to kill Hoffman? The effect of this testimony was magnified because it called the jury's attention to the Wells Fargo heists at Canadian and Woodward and the murder of Sheriff McGee (when otherwise both would have been irrelevant and thus inadmissible), plus it implicated Alfred Son in both crimes.

The Oklahoma Supreme Court agreed with Houston's argument and reversed the trial court in June 1897. The case was remanded back to the court for yet another trial.[68] Son was returned from prison in Kansas that August and was released on bond pending his third trial, which was set for the November 1897 term of court in El Reno. The streets of El Reno were jammed, and the courthouse was packed when the Alfred Son murder case was called for trial the third time.

This time, as a result of the appellate court's decision in the second trial, the prosecution was not allowed to introduce the damning evidence of Hoffman's investigation or that Alfred Son was their target suspect. The prosecution was still unable to lay the proper predicate for this evidence because, apparently, it could not provide proof that Alfred Son, prior to the killing, had been informed of Hoffman's potentially incriminating investigation. This omission allowed Houston to run wild in his jury argument, dramatically calling attention to the fact that the terri-

Woodward, Oklahoma Territory, in the early 1890s. Woodward was the site of a Wells Fargo heist when, on the night of March 13, 1984, masked bandits woke up the station agent and relieved him of the U.S. Army's Fort Supply payroll. Fred Hoffman was investigating this crime as well as the attempted Wells Fargo robbery and subsequent murder of sheriff Tom T. McGee at Canadian, Texas, on November 23, 1894, when Hoffman was ambushed and murdered near Taloga, Oklahoma Territory, on January 22, 1895.
(Courtesy of the Western History Collections, University of Oklahoma.)

tory had failed to provide any motive for Alfred Son to kill Fred Hoffman. He held the jury spellbound, and they drank in every word. The following is a sample:

Gentlemen, as I told you in the beginning, the Territory has shown no motive for the commission of such a crime; and we have given you a reasonable—a true—explanation of every act and utterance of the defendant—even for his trip in that fatal direction. He went only to woo-and-win one of the daughters of the land, tender-eyed, fair to look upon, and how like a boy, to take the shortest route to see his sweetheart, and seeing her, take her back by the longest. The life of this boy, up to the instance of his accusation, has been faultless; and do you believe that he took this sudden and awful plunge from innocence into fathomless depths of crime—from childlike purity into hideous murder?

When asked to believe such a supposition, refer to your duties, as given you in His Honor's charge; apply the law as there laid down to the proof, and then follow the dictates of your conscience, and I do not fear the result.

This brave boy asked me to say to you that, to him, honor is dearer than life, and as the old exemplar of purest patriotism thundered in the ears of his country's oppressors, he says in this, his hour of trial, "give me liberty or give me death!" He demands that you free him or inflict the death penalty. Rather than that, you should fix upon his boyish brow the brand of felon, he would prefer to walk from your presence with his body polluted with the scales of whitest leprosy. He appeals to no sentiment of pity; only to the justice of his country's laws, which you are so solemnly charged to administer.

You came into that jury box with light hearts and consciences clear. Oh, may you leave there thus! Untortured with the curse of having wrecked the life of him whose life you hold in the hollow of your hands. And he is so young, too. Boyhood's down still softens upon his childlike face. You will not be here long now. Your homes where loved ones are even now watching, waiting, to greet you, and when you clasp them to your manly breasts may the rapture at that moment be not embittered by the memory of having wrecked the life of yonder boy, whom all law and righteousness plead with you to save.

Gentlemen, be just; heed not the perjured fiends who thirst for this boy's blood, and in the years yet to come, when the pall messenger summons you before the court where you shall be tried alongside the kings of the earth, each memorized hour of life shall come back to you with awful distinctness, then happily can you recall that when you judged here, you judged with justice, and in the very spirit of Him who said: "Even as you did it unto the least of these, so you did it unto me." So that in the perfection of righteousness you tried the stranger within your gates—for he never saw one of you until he fearlessly placed his fate in your hands—even as you would be tried yourselves.

He has a Texas home far across the southern prairies, where the skies are a deeper purple, where the dawn has a brighter glow and the sunset wears a softer gold; where midnight stars look down upon us in a more unspeakable splendor. His loved ones, like yours, are waiting—no! no! not like yours—for his life is darkened even now by the awful shadow of death; and who shall tell what he feels?

Gentleman, break the suspense; dry those tears; bind up these almost broken hearts, for now no power but you can do so. This noble duty done, each hour of your life thereafter will grow proud with this recollection![69]

It didn't take the jury long to acquit the defendant—the verdict was returned on November 17, 1897. It was greeted with wild cheering, and it was reported that, but for the interference of the judge, the crowd would have hoisted the defendant, the defense attorneys, and the jury on their shoulders and paraded them about in the street.[70]

Aftermath and Ruminations

With the collapse of its strongest case for the murder of Fred Hoffman—*The Territory of Oklahoma v. Alfred Son*—along with the understandable reluctance of any "D" County witness to come forward and "bell the buzzards," the prosecution, deflated, dismissed the indictments against the others: Zip Wyatt (who, by that time had been hunted down and killed), Dan McKenzie, Bailey Son, and the ubiquitous Grant Pettyjohn.

While the flamboyant Houston's rhetorical tour de force may have mesmerized the El Reno jury, the evidence against Alfred Son was still damning. Damning to the extent that it placed Son at the scene of the killing, although it would seem more likely that the older and hardened Bert Collins was the actual triggerman. Local historians seem to agree that "Bert Collins" was Red Buck Weightman and that Red Buck was, in fact, the killer. In reminiscences penned years later, George E. Black, who was the "D" County assistant attorney at the time, flatly stated:

Red Buck killed Fred Hoffman. Alford [*sic*] Son had no part in it, but was with Red Buck at the time. After Red Buck was killed, Son disclosed the true facts.[71]

However, if Alfred Son disclosed all the "true facts" they have not been recorded. Officers found four sets of footprints around the crime scene, indicating that at least two additional men were present. But nowhere is there a mention of the names of the other two parties. Some hints of what must have been going on behind the scenes, as well as the motive for Hoffman's termination, remain. Hoffman was killed, and the killer then took pains to shoot him again in the mouth—a clear message that he was executed not only to silence him but also to discourage anyone else who might get the urge to start wagging their tongues. The killing was most likely an attempt to cover up someone's involvement in the Canadian and/or Woodward robberies. But who had the motive to cover up these heists? More to the point, the first question that should be asked is, Who *didn't* have a motive to cover up their role in these crimes?

Bill Doolin, Zip Wyatt, Red Buck Weightman, Tulsa Jack Blake, Bitter Creek Newcomb, Charlie Pierce, and other Doolin gang members were already well known and had sizeable bounties on their heads. In fact, they seemed to revel in their respective reputations as brazen outlaws. These major outlaws didn't give a flip about a cover up, because their principal concerns were to outrun the posses. It would seem much more likely that the man in need of a cover up was a man not known as an infamous outlaw, one who was instead a man (or men), perhaps prominent, who was involved behind the scenes as a mastermind or at least as an informant for the actual bandits. Someone who might concoct a bizarre phony money-packet scheme, or reveal when and where a large money shipment could be found in a Wells Fargo safe, or furnish the cattle George Isaacs shipped to Kansas City. Logic further suggests that if, as is believed by most, Red Buck was the actual triggerman, then he must have been a paid assassin—paid by whomever needed the cover up.

County attorney George E. Black stated that shortly before he was killed, Hoffman mailed a letter at the Taloga post office that was apparently addressed to either a Wells Fargo official or a federal law enforcement official, which contained incriminating information discovered during his investigation. According to Black, a "D" County official named Cicero Davis saw the letter and stole it from the Taloga post office. Black further relates:

Another Bill Doolin gang regular, Charley Pierce, was a near neighbor of Fred and Florence Hoffman in "D" County, Oklahoma Territory. Pierce was half-brother to Joe and Will "Tulsa Jack" Blake. (From *West of Hell's Fringe: Crime, Criminals, and the Federal Peace Officer in Oklahoma Territory, 1889–1907*, by Glenn Shirley, Oklahoma University Press, 1978.)

[Davis] took [Hoffman's letter] to a man who lived near Lenora, and he and a man who lived near Seiling together paid Red Buck $500 to kill Hoffman. Lee Moore paid this money to Red Buck, and there was an eye-witness to the payoff.[72]

"The man who lived near Lenora" appears to be a thinly veiled reference to Jim Riley, a known outlaw colleague whose ranch headquarters was located about a mile east of Lenora, while "the man who lived near Seiling" is almost certainly a reference to Lee Moore, Amos Chapman's son-in-law and the foreman of the Chapman Ranch near Seiling—or, perhaps, even to Amos Chapman himself. Moore and Riley, close friends and business associates, provided both refuge and fresh horses for the Doolin gang and perhaps other outlaws, and they were partners in establishing Taloga's most active saloon, which later became known as the infamous McFadden Saloon.[73] Court records reflect numerous charges were brought against Moore during this time for assault, receiving and handling stolen property, public intoxication, carrying a firearm in the city limits and grand larceny. Although Moore was never convicted of any felonies, "D" County probate records further reveal that several months after the Fred Hoffman murder, Moore and his famous father-in-law, Amos Chapman, pled guilty to assaulting and pistol-whipping Morris Black.[74] If, as it appears from the accounts of local historians, Lee Moore was more or less openly associating with known outlaws and sometimes harboring them on Chapman's ranch, it would seem unlikely that Chapman was unaware of these facts.[75] We can only wonder what role, if any, Jim Riley, Lee Moore, Amos Chapman, Sam Isaacs, or Bill Isaacs played in the Hoffman and McGee murders and the Wells Fargo robberies.

One of the last questions that remains unanswered is whether the bandits who attempted the Canadian heist were the same ones who, a few months earlier, pulled off the Woodward caper? It's a likely possibility since the robberies were similar in design and since they were closely related in terms of time and place. It appears that the Canadian gang consisted of Jim Harbolt, Joe Blake, Will "Tulsa Jack" Blake, and the mysterious "Jim Stanley" and that these men were joined shortly afterward at Dan McKenzie's cabin by Bitter Creek Newcomb and Sam Blake.

Of the four who rode over to Canadian that day, two—Jim Harbolt and Joe Blake, not known outlaws at that time—were seen socializing in Paul Hoefler's saloon that afternoon. A safe bet was that the other two avoided being seen in public because they were known outlaws. We know that Tulsa Jack was a notorious member of Doolin's gang and can surmise that "Jim Stanley" must have also been a known outlaw, and can further conclude that "Jim Stanley" was an alias. Testimony from independent witnesses described "Jim Stanley" as a tall man with a fair complexion, mustache, and sideburns.[76] The candidate that best fits the description was Doolin gang member Charley Pierce—half-brother of Tulsa Jack Blake, Joe Blake, Sam Blake, and close friend of Bitter Creek Newcomb.[77] In fact, shortly after the Canadian heist and the Woodward caper on the night of May 1, 1895, Bitter Creek and Charley Pierce were together when they were both assassinated while sleeping in the home of trusted friends turned bounty hunters. Yet another similarity exists between the Canadian and the Woodward operations: both were initi-

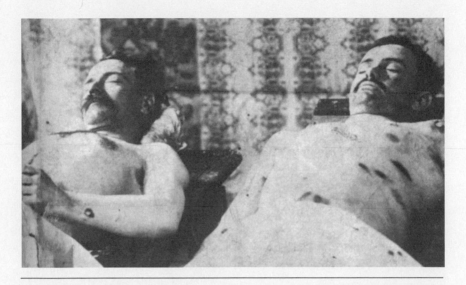

George "Bitter Creek" Newcomb (*left*) and Charley Pierce at the undertaker's parlor
in Guthrie, Oklahoma Territory, after being murdered in their sleep on May 2, 1895.
A "friend," motivated by a keen desire to save his own skin, was
responsible for the murder.
(From *West of Hell's Fringe: Crime, Criminals, and the Federal Peace Officer in Oklahoma
Territory, 1889–1907*, by Glenn Shirley, Oklahoma University Press, 1978.)

ated by two unmasked bandits, who were soon joined by several other
riders who preferred to remain in the shadows.

No indictment was ever returned against the suspects in the Woodward robbery. More than a century later, this is just one of the intriguing
mysteries that remain to tantalize us.

Epilogue

The days of rampant outlawry in Oklahoma Territory were slowly
drawing to a close. Until 1892, when the Cheyenne-Arapaho Indian
Reservation was opened for settlement, the western part of Oklahoma
Territory had been the almost unchallenged domain of outlaws. And
even for quite a spell thereafter, as honest settlers rushed in and staked
their claims, the outlaws were seldom bothered or reported. The intimidating presence of these violent hardcases was one reason. But there was

also another good reason: the hard-scrabble settlers had their hands full simply trying to eke out a living and survive. Trouble with outlaws was the last thing they needed, and thus an uneasy truce between the settlers and the outlaws developed during the early settlement years. Dewey County historian Robert E. King calls it "an unwritten treaty," or "leave us alone and we'll leave you alone." As time went along tensions increased. The outlaws became more arrogant, and the settlers became more numerous and more resentful—resentful because many of their county officials were not only unresponsive to their needs but also corrupt and tucked securely in the pockets of the outlaws. Once Fred Hoffman dared to speak out against the outlaw faction—and paid the price—the "unwritten treaty" was broken. His shocking murder alarmed the ever-increasing number of law-abiding settlers and galvanized them into action. As a result, according to King, within two or three months after Hoffman's murder, the settlers formed a vigilante group known as "the Anti–Horse Thief Association." The group never lynched any outlaws, but they did succeed in running a number of thieves out of the country as well as serving as a bridge between "no law" and the fledgling system of "justice under enacted law."[78] In addition to the citizens, deputy U.S. marshals and bounty hunters began taking a toll on the outlaw numbers.

Within two years of the Hoffman murder, Bill Doolin and the main members of his gang—Bitter Creek Newcomb, Tulsa Jack Blake, Charlie Pierce, Red Buck Weightman, Bill Dalton, Zip Wyatt, and others were dead by violent means. Jim Harbolt, a killer himself, was shot to death on December 8, 1903, by Oscar Donahoe near Siboney in Tillman County, Oklahoma.[79] Grant Pettyjohn got his come-uppance on August 30, 1906, when O. J. Young, a disgruntled speculator in one of Pettyjohn's get-rich-quick schemes, gunned him down on the streets of McCracken, Kansas.[80] It appears that Joe Blake, Dan McKenzie, and Alfred Son not only avoided conviction and incarceration for the murders of McGee and Hoffman as well as their participation in the Wells Fargo robberies but they also escaped the death-by-the-sword fate of their colleagues.[81]

Meanwhile, back in the Texas pen at Huntsville, dull-witted George Isaacs, the only poor soul who ended up doing time for any of these robberies or murders was facing a decidedly bleak future: life imprisonment busting rocks and picking cotton for the warden. But fate, and a very imaginative fellow by the name of William J. Dent, provided George Isaacs with one last shot at avoiding the payment of his debt to society, the details of which are chronicled in the next chapter.

Off the Record

The Oklahoma Supreme Court was correct in reversing Alfred Son's conviction (obtained during the second trial) because the trial court allowed the prosecution ("the territory") to introduce damaging testimony from two Wells Fargo officers that should not have been not admissible.

In a murder case the prosecution is not required to prove, as a part of its case, the motive for the killing. Still, sometimes (and particularly if the state's case is not all that compelling or if, as in the Alfred Son case, it depends solely upon circumstantial evidence) it becomes a practical necessity for the state to give the jury an explanation as to why Joe Defendant killed his victim. The jury always wants to know why, and if the state's case is not overwhelming, the lack of a motive might well lead the jury to develop a "reasonable doubt" as to the defendant's guilt. Indeed, the inability of the territory in Alfred Son's third trial to provide any evidence of motive (because of the state supreme court's ruling in the second trial) was the key to Houston's successful defense. The prosecution couldn't give evidence of a motive because it couldn't prove Alfred Son knew of Hoffman's potentially incriminating investigation.

The above story also suggests the rather laissez faire attitude of frontier trial lawyers toward legal ethics—and even outright highjinks. To many lawyers it was "All's fair in love and war." And "war" was defined broadly enough to include courtroom battles. Suborning perjury (the favorite in this case), buying witnesses, and another all-time favorite— buying a juror—were more or less looked upon by many as acceptable weapons in the trial lawyer's arsenal.

Seeking Salvation in Various Ways

TALES OF FINAGLED, FORGED, AND OTHER "FUNNY" PARDONS

WHEN THE appellate court upheld the conviction of George Isaacs for murdering sheriff Tom T. McGee, it looked like the end of the line for George. Looked like he was doomed to making very small rocks out of very large rocks and doing so for a very long time—for life.

There was just one last possibility of escaping such a dismal prospect: a pardon. On the surface, that certainly appeared to be a *remote* possibility. After all, George Isaacs was an unappealing and unlikely candidate for a pardon, having been convicted of the unprovoked and greed-motivated murder of a popular sheriff. Besides that, he was an admitted (would-be) swindler and a confessed co-conspirator with the worst of the Oklahoma Territory outlaws.

But then, as we shall soon see, a lot of funny things happened when it came to the business of finagling pardons in the great state of Texas.[1]

George Isaacs had not suffered the harsh regimen and the back-breaking labor that were a part of prison life in that era for very long when he met a fellow inmate named William J. Dent. Dent proved to be just about everything that poor old George wasn't—brilliant (at least in his own nefarious way), imaginative, articulate, and, most of all, audacious.

Those who knew him best said this: if you give William J. Dent a drink and a little ink . . . well, stand back! No telling what kind of devilment might result. When fueled by a toddy or two, his already fertile imagination, as well as his impressive skills as a conman and forger, would kick into overdrive.

To those who knew of his impressive lineage, the felonious shenanigans of W.J. must have seemed very incongruous indeed. His family back in Virginia and West Virginia were Old South royalty—and were well connected. W.J. himself was a first cousin of the famous Confederate hero General Stonewall Jackson. But W. J. Dent was never one for lounging around the plantation veranda, sipping mint juleps, and basking in reflected family glory. Instead he preferred to live life in the fast lane. In fact, by the time he was thirty years old, he had already served prison terms in Missouri and Colorado.

He came to Texas in 1896, began introducing himself as "J. W. Brown," and settled in Fort Worth, where he immediately got down to business—funny business. W.J. claimed to be an accountant by trade, with fifteen years of schooling in that field. Before long he had talked himself into a position as secretary and treasurer of the Flury Cattle Company. He soon began drawing sizeable drafts on the company, which, because they were paid, no doubt increased his credibility.

On August 26, 1896, he went into a Fort Worth jewelry store, bought a ring for $175, and gave the proprietor a check for that amount on a Missouri bank. Later in the day he came back to the jewelry store, returned the ring, and got his check back. But before he left, he suddenly got interested in other jewelry and bought a diamond ring and pin for $500, giving the proprietor another check on the same Missouri bank. He showed the proprietor a $20,000 certificate of deposit in a Fort Worth bank for the Flury Cattle Company, but he explained that, since that was the firm's money, he'd prefer to give a check from his own account at the Missouri bank. Of course the check bounced, and W.J. was indicted for swindling. He was tried, convicted, and sentenced to ten years in the pen. He beat the conviction on appeal when the appellate court (in a decision devoid of logic or common sense) held that, although Dent had given the victim a worthless check (and knew it to be worthless), the action somehow did not, in and of itself, amount to a "fraudulent mis-representation"—an essential element in the definition of swindling.[2] So explained the appellate court. Supposedly, in order to satisfy the appellate court's criteria, Dent would have had to formally assure the jeweler, "I now represent to you that this is a valid and genuine check on my account and will be duly paid when presented."

So W. J. Dent (still going under the pseudonym of "J. W. Brown") went merrily upon his diamond-studded way—but not for long. When he tried a similar scam, the jury convicted him, and the appellate court got it right. During this appeal Dent had the audacity to argue that his conviction should be reversed because he had signed the worthless check "J. W. Brown," which was not his real name, so it didn't count! The appellate court, however, summarily disposed of this sophistic nonsense, "This view is too absurd for discussion."[3] And so on March 17, 1898, Dent was sent to the Huntsville, Texas, state prison for six years. This is where he met fellow inmate, George Isaacs, who arrived at about the same time to begin serving his life sentence.

W. J. Dent wasted no time before talking himself into a cushy job as a bookkeeper in the prison's financial office. That accomplished, he immediately launched a vigorous campaign to get himself pardoned. And, as reflected in Dent's prison records, W.J. pulled out all the stops. He even enlisted the support of his illustrious Old South family members. Soon the Texas governor, Joseph D. Sayers, was bombarded with letters urging him to pardon their poor, misguided relative.

It would seem that the "name thing" might have presented a problem. They were urging the governor to pardon "W. J. Dent," but he had been convicted and was serving time under his pseudonym "J. W. Brown." That was not much of a hill for a stepper like W. J. Dent to climb. Dent himself wrote a letter directly to Governor Sayers explaining that he had been going under the name "J. W. Brown" because he didn't want to besmirch the name of his honored family back in the Virginias. However, at another point in the same letter, he took a contradictory position: that he was actually innocent of any wrongdoing in the first place. W.J. was also a couple of clicks shy of candor with the governor about another minor matter. Before assuming the pseudonym "J. W. Brown" and heading for Texas, he had been convicted of felonies in two

Governor Joseph D. Sayers rued the day in 1899 when he granted a pardon to conman and forger William J. Dent. Sayers, a twice-wounded Confederate veteran, was governor of Texas from 1898 to 1902. Previously he had served as a U.S. congressman for fourteen years and spent one term as lieutenant governor. After his term as governor he developed a lucrative private law practice and served as chairman of the Texas Industrial Accident Board and as a regent of the University of Texas.
(Photo detail from PICB 07896, Austin Historic Center, Austin Public Library.)

other states—colorful little adventures of which neither the governor nor the prison officials were yet aware.[4] Thoughtfully, W.J. didn't see fit to burden the governor with this extraneous stuff.

Dent's plea to the governor was indeed a thing of beauty. He wrote it on the official stationery of his boss, William G. Hill, who was the financial agent for J. S. Rice, the Texas prison system's superintendent. Dent's letter was long, eloquent, and cleverly worded. He informed Governor Sayers that he had been orphaned at an early age and thus deprived of the "wise guidance which a boy can only receive from a mother." He acknowledged that at times in the past he had been "wayward and dissipated," but assured the governor that he had learned his lesson well. W.J. ended his plea for mercy with the following words (words that Governor Sayers would doubtless recall with rue many times in the future):

I most solemnly promise by those things which I hold most sacred and holy, by the honor of my family . . . that, should you find it possible to grant the executive clemency asked for, I will never, so long as

I live, commit any action which might cause you to feel a pang of regret for having shown mercy which was undeserved. With inward trembling, but with great hope . . . etc., etc.[5]

The governor received a second letter on the same stationery as the first, purporting (at least) to be from and signed by Dent's boss, William G. Hill. The letter stated that Hill was writing the governor upon behalf of Prison Superintendent Rice, who was "absent." The governor was informed as follows:

> As per request from you, directed to Sup't. J. S. Rice, in regard to convict J. W. Brown, would state that said convict was transferred to my office as bookkeeper. His conduct has been first-class in every particular. He has proven very efficient and attentive to his duties. He evidently has good breeding, and he tells me that his correct name is William J. Dent, and that he abandoned his correct name because he had disgraced his family and name.
>
> I write you because Mr. Rice is absent. Brown has every appearance of, and his conduct is that of, a gentleman, and I learn that he has never given officials any trouble since he has been in prison.[6]

Governor Sayers next received a letter directly from Dent's uncle, U.S. district judge J. J. Jackson of West Virginia. Judge Jackson beseeched Governor Sayers to extend leniency to his nephew and grant him a full pardon. His Honor conceded that Dent's career "has been a wild one," but attributed this to a head injury that, the judge explained, affected Dent's brain so that "the moment he takes a drink, it sets him crazy and his inclination is to be wielding a pen and trying to counterfeit names." Nevertheless, Judge Jackson assured Governor Sayers that Dent came from one of the finest families in the Virginias and that he had learned his lesson. He added that Dent was seeking a full pardon so he could "enlist in the public services under the call for soldiers for the Philippine War."[7]

The next luminary to weigh in on W.J.'s behalf was no less than the governor of West Virginia himself, the Honorable George W. Atkinson. He wrote that he had personally known Dent since childhood. He attested to the fact that W.J. was "of good stock," being a member of the "the great Jackson family" and first cousin to the legendary General Stonewall Jackson. He also attributed W.J.'s "wild methods of living" to his head injury, which Governor Atkinson speculated was the cause of Dent's "weakness in forging names."[8]

Governor Sayers eventually threw up his hands and yielded to this impressive barrage. On August 28, 1899 (slightly more than one year after Dent's arrival at the prison), Governor Sayers granted William J. Dent a full and unconditional pardon.[9]

W.J. was overjoyed when he heard the news of his impending release. But first he had some business to attend to. Dent saw a golden opportunity, and he didn't hesitate to exploit it. He sat down with his good buddy George Isaacs and let him in on the good news. We can assume that Dent had, by this time, learned that his pal Isaacs came from a relatively wealthy and supportive family. On the other hand, George was no doubt mightily impressed by Dent's demonstrated political clout. Dent expressed his sorrow that he would soon be forced to leave his dear friend behind. Suddenly it occurred to W.J. that perhaps he could use his political connections to do good old George a favor by obtaining a pardon for him, too! All for a mere five thousand dollars. And so the deal was struck. We may believe, with great assurance, that the Isaacs brothers, or whoever bankrolled the five thousand dollars for George, had at least enough sense not to give Dent the five thousand dollars until *after* the promised pardon was secured.

At any rate, as soon as the prison gate swung open, Dent hit the ground running—headed straight for the governor's office in Austin. However, when he got there he did not appeal to Governor Sayers to pardon his good friend George Isaacs. Instead he managed to purloin some of Governor Sayers's official stationery. That was all Dent needed. He then put his talented pen to work and either forged a pardon for George using his own pardon as a pattern, or, more likely, he made a few significant alterations on his own pardon. The missive was enclosed in Governor Sayers's official envelope and included a forged cover letter from the governor written on his official letterhead and appeared to be signed by Governor Sayers. Then he forwarded this by mail to Prison Superintendent Rice in Huntsville, Texas.

The warden received this letter, examined it, and, since it all appeared to be in order, he, on September 30, 1899 (only a month and two days after he had turned Dent out), recorded on the official prison records that George Isaacs had been pardoned by the governor. A joyful George grabbed his pardon and lit out for his old haunts in Indian Territory and the Canadian, Texas, area, where he openly bragged about his good fortune and proudly displayed his pardon from Governor Sayers. The good folks around Canadian were flabbergasted—and then enraged—by the temerity of Governor Sayers in freeing the only outlaw convicted of the murder of their beloved sheriff—and after such a brief stint in prison. Their outrage soon reached the ears of the baffled governor, who immediately ordered an investigation.

George Isaacs's prison records were quickly altered. The word *pardoned* was scratched out, and the word *escaped* was inserted next to George's name.[10] A warrant was issued for his arrest, but by this time, George (or more probably his astute brothers) knew what was headed his way. Therefore, when the warrant for George's arrest arrived in the Panhandle, George was gone—long gone and gone for good. Rumor had it that he took a permanent vacation to South America. Wherever he went, he was never heard from again, and so George (with a little help from his friends) cheated the Texas justice system and never served another day of his sentence.

Another arrest warrant was issued at the same time for the wiley William J. Dent. Dent was tracked down and arrested in Arizona, no doubt still enjoying the fruits of the George Isaacs scam. The State of Texas summoned Dent to a command performance in order to afford him the opportunity of explaining the matter of the "funny" pardon. As ever, Dent was not at a loss for words. Simple, he explained, it was not forged at all! Governor Sayers had actually signed it, but he was drunk at the time and just disremembered signing it. The explanation, unsurprisingly, enraged Governor Sayers, who was already embarrassed to the high side of irate.

Harry Koch was a pioneer newsman who owned, published, and edited the *Quanah Tribune-Chief* when, in 1895, George Isaacs was convicted of the murder of Sheriff McGee. Years later, in the February 17, 1931, edition of his paper, Harry Koch wrote his memoirs and recollected the George Isaacs murder trial as well as the ensuing flap over the forged pardon. After giving an account of the murder trial, Harry Koch wrote the following on the forged pardon episode:

> Dent stoutly maintained that the pardon was genuine, and that he got Sayers to sign it when the old governor was drunk. Judge W. B. Plemons [famous Amarillo trial lawyer] who told me about it said that it was whispered around Austin that Sayers did go on a "high lonesome" once in a while, and the Governor, knowing about such talk, was not a little incensed. He swore that if there was any law by which he could have Dent hung, he certainly was going to let him swing for it, and uttered a number of threats which amused Plemons greatly. While Dent was not executed, he did have to board in Huntsville for several years thereafter.[11]

In a strange legal twist, William J. Dent was not indicted for forging an official governmental document (the pardon), as we might expect. The district attorney obtained an indictment against Dent for murder— the murder of sheriff Tom McGee in Canadian, Texas, in the foiled Wells Fargo robbery of 1894! Never mind that Dent had nothing to do with the incident, nor was he ever, so far as we know, anywhere near Canadian, Texas, in his whole life. Most likely the district attorney went for the jugular when prosecuting Dent because of a little behind-the-scenes arm-twisting from Governor Sayers. The Texas statute then in effect, upon which the prosecution relied (Article 86, *Texas Penal Code*), read as follows:

> *An accessory is one who* knowing that an offense has been committed, conceals the offender or *gives* him any other *aid, in order that he may evade* an arrest or trial, or the *execution of his sentence.*

The punishment prescribed for being an accessory was the same as for the principal. The novel case was called for trial in the Cherokee County District Court, where W. J. Dent told his tale of the tipsy governor. Perhaps it was the setting (the cold, stern, sober ambience of a court of law is certainly not congenial for a conman), but W.J.'s flim-flam artistry finally failed him. The jury, having considered the evidence, did not believe that Governor Sayers signed George Isaacs's pardon—drunk, sober, or anywhere in-between—and found Dent guilty. They decided that since he had cheated the Texas justice system out of Isaacs's life sentence, Dent might just as well serve it himself.

Dent, of course, appealed. The main point his lawyers argued on appeal was that the prosecution (for a purely punitive reason) had over-reached by stretching the legal definition of accessory to unconscionable lengths. Such a tortured interpretation of the accessory statute, he argued, brought about the ridiculous result of his conviction. Dent, a mere forger at worst, was convicted of the murder of a Panhandle sheriff way back in 1894 during an incident in which he had absolutely no part. He didn't even know the deceased or any of the parties involved (including George Isaacs) until years after the event.

The appellate court wrestled mightily with this argument, but, in the end (albeit in a split decision), affirmed Dent's conviction.[12] Governor Sayers must have taken great delight in that result.[13] And so, despite his heavy-hitter connections and famous relatives, William J. Dent went back to his recently vacated prison cell, this time for life. On the prison intake records, in the space for "Expiration of Sentence" the warden made this chilling entry: "Death."

But the irrepressible Dent was not through just yet. He prudently waited until Governor Sayers left the Austin stage and then applied again for a pardon. He once again leaned on his influential connections. In May 1911, after serving ten years of his life sentence, Governor O. B. Colquitt, for whatever reasons, granted Dent yet another pardon—even after the Texas authorities had finally learned of Dent's two prior felony convictions in Missouri and Colorado. One is tempted to speculate that Governor Colquitt might have concluded that a murder conviction, carrying an attendant life sentence, was a bit much in view of the fact that the real violation of Texas penal law was the nonviolent forging of an official document. Maybe he believed ten years of hard time, despite Dent's prior record and despite the understandably bilious reaction of his predecessor, Governor Sayers, was sufficient punishment for a forger. Governor Colquitt's official statement of grounds for granting Dent a pardon was this:

Whereas, it appears that Applicant has an Aunt residing in West Virginia, who raised him from an infant, who now pleads for his release on grounds that he has been sufficiently punished for the crime committed, and, if released, will take him to her home and do all in her power to make his reformation complete.

However, Governor Colquitt was somewhat more circumspect than Governor Sayers had been. He did not grant Dent a full pardon, but a conditional pardon. The principal condition being that "he shall go to his Aunt in West Virginia and remain outside of this State."[14]

So, insofar as the record shows, Texas finally got rid of William J. Dent. Perhaps Mr. Dent's "reformation was completed" in West Virginia amongst his esteemed relatives; and perhaps Mr. Isaacs began earning a livelihood through honest labor in South America . . . anything is possible.

. . . And Still More Funny Pardons

Pardons by the bushel-basketful were cranked out of Austin during the gubernatorial administrations of James E. "Pa" Ferguson (January 19, 1915, to August 25, 1917) and his wife, Miriam A. "Ma" Ferguson (January 20, 1925, to January 17, 1927, and January 17, 1933, to January 15, 1935). The often outrageously hambone antics of Ma and Pa liberally spiced Texas politics for more than a quarter of a century. Although the Fergusons made blatant appeals to the uneducated, the unenlightened, and the unwashed, they nevertheless were ahead of their time in two respects: they bucked the two popular trends of their time—the revival of the Ku Klux Klan and the push for Prohibition. However, their liberal pardon policy and their support of the liquor industry may not have been entirely motivated by lofty principles. Pa was impeached and booted out of office in 1917 for enhancing his $4,000 salary with an anonymous donation of $156,000 from bashfully nameless brewers (not to mention a few other financial indiscretions).[15] But the Fergusons' motto was "Never say die, say damn!" and Pa responded to his ouster by promoting Ma's candidacy for governor. "Two governors for the price of one," he crowed. Astounding their enemies and confounding the political pundits, Ma managed to win the 1924 gubernatorial race and

Miriam A. "Ma" Ferguson became the first woman to be elected governor of any state in the United States in 1924. Her husband, J. E. "Pa" Ferguson, had previously served as governor of Texas but was removed from office in 1917 for malfeasance. Both pursued lenient (and suspect) pardon policies. (From *The Texas Women's Hall of Fame*, by Sinclair Moreland, Biographical Press, 1917.)

Although a college-educated woman, Ma Ferguson played a "hayseed" role during her political campaigns for the benefit of the basically rural electorate. In this campaign photo she is posed with her daughter and a Democrat donkey. Like many farm women of the time, she donned a borrowed bonnet, which became a symbol of her political career. (Courtesy of the San Antonio Light Collection, the University of Texas Institute of Texas Cultures at San Antonio.)

become the first woman elected governor of any state in the union.[16]

Ma immediately revived Pa's liberal pardon policies and again opened the prison gates. Her actions fueled rumors that Pa was selling pardons.[17] During the years of 1925 and 1926, at a time when the population of Texas was less than a fifth of what it is today, Ma Ferguson granted executive clemency to 3,595 convicts.[18] Austin insiders at the time chuckled over one supposed encounter. A gentleman was riding an elevator in the governor's mansion with Governor Ma. He accidentally stepped on her foot. "Oh, pardon me, please!" he exclaimed. Without batting an eye Ma replied, "Well, you'll have to see Pa about that!"[19] Another anecdote making the rounds in Austin went this way: the father of a convicted criminal pleaded with Pa Ferguson to pardon his son. Pa didn't give him a direct answer, and instead kept changing the subject to a horse he wanted to sell for five thousand dollars. Finally the exasperated father blurted out, "What on earth would I want with a five thousand dollars horse?" To which Pa responded, "Well, I figure your son might ride him home from the penitentiary if you bought him."[20]

Still, for those unfortunates who were unable to bend the ear of a sympathetic governor . . . well, maybe a lieutenant governor would do. Under the Texas constitution, if the Texas governor takes a trip outside the state, then the lieutenant governor is empowered to act for him, including the power to grant pardons.

In 1900 J. N. Browning, an Amarillo lawyer, was serving his first term as lieutenant governor of Texas and running for re-election. The term "laid-back" was not yet common vocabulary, but that was what J. N. Browning was. He was also a consummate and comical storyteller. Browning's opponent in the race for lieutenant governor was making some headway in his campaign by telling a tale on Browning. Problem was, the accusation was the flat truth. Browning's opponent told anyone who would listen that one day when Governor Joe Sayers had gone up to Washington to "hob-nob with the big bugs," Lieutenant Governor Browning took the occasion to pardon one of his very own kinfolk from the state pen at Huntsville. Browning also applied that opportunity to a number of his kin's fellow jailbirds.

Browning met the problem head on. At an election rally in the Dick-

Lieutenant governor J. N. "Honest Jim" Browning, genial, loquacious, and always ready with an appropriate joke or a tall tale, was a noted Texas Panhandle pioneer lawyer. He was the first district attorney of the huge Panhandle District in 1881, and he successfully challenged the rough and lawless element. He was later elected lieutenant governor of Texas and then served as a district judge in Amarillo.
(Courtesy of the Panhandle-Plains Historical Museum, Canyon, Texas.)

ens County Courthouse Browning "adjusted his diction as the occasion and audience demanded," and said this:

My Fellow Citizens—Me and Bud [his brother] began our career together in the cattle business. We spent most of our time in jail. Bud said to me one day, "Jim! You ain't worth a damn for anything else, why don't you make a lawyer out of yourself?" Well, I sent down to our lawyer's office and got a law book and when I got out of jail I was a full-fledged lawyer. From then on we had no more trouble. Bud ran the cattle business and I kept him out of jail and we both succeeded. I then began to dabble in politics. I held various offices about which I knew very little before I became Lieutenant Governor. Perhaps you don't know nothing about what the duties are of a Lieutenant Governor. Well, he presides over the Senate when it is in session until some knotty problem comes up he don't know nothing about, and then calls the President Pro Tem to the chair and goes out and takes a drink and loiters around with the lobbyists until the fuss is over. When the Governor leaves the State, he becomes acting Governor. During my term as Lieutenant Governor, now closing, Governor Sayers left the State and went to Washington to hob-nob with the big bugs. That left me in charge. By jinks I was Governor of Texas for a little while! Now ain't that a hell of a note? But, my fellow citizens, I am going to take you into my confidence. I wasn't Governor long, but while I was, I was true to my kind and the records will bear me out in that assertion. The records will show I pardoned more men out of the penitentiary than any Governor in Texas has ever done during the same length of time. I didn't know whether I would ever have another opportunity and I got busy while the getting was good. And I thought while I was giving an account of my stewardship, I had better tell you about my loyalty to my friends for fear you might not otherwise hear about it.

The crowded courtroom "resounded with applause," and one observer dryly added that he figured "some of the audience had already been in the pen and others expected to go."[21] Browning was re-elected lieutenant governor.

What about those unfortunate penitents who were unable to bend the ear of a sympathetic governor or a sympathetic lieutenant governor . . . who was there for them? Well, it so happens that under the Texas constitution, if both the governor and the lieutenant governor are absent from the state, then the president pro-tempore of the Texas senate is The Man—empowered to act as governor of Texas, complete with the power to grant pardons. This power brings us to the scandalous case of Miss Ruby Britain, the subtitle of which has to be "Hell Hath No Fury Like . . ." Especially if the scorning involves a much younger, and perhaps prettier, female.[22]

In 1934 Miss Ruby was an attractive forty-year-old brunette. Never married, she lived with her mother on the rolling plains of northwest Texas in the small town of Seymour. The Britains were one of the most prominent families in that area. Two of Ruby's brothers were well-known and respected lawyers who had outgrown Seymour and moved to larger cities. B. M. Britain went to Amarillo and A. H. Britain (actually a half-brother) went to Wichita Falls. In fact, A. H. Britain was not only one of Wichita Falls's leading lawyers but was also a former mayor of that town.

Meanwhile, Horace E. Nichols, thirty-eight and vice president of the

First National Bank, also came from one of the leading families. The Nichols family were early-day residents of Baylor County, settled around the Red Springs community, a few miles west of Seymour. Handsome Horace stood about six feet tall, had dark, wavy hair, and was very "romantic looking." And he had an eye for the ladies. Although Nichols was married and the father of two children, the small-town gossip was that Miss Ruby and Horace were "involved."[23]

As it turned out (unfortunately for Horace), his amorous interests were apparently not limited to his wife and Ruby. In August 1934 nineteen-year-old Miss Willie Mae Couch of Portales, New Mexico, came to town to visit her sister. She soon became very well acquainted with Horace Nichols . . . and Miss Ruby got wind of it. One hot August night Miss Ruby caught Horace and Miss Willie Mae parked in Horace's car on a country road a few miles from Seymour. Miss Ruby drove her car along side of Horace's car, and, without so much as a "howdy-do" or other preliminary, opened up on Horace with a .380 automatic pistol. Horace jumped out of the car and attempted to run off, but he got only about seventy yards before Miss Ruby nailed him—fatally. Miss Willie Mae suffered a deep facial cut from the splintered windshield of Horace's car. However, she had presence of mind enough to crank up Horace's car and make her getaway while Ruby focused her firepower on Horace. Willie Mae's quick action saved her, and she lived to tell the tale.

That tale was bolstered by other independent evidence. In Ruby's haste to flee, she ran her car into a ditch about a half mile from the shooting site. She made a frantic midnight jog back to Seymour where she rousted a relative, Ambrose Bowie, out of bed, and, together, they returned to Ruby's abandoned car intending to drag it out of the ditch. Meanwhile, however, the terrified Miss Willie Mae had blurted the story to the Baylor County authorities, and they were already on the scene. They had discovered Horace's body and, not far down the road, still in the ditch, Ruby's car. So when Ruby and Bowie showed up, the lawmen arrested her and charged her with the murder of Horace Nichols. An empty .380 automatic shell casing was found in Ruby's car, which matched other empty shell casings found at the crime scene.

When Ruby came to court, she was flanked by a formidable array of lawyers, thanks no doubt to her distinguished brothers. She would need them! Ruby took the stand in her own behalf and struggled to raise the issue of self-defense. Alas, it was about as thin as a bowl of bus station chili. First, she had to admit that she'd had an affair with a married man—Horace. But, she went on, he'd practically dragged her down the primrose path kicking and screaming all the way, "manifesting his affections for her in many ways." It was the stuff of a great B-grade movie: he loved her desperately; his wife didn't understand him; his home life was unhappy, but he could be so happy with her; more than anything in life he wanted to divorce his wife and marry her . . . but then there were the dear children to consider, etc. So . . . finally . . . the inevitable.

And then along came Miss Willie Mae—pretty, nineteen-year-old Miss Willie Mae. And, according to Ruby's tale, it was also about that time that she learned Horace was having clandestine flings with other young things. She tried, she tearfully continued, to persuade Horace to "straighten up," but her tearful persuasion didn't work. She then tried threats: she would "spill the beans" to Horace's wife, and she would also go to all his young girlfriends and "warn them of the pitfalls into which he was leading them." That, Ruby said, was when he threatened to kill her if she exposed him.

Such was the state of affairs preceding Horace's untimely demise. Ruby's persuasion had failed, and the threats hadn't worked. Ruby testified that on August 15, 1934, she suspected Horace was out with Miss Willie Mae, and therefore (at about midnight, packing a loaded .380 pistol) she set out to find them—but, according to Ruby, her laudable mission was to warn Miss Willie Mae "against Harold's blandishments, insincerity and duplicity."

But things didn't quite work out as planned. When Horace surfaced to window level, he made what Ruby contended was an alarming gesture. Although not a word was spoken by anybody, she told the jury that she thought that Horace was attempting to carry out his earlier threat to kill her, and so that's when, purely in self-defense, she whipped out her .380 and cut him down. She somehow shot him twice in the back (in self-defense) as he was sprinting away from her about seventy yards down the road. Thus ended Miss Ruby's tale.

To gild the lily a bit, however, the defense called one of the local doctors who (doctor-patient confidentiality nowithstanding) told the jury a dirty little secret on Horace: he had treated Horace about a year earlier for gonorrhea. This testimony, however titillating, was clearly inadmissible as it was not relevant to the single issue in the case: self-defense. For that reason, the trial judge later instructed the jury not to consider that juicy tidbit in reaching its verdict, which, no doubt, was about as efficacious as allowing the defense to throw a skunk into the jury box and then ordering them not to smell it.

Despite the efforts of Ruby's illustrious defense team, the jury found her guilty and sentenced her to a twelve-year prison term. How the jury arrived at a twelve-year sentence is the subject of local legend, as described by Jack Jones, longtime Seymour resident and historian laureate of Baylor County.[24] The legend holds that one of the prominent, married jurors (all of whom were men, of course), was also one of Ruby's lovers. Despite Ruby's performance before the jury, it appears she just might not have been quite the choir girl (albeit slightly tarnished) she pretended to be. Although he was not initially inclined to convict at all (which raised interesting speculations as to his motives: love, lust, fear of exposure), he finally agreed to a guilty verdict. But then he dug his heels in the dirt and decreed that he would hang the jury if the others insisted on anything longer than twelve years for poor Ruby. That part is legend. What is known for a fact, however, is that the very next day after Miss Ruby terminated Horace, another rather prominent, married Seymourite (who was rumored to have had more than a nodding acquaintance with Miss Ruby) hastily rounded up his whole herd of cattle and, even though every last one was mortgaged to the bank, sold them off to purchase his wife a brand new Oldsmobile.[25] Bone-deep fear of exposure seemed to be reaching an epidemic level in those parts.

Ruby Britain was convicted in the Baylor County District Court on September 28, 1934, and the sheriff escorted her to prison to begin serving her sentence. She later appealed, but to no avail. But Ruby didn't stay there very long. At that time, unfortunately for Ruby, Pa and Ma Ferguson (and their liberal pardon policies) were already history. But never mind, the prominent Britains had friends in high places, one of whom was state senator John S. Redditt of Lufkin over in east Texas. Senator Redditt happened to be president pro-tempore of the Texas senate at the time. And it just so happened that one day (September 12, 1935, to be exact) both the governor and the lieutenant governor decided to take short, out-of-state vacations, thus leaving Senator Redditt to mind the state store. On that day, less than a year after Ruby Britain began serving her sentence, acting governor John S. Redditt, signed official Texas Proclamation No. 28037: a pardon for Ruby Britain. As justification, the pardon cited the poor health of her seventy-eight-year-old mother. Redditt then added this intriguing recital: "I am further advised that there are other extenuating circumstances in favor of Ruby Britain, but public policy would not be served by making said matters a part of a public record."[26]

Still, there appears to be a bit more to the pardon tale than yet told. It's the subject of another local legend that, according to Jack Jones, enjoyed considerable currency in its day.[27] A little more background will help. As mentioned earlier, Ruby's two brothers were prominent lawyers. Brother A. H. Britain was also the very close friend and associate of another prominent Wichita Falls lawyer named James V. Allred, the same James V. Allred who just happened to be the governor of Texas.

In September 1935 Governor Allred was serving his first term, but he was also tooling up to run for re-election in the fall of 1936. (He did, and he won.) Even a country constable has enough savvy to recognize that Governor Allred would have been weighted with a political millstone had he pardoned a sensational murderess who had barely gotten her suitcase unpacked at the state pen. Especially if the murderess was the sister of a close friend who lived in the governor's own hometown. Moreover, it can be safely assumed that the lieutenant governor had similar political ambitions and didn't care to take on any unnecessary political liabilities. But those limitations didn't apply to senator John Redditt from east Texas. His senatorial district was many miles from Seymour. Also, we may deduce that since Redditt was the president pro-tempore of the Texas senate, he had considerable seniority and a "safe" seat in that body.

As the legend goes, the Britains, Senator Redditt, and Governor Allred engineered the whole pardon scenario. Governor Allred waited until the lieutenant governor took a vacation, and then he took a little trip to get out of the way so that Senator Redditt could do the deed. He did the deed, and Miss Ruby returned to Seymour to care for her aged mother . . . and perhaps other matters.

Off the Record

The authority of a chief governmental executive to issue pardons to convicts is a power that is intended to correct injustices. Typically it is invoked when exonerating evidence comes to light long after the judicial system has played out its role and pronounced the convict guilty. Or, often, for a myriad of reasons (the defendant's conduct before or after conviction, serious illness of the defendant, or a variety of other considerations) it appears that the punishment fixed by the judicial system was too harsh. The governor or president can then, depending on applicable law, pardon the convict outright and re-establish his rights as a citizen or commute the sentence (leaving the conviction standing) and order the convict's release from prison. These are all legitimate exercises of the executive power to play "Monday morning quarterback" to the judicial system and thus rectify errors or excesses. Trouble is, the power to pardon or commute has proven to be, and still is, readily subject to abuse, and it is the type of abuse that is almost impossible to prove and prosecute.

Lizzie Continues the Black Sheep Tradition

THE SONS OF GEORGE AND LIZZIE
TRIED FOR MURDER

WHEN, IN 1896, Lizzie Isaacs's husband, George, was sentenced to life in prison for killing the county sheriff in Canadian, Texas, she, at age twenty-nine, was still a young woman. Not only young, but also headstrong and rambunctious—and not the least inclined to squander the rest of her days sitting about moping and pining for her departed mate.

Born April 21, 1867, in Tishomingo County, Mississippi, Lizzie was one of eight children born to William Rufus Ellis and his wife, Mary Weton Horton Ellis, folks molded from the common clay of most hardscrabble, hardworking rural people of the time.[1] They were apparently a respectable family—no reports of outlawry among the clan has been discovered. Except, that is, for their third child, Mary Elizabeth "Lizzie" Ellis, the black sheep of the family. (Well, as we shall soon see, Lizzie's brother John might also fall into that category.) Therefore, when Lizzie hooked up with George Isaacs, the black sheep of his family, no one was very surprised at the match.

• • •

The Ellis family migrated westward to the north-central Texas area around Gainseville in Cooke County. This land,

Lizzie Ellis Isaacs was the black sheep of the Ellis family. She left her first husband to marry the black sheep of the Isaacs family, George Isaacs. Before it was all said and done, both had been convicted of separate murders.
(Courtesy of Carol Morse.)

just south of the Red River boundary of Indian Territory, was where six-teen-year-old Lizzie married her first husband, John L. Byrne, on November 7, 1883. Byrne was ten years her elder, and it was just ten months later when their son, Wiley Francis Washington Byrne, was born. But sedate married life was just not Lizzie's cup of tea. Or maybe she succumbed to a bad case of the seven-year itch, as sometime around 1890 she ignited a star-crossed romance with George Isaacs. She and George married in El Reno, Oklahoma Territory, on April 12, 1891, and then settled down near Chickasha, Indian Territory. Their son, Richard "Dick" Isaacs, was born in El Reno in April 1892.

As mentioned in a previous chapter, the Chickasha honeymoon cabin soon became known to lawmen as the haunt of some of Indian Territory's worst outlaws, including Bill Doolin and his gang. Chickasha is where George and his outlaw friends cooked up the ill-fated scheme to defraud Wells Fargo, which, in turn, led to the killing of the Canadian sheriff, Tom T. McGee. George was arrested on that murder charge on November

25, 1894. He immediately filed a habeas corpus petition seeking release pending trial. The judge denied it, and George was returned to his jail cell. While George was incarcerated Lizzie gave birth to a third son, Roy, on October 22, 1895.

Meanwhile, even before George's trial, Lizzie didn't waste much time getting herself into a peck of trouble. On May 30, 1895, while she was still pregnant with Roy, she and her brother John Ellis got into a squabble with neighbors Mr. and Mrs. Sterling Elder over the grazing of some cattle near Chickasha. Lizzie started a screaming, scratching, hair-pulling cat-fight with Mrs. Elder while John and Sterling looked on. But they did not remain spectators for long, and during the melee John pulled his pistol and killed Sterling Elder—an indiscretion for which Lizzie and her brother were jailed and charged with murder.

On February 10, 1898, Lizzie was tried and convicted in the federal district court in Chickasha, Indian Territory, for the murder of Sterling Elder. Although the old Indian Territory court records of the trial are not in the federal archives and have not been located, the jury's verdict was reported in the February 11, 1898, edition of the *Daily Oklahoman*. The reporter's statement was: "The penalty is death, but the jury recommended a life sentence." The story concluded with the observation "The verdict of the jury in the Lizzie Isaacs case is considered by the public as being very severe."[2]

Since the court records are not available, it is not clear what sentence, if any, was eventually imposed. It is clear, however, that she was not hanged, and that if a prison sentence was imposed, she spent little, if any, time serving it. We know this because the 1910 federal census lists Lizzie and her two sons, Richard and Roy, as residents of Clinton in Custer County, Oklahoma.

What became of the scandalous Lizzie after 1910 has remained a tantalizing and unsolved mystery—until recently. A curtain of silence seems to have been brought down by the mutual consent of the families of George and Lizzie, who, no doubt, felt there had already been way too much dirty family laundry aired in public. Unlike today, when hordes clamor to win five minutes of national television exposure by publicly regurgitating the most heinous of their sins and the most sordid of their aberrations, nineteenth-century family scandals were taken very seriously and were guarded for years afterward. Despite the attempt at secrecy, whispers spread throughout the Ellis and Isaacs families. One descendant, Carol Morse of Ardmore, Oklahoma, great-graddaughter of Lizzie and her first husband, John Byrne, grew up with tales of two more murders and a barn burning that brought an end to Lizzie's story.[3] Ms. Morse spent years combing through Oklahoma records to verify and tease out the details, but found little success—she couldn't even discover where Lizzie was buried. Then, in 2006 the author discovered a clue in Texas and redirected the search. The rest of the story was finally told. And what a tale it was!

Lizzie's youngest sister, Helen Gertrude Ellis, married Thomas N. Sparks on Christmas Day, 1903, in Carter County, Indian Territory. The Sparks were a prominent pioneer family, and several family members settled in and around the northwest-central Texas town of Crowell in Foard County. Thomas owned a farm several miles southwest of Crowell in the Foard City community. Apparently the marriage went well, and by 1914 Thomas and Helen were the proud parents of four children. But their marriage ended in tragedy when Helen, at age thirty-three, died on April 29, 1915, as a result of complications in childbirth. Their fifth child also died during the birth.[4]

Then along came Lizzie. She soon took up with Sparks and began living with him, going under the name Mrs. Jessie Sparks. She was forty-eight years old, and Sparks was thirty-six. No record of a marriage between them has been found, nor has a record of divorce between Lizzie and George Isaacs. Nevertheless, they presented themselves to the community as husband and wife. The fact that Lizzie called herself "Jessie" when she moved in with Sparks leads to the conclusion that she was trying to escape her checkered past and save the respectable Sparks family from any embarrassment.

The union, whatever its exact nature, was not by any stretch a marriage made in heaven, and it certainly did not last long. On January 3, 1916, an enraged Lizzie burned down Tom Sparks's barn. (The barn just happened to be insured for the enormous sum of four thousand dollars.)[5] What enraged Lizzie? According to Carol Morse, family legend holds that Sparks had exhibited unseemly interest in another woman—or, at least, Lizzie suspected that he had. Whatever her motives might have been, Sparks did not take this barn-burning business lightly. The next day he drove into Crowell and filed criminal charges against Lizzie and had her

Lizzie Byrne Isaacs Sparks, between her sons Richard Isaacs, age twenty-three (*left*) and Roy Isaacs, age twenty (*right*). The baby picture of Lizzie's first husband, John L. Byrne, is partially visible in the upper left. A few days later, on January 4, 1916, Lizzie was killed by her third husband, Tom Sparks.
(Courtesy of Carol Morse.)

arrested. But neither Tom Sparks nor the local constabulary could keep the infuriated Lizzie caged for long. She promptly posted bond, borrowed a car, and took her son Roy out to the Sparks farm to confront Tom.

It was a fatal mistake. Sparks ordered them not to get out of the car. Lizzie, of course, was not the kind to take orders from anybody—and especially not from Tom Sparks! When she and Roy stepped out, Sparks opened fire. He shot Lizzie in the chest with a large-caliber revolver, killing her instantly. Then he opened up on Roy with a shotgun. Roy was wounded, but not seriously. Sparks was quickly arrested but then released on a five-thousand-dollar bond.[6]

Lizzie was killed on January 4, 1916, less than nine months after her sister, Helen Sparks, died. Roy bought a plot in the Crowell, Texas, cemetery and erected a large and impressive tombstone over her grave. She was buried under the name Mrs. Jessie Sparks, and the epitaph Roy had carved reads: "No love like a mother's love ever was known." While such an extravagant expression of emotion may not be all that unusual for a child upon the loss of a mother, it hints at another side—perhaps gentler—of Lizzie's character. Moving in with Sparks only a few months after her sister's death may well have been motivated, at least in part, by her love and concern for Helen's four small children.

Meanwhile, Tom Sparks was indicted for murder, and the trial was set to begin on April 4, 1916, exactly three months after he killed Lizzie. On that day Lizzie's sons, twenty-year-old Roy and twenty-three-year-old Dick, who were living in Oklahoma City, drove to Crowell to appear as witnesses for the prosecution. But they were not satisfied with playing that role. Whether they doubted a jury in Foard County (a place where the Sparks family was prominent) would convict Tom or whether they considered any court-administered justice unsatisfactory even when a conviction was assured, we will never know. What we do know is that Roy and Dick decided to personally administer a full measure of Old Testament justice and thus ensure Tom Sparks paid the ultimate penalty for killing their mother. On April 4, 1916, they confronted Sparks in downtown Crowell in front of the Bank of Crowell, across the street to the west of the Foard County Courthouse. Both men opened fire on their stepfather, and he was fatally wounded in a hail of bullets.[7] (Family legend has it that Roy and Dick pumped as many as forty-eight slugs into Tom's body.) Although the Bank of Crowell went defunct many years ago, the building still stands, and two bullet indentions can be seen clearly in the granite slab on the building's northeast corner—evidence that Roy or Dick aimed a bit too high and missed their target at least twice. Sparks was also armed, and, before falling, he once again managed to hit Roy in the arm, but the wound was once again not serious.

Dick and Roy Isaacs were indicted for the murder of Tom Sparks. On November 9, 1916, they were tried jointly in the district court in Crowell. There was a final note of irony in that. The town of Crowell is located only twenty miles south of Quanah, Texas. And it was in the town of Quanah where some twenty-one years earlier (almost to the day) their father, George Isaacs, was tried, convicted, and sentenced to life imprisonment for the murder of Canadian, Texas, sheriff Tom McGee. Roy and Dick were more fortunate, however, when they stood before the bar of justice. The Foard County jury that heard the murder case took only eight minutes to declare them "not guilty."[8]

Off the Record

The Isaacs brothers, Dick and Roy, were called by the prosecution to testify in the murder trial of Tom Sparks for killing their mother. On the morning the trial was to begin they arrived in Crowell, Texas. But they didn't come to testify. They came to administer their own brand of justice.

And that they did. Right across the street from the Foard County courthouse they both opened up on Tom Sparks, pistols blazing.

That they were determined to ensure that Tom Sparks paid the full price for killing their mother is beyond question. Yet why kill Tom Sparks *before* the trial? Perhaps they doubted that a Crowell jury would find Tom Sparks guilty and exact a satisfactory sentence. After all, the Sparks family was well respected in the community while Lizzie's past was checkered, to put the best face on it. Still, why risk a cell for life or a trip to the gallows by killing Tom Sparks—at least before the trial? Why not wait and see what the court would do to Sparks? Even if he were exonerated or a lenient sentence were imposed, the brothers could then bring their pistols into play.

Of course, logic had little to do with it; possible consequences of their acts were given little consideration. In that place and time—even after the turn of the century—subliminal echoes of the Old South's code of honor still resonated powerfully in the sons of the southwest. As President Andrew Jackson's mother told him when he was still a boy, there are some crimes so personal and so outrageous that court justice is simply too tepid to yield full satisfaction. By that doctrine, a man—if he is to call himself a man—has to personally avenge the wrong and thus restore honor to himself and his family. Or, as a typical frontiersman might have put it: a man has to kill his own snakes.

And that was the mindset of the brothers Isaacs. Whatever a judge or a jury might do to Tom Sparks, it simply would not be enough. Even if the law hung him, it would not be enough. Not enough because the noose would not have been tied, nor the trap sprung, by the sons of Lizzie Isaacs.

Even today, however civilized and humane we may like to believe we have become, there yet simmers just below the surface an all-too-human gut instinct that demands personal revenge when heinous crimes are perpetrated against us or our families—a powerful human factor that continues to challenge the supremacy of court-administered justice.

MURDER AND MAYHEM IN THE KNOX COUNTY COURTHOUSE

Dr. Jones Attacks the County Attorney

PLUS, THE GAMBLER, THE SHERIFF, AND THE MAIL-ORDER BRIDE

COURTHOUSES are supposed to be temples of justice, places where disputes are peaceably resolved by reliance on reason, logic, and law, places where violent crimes are punished—not perpetrated. But alas, on several occasions near the turn of the century in the tiny northwest Texas town of Benjamin, the Knox County Courthouse more nearly resembled Tombstone's famous OK Corral rather than a dispassionate temple of justice. "Bloody Knox" became an apt nickname for the stately old courthouse. (Could the bloody curse have had anything to do with the fact that the county was named in honor of Henry Knox, the first U.S. secretary of war?)

If the courthouse itself was cursed by repeated incidents of violence within its walls, did the same curse attach itself to pioneer Knox County lawyer D. J. Brookerson? Maybe so, for nearly every time blood was let in the Knox County Courthouse, it seemed that somehow Brookerson was always present. As you might guess, some of that blood came from the body of D. J. Brookerson himself.

The original Knox County Courthouse built in Benjamin, Texas, in 1887 was the site of much murder and mayhem. It was torn down in 1935 and replaced with a more modern and efficient—but not nearly as artistic and impressive—structure.
(Courtesy of the Knox County Historical Commission.)

Dr. Jones Attacks the County Attorney

D. J. Brookerson is remembered as an esteemed stalwart of the Northwest Texas Bar Association from its formative years, in addition to being a quite a colorful character. In the twilight years of the nineteenth century, D.J.'s dad and uncle migrated to America from Holland. When their ship dropped anchor off Galveston Island, they didn't have much of a struggle toting ashore the two trunks that held all their worldly possessions. The brothers soon obtained employment washing dishes in a Galveston cafe. The brothers eventually saved a few dollars and drifted northward in search of better employment, finally ending up in San Antonio, where the brothers went their separate ways. D.J.'s father found an American bride, and D.J. was born in 1875 in San Saba County, Texas.

Young D.J., still wet behind the ears, eventually wandered westward, where he first got a job cowboying on a West Texas ranch and later assisted a land surveying crew. At night, however, he poured over borrowed law books by the light of a kerosene lamp and became a self-educated lawyer. D.J. not only learned to read law books; he also learned to read people. He followed the typical path (apprenticeship) to earning his law license in 1900 without ever darkening the door of a law school, and in 1901 he managed to get himself elected county attorney of Knox County.[1]

Like most other cub lawyers of his day, Brookerson was young, single, and poorly paid, struggling to survive while establishing his reputation and a meager civil practice. Brookerson not only practiced law out of the county attorney's office; he also, in order to save money, lived there. Rural county attorneys, in addition to performing their official duties, were allowed to accept employment in private civil matters such as probate, divorce, damage suits, and land title suits. However, as mentioned earlier, not much civil practice was to be had until well into the twentieth century. Still, Brookerson managed to establish a modest and slowly increasing civil practice. He was eventually elected county judge of Knox County and later he became district judge for the four-county district.

Brookerson proved to be a consummate country politician. In addition to his native "people-smart" astuteness and general likeability, Brookerson devoted considerable time and effort to befriending nearly every family in that sparsely populated, multi-county district. He reaped a bountiful harvest from tireless fraternization with the common folks—not only in terms of his eventual political ascendancy, but, more immediately, in achieving an impressive record of courtroom victories in jury trials. As often as not, the canny Brookerson had a jury trial won as soon as they were seated, for he knew most prospective jurors personally, knew their biases and proclivities, and knew their community and familial relationships. He could therefore predict with a fair degree of accuracy how each person was likely to interact with others on the panel and how each was likely to react to the witnesses, the victim, the judge, the applicable law, and the opposing counsel. Lawyer Brookerson was hard as hell to beat on his home turf.[2]

In 1904, however, Brookerson accepted employment that almost ended his career before it got off the ground. He was hired to represent

D. J. Brookerson was a prominent and colorful jurist and trial lawyer at the turn of the century. Dr. L. P. Jones, whose wife Brookerson was representing in a pending divorce suit, attacked Brookerson with a knife in the Knox County Courthouse.
(Courtesy of Jack Jones, resident historian of Knox and Baylor counties and David Lott, grandson of D. J. Brookerson.)

the wife of Dr. L. P. Jones, a prominent doctor and rancher, in a bitter divorce proceeding.[3] Dr. Jones apparently suspected that his wife had become something more than just a client to lawyer Brookerson, and he threatened to kill Brookerson.

After separating from his wife, Dr. Jones moved out of their home in Benjamin to a ranch he owned some seven miles north of town on the Wichita River. As the divorce proceedings dragged on, the bitterness escalated. Dr. Jones ultimately decided to kill his wife, but of course he didn't intend to take the rap for it. To put his heinous plan into action, he surreptitiously obtained two bottles of chloroform. On Saturday night, August 19, 1904, he went to bed as usual in his ranchhouse. At about 3:00 in the morning, he got up, placed the pillows lengthwise on the bed and covered them with a quilt, saddled his horse, and headed for Benjamin. Before he got there, he stopped, donned a mask, replaced his boots with slippers, and muffled his horse's feet with rags. Later, with the chloroform in his pocket, he stealthily pried open a window to his wife's bedroom and entered.

At that point his plan went all to hell.

His wife awakened and began screaming. Abandoning the chloroform, he pulled out his long-bladed pocketknife and commenced upon a work of butchery. He dragged her from the bed and was in the act of stabbing her repeatedly when her cries awoke their three children. The eldest, L.P. Jr., age fourteen, and his younger brother, John Edd, rushed into their mother's room, grabbed their (still disguised) father, and pulled him off of their mother. L.P. Jr. yelled for John Edd to go get the pistol. Dr. Jones then pulled the mask from his face and exclaimed: "No, don't do that, this is your papa!" The children terrorized and confused— fled. Meanwhile, Mrs. Jones managed to crawl out of the window and attempted to reach the safety of a neighbor. But Dr. Jones overtook her at the yard gate and continued his murderous knife work. She fell just outside the gate and died.

By this time, L.P. Jr. had regained his nerve and came out to the scene of the carnage. He went with Dr. Jones to where the doctor's horse was tied and asked his father why he had attacked his mother. Dr. Jones replied that he was crazy. He kissed his son goodbye and told him to kiss the other two children for him, as he would never see them again. Mounting his horse, he fled. When L.P. Jr. returned to the scene where his mother lay, John Edd was there. "Mama is dead," John Edd sobbed. They covered their mother's body with a blanket and sat down beside her until neighbors arrived. An examination of Mrs. Jones's body revealed that she had suffered more than twenty stab wounds, several of which had penetrated her heart and other vital organs.[4]

Dr. Jones's blood lust was far from quenched, however. No doubt realizing that his plan had badly misfired and that he would be hunted down and probably hung for the brutal murder of his wife, he decided that he might as well even the score with D. J. Brookerson while he still had the opportunity. Dr. Jones rode to the courthouse. The courthouse doors were never locked, so he easily entered and climbed the stairs to the third-floor room where county attorney Brookerson was sleeping. When he found that door locked, he called out to Brookerson. Brushing the cobwebs of sleep from his brain, Brookerson asked, "Who's there?" Jones replied that he was Rufe Browder and that he had important business with him. Brookerson partially dressed, lit a lamp, and opened the door. Jones immediately sprang at Brookerson, brandishing his knife, and cursed: "Now I've got you!" Brookerson grabbed Jones by the arm and partly averted the blow, but he received a cut on his shoulder. In the ensuing life-or-death struggle, Jones moved the knife to his other hand and managed to cut a foot-long gash across Brookerson's right hip. Brookerson made several attempts to throw Jones out the window but failed. However, in a burst of panic-fueled strength, Brookerson forced Jones outside the door and into the hall corridor. He finally succeeded in throwing Jones over the stairwell banister. One hip was crushed in the fall, disabling Jones, but his injuries did not appear to be fatal. Nevertheless and in spite of a close watch by the jailers, Jones frustrated their vigilance. He persuaded a guard to bring him his doctor's satchel. When the guard's back was turned, Dr. Jones withdrew a scapel. At 8:00 Tuesday night he committed suicide by slashing his juglar vein.[5]

Brookerson, in later years, became a renowned raconteur whose habit, on pleasant mornings, was to hold court in the planter box in front of his office. One of his favorite stories was "The Time Dr. Jones Tried to Kill Me," and with little or no encouragement Brookerson would strip down and display the resultant scars on his posterior.[6]

Long before Brookerson reached his golden, yarn-spinning days, however, he was involved in yet another Knox County Courthouse bloodletting that made the 1904 episode look like touch football. Ten years after Brookerson's battle with Dr. Jones, another young, broke, and single lawyer moved to Benjamin and took over the reins as county attorney. He lived in the same county attorney office/apartment that Brookerson had occupied. Born September 9, 1890, in Rusk, Texas, John Bunyon Rhea graduated from Goree High School in Knox County and then went on to the University of Texas law school, where he graduated in 1914.[7] Rhea and Brookerson were both in the Knox County District courtroom on March 20, 1917, participating in a murder trial when a wild shootout erupted. However, the seed that produced this violent episode was sown years earlier.

J. J. "Red" Mitchell was a huge man with red hair and a bristling red mustache—a rugged westerner, a "man's man," and a turn-of-the-century West Texas sheriff who feared little in the way of man or beast.

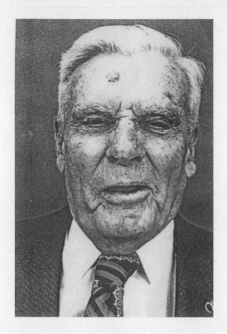

John Bunyon Rhea was the Knox County attorney in Benjamin, Texas, in 1917. He was assistant prosecutor during the murder trial of George Douglas when Will Mitchell, brother of the murdered sheriff Red Mitchell, came out of the courtroom crowd and shot Douglas dead. He also wounded Douglas's attorney, J. F. Cunningham, and witness Henry Delk.
(From the *Wichita Daily Times*, May 2, 1976.)

However, the task he was so earnestly engaged in when we pick up his story caused sweat to pop out on his forehead. Hunched over the kitchen table in his modest ranch cabin, he tightly gripped a pencil and concentrated by the flickering light of a kerosene lamp on the words he was marking on his tablet. Writing anything was a stretch for the sheriff because he had had very little formal schooling, but that was the least of his problems. What caused him to agonize over each word was the nature of the message he was attempting to compose.

By the time Red reached middle-age he had achieved a fair amount of success. He was the elected sheriff of King County, Texas, and he had a good-sized ranch (a respectable five-thousand-acre spread, unfortunately dwarfed by Burk Burnett's adjoining 6666 Ranch, which covered about a quarter-million acres). Red, who had lived alone all his adult life, felt something was still missing. He was lonely, and he wanted a wife and children to fill the vacuum.

Attaining that goal presented some mighty big challenges. For one thing, no one ever accused Red of being handsome or even close to cute. Also, very few folks called the windswept prairies of King County home in the late 1890s, and not many of them were women. Those who were, were already taken. Finally, Red, who knew a lot about how to handle ornery broncs and wild cattle and rough men, was woefully ignorant when it came to social graces, the rituals of courtship, or women in general. Someone—who probably had no more sophistication in these matters than did Red—suggested that he should place an advertisement for a mail-order bride in a publication back East.

And that was the document Red was struggling so mightily to compose. Having no guidance in such matters, he must have felt like a rudderless ship adrift in heavy seas. Nevertheless, he persevered, got it in as good shape as he could, and mailed it.

Amazingly enough, it worked!

He soon received a response from a Tennessee school marm named Ellen Douglas. Very shortly thereafter Red caught a train headed east, and on September 26, 1906, he married Miss Douglas in Warren County, Tennessee. Ellen was described as a "good-looking, though somewhat buxom, dark-haired young woman in her twenties or early thirties." She was no small woman, and she was certainly no shrinking violet. She proved adaptable to her new environment—a hard-scrabble existence on the stark and desolate plains of King County, Texas. Soon after her arrival, Ellen developed quite a talent in the use of firearms and became an expert shot with both pistol and rifle. If Ellen was packing her .45 pistol, it was said that a jackrabbit's chances of survival at thirty paces were slim to none.[8]

For quite some time things went well, and it appeared that Red had stumbled upon an ideal mate. Within a couple of years their first daughter, Annie May, was born, followed by a sister, Sallie Lee, the next year, and then a son, J.P., five years later. Sheriff Mitchell adored his children and, in his crude way, loved his wife.

Not very long after J.P. was born, however, dark storm clouds began to gather, and Red's days of peace and paradise on this earth were fast counting down. When those storm clouds broke, a bitter divorce battle erupted in the Knox County Courthouse. Worse yet, a trail of fresh blood and dead bodies would soon lead directly back to, and into, the same Knox County courtroom.

The trouble between the Mitchells began when their children reached school age. King County was so sparsely populated that its school system was sadly inadequate. The nearest "city" that afforded adequate schooling opportunities was Knox City, a village of 2,500 or so inhabitants about thirty-five miles east of Red's ranch. (Knox City is located in Knox County, which adjoins King County on the east.) In order to facilitate their plan to educate the children, Red bought a hotel in Knox City and established Ellen as the manager. He reckoned that this would not only assure a good education for their children, but it would also provide additional family income. Once the hotel was established, Red returned to his ranch and came to town only on weekends. The new arrangement worked out pretty well—for a time.

Knox City was the center of a rich farming area. Cotton was the chief crop, which at that time was picked by hand. For three or four months each fall a great influx of transient cotton-pickers—mostly Mexican aliens—came to town. The season gave the little burgh a boomtown atmosphere, which attracted bootleggers, prostitutes, and gamblers in search of a quick, easy buck. Among the latter was a professional gambler by the name of Sil Morton, who found conditions in Knox City so favorable for his occupation that he settled down for an indefinite stay. He also found the Mitchell Hotel to be a convenient headquarters from which to operate. Not only were there many transients, but plenty of young, local amateur gamblers were available, all of which made for a rather lucrative year-round environment.

In his early forties, a good dresser, a smooth talker, and a handsome fellow, Morton's prosperous and easy lifestyle, despite the absence of a visible means of support, occasionally evoked raised eyebrows, and his increasingly apparent efforts to ingratiate himself with Ellen Mitchell started whispers from residents. Sometime in the first part of 1915 it became obvious that Ellen Mitchell was providing amenities to Sil Morton over and above those furnished to other guests of the Mitchell Hotel, and the whispers grew louder and pervasive enough to reach the ears of Red Mitchell—who wasted no time in addressing the matter.[9] The Mitchells were separated shortly before Christmas 1915. On December 27, 1915, Red and Ellen sat down and wrote a homemade "contract," which they recorded in the King County Deed Records. It stated that Red sold Ellen his undivided one-half (community) ownership in the Mitchell Hotel in Knox City for $2,500. The contract states that it was made in contemplation of a divorce between the parties because "we have lost proper love and respect for each other."[10]

On January 9, 1916, Mitchell, nursing a badly bruised ego and with

W. S. BRITTON

SHERIFF AND TAX COLLECTOR
OF KNOX COUNTY

WHEN WRITING OF LAND DON'T FAIL TO GIVE ABSTRACT NUMBER

A. E. PROPPS, OFFICE DEPUTY.   BENJAMIN, TEXAS, 8-28   1916

Received of W. S. Britton 1 $0 32 automatic Colts pistol, the property which was taken off the diceesed Sil Morton.

C. L. morton

King County sheriff Red Mitchell shot and killed his wife's lover, professional gambler Sil Morton, in Knox City on January 16, 1916. Morton had been expecting trouble
from Sheriff Mitchell and was armed with a pistol. After the murder, Knox County
sheriff W. S. Britton delivered Sil Morton's .32 caliber automatic Colt pistol to
C. L. Morton, a relative of the deceased, who received this receipt.
(Official court records of Knox County, Cause No. 987, Knox County District Court.)

blood in his eye, left his King County ranch for Knox City, where he confronted Sil Morton with an ultimatum. The town was not big enough for
both of them, and he expected Morton to be gone by sunrise. Sil Morton
made a very serious and unwise career move at that point. He told Red,
"No S.O.B. is going to run me out of this town."[11] Both men spent what
must have been a restless night at the hotel, and both ate breakfast there
on January 10, 1916. The typical small West Texas hotel served family-
style meals in a dining room that opened directly off the lobby. Morton
arrived first and entered the dining room. Mitchell came in a few minutes later and took a seat at the other end of the long table. Only two or
three others were having breakfast at this early hour, but seeing the
tense situation, they hurriedly choked down a few bites and departed.

Not a word was spoken by either of the men, who must have realized
that their little drama was rapidly approaching a deadly climax. Upon
Mitchell's entry, Morton had shifted his .32 Colt automatic from its concealed location to the seat of his chair, directly between his legs. Despite
the fact that Morton was the first to arrive, Mitchell was the first to fin-

ish breakfast and leave. He then hid in the lobby . . . and waited.

When Morton entered the hotel lobby Mitchell ambushed him and shot him dead.[12]

Knox County sheriff W. S. Britton in Benjamin, the county seat about fifteen miles north of Knox City, was called. He, together with county attorney John Bunyon Rhea, immediately drove to the scene. Many years later, Rhea wrote an account of what happened next:

> Within thirty minutes we were in Knox City, traveling over the unpaved road. [I still remember what] a rough ride a 1914 Dodge with its rigid springs [gave] a passenger. The sheriff was an emotional person, capable and efficient, he knew everybody, was a friend to everybody and he took others' troubles personally. Hardly a word was spoken between us. . . . We found Morton's body lying just outside the dining room door but within the lobby. Morton had fallen face-down with his right hand beneath his body. . . . We turned it over and found in the right hand a .32 caliber automatic pistol. It had not been fired recently and was still on safety. A search of his pockets revealed only a pocketknife, some small coins, and a rabbit's foot. I never again had much respect for that supposedly good luck charm. . . . Red hired D. J. Brookerson to defend him. Action then turned briefly to the civil courts.[13]

Ellen wasted no time in filing for divorce. On January 12, 1916, two days after her husband killed Sil Morton, she filed a divorce suit in the King County District Court in Guthrie seeking a healthy property division including an interest in their five-thousand-acre ranch and custody of the three children.[14] Red, out on bond and awaiting trial for the murder of Sil Morton, countered by filing a divorce suit against Ellen on June 24, 1916, in the Knox County District Court in Benjamin. He also sought custody of the children. It is interesting to speculate why each chose the county he or she did. We might think that Ellen would have preferred Knox County—the county in which she resided and the county in which her husband had just killed a man. And it would seem logical that Red would have preferred to file his suit in King County—the county where he lived, owned a ranch, and was the sheriff. But, for whatever reasons, each chose otherwise. Filing in different courts created an additional issue: which court would ultimately decide the case? Red's petition hung out all the dirty laundry. In his petition he alleged that Ellen

> ... in total disregard of her marital obligations began a course of unwomanlike conduct with one Sil Morton who was a libertine and associate of lewd women ... [and that Ellen, over his protest] ... continued to associate with said Sil Morton and show affection toward him ... and ... during the fall of 1915 [she] also began to associate with vulgar, indecent and lewd women and to harbor such women in and about the [Knox City hotel] home of plaintiff [Red Mitchell] and to permit women of lewd character to ply their vocations in the [hotel] home of plaintiff ... and that the defendant continued to associate with Sil Morton ... and to permit him to enter and remain in [her] private room ... at unseasonable hours of the night and by reason of the remonstrance of plaintiff against such acts he is informed and believes ... that the defendant, acting together with Sil Morton and other persons, entered into conspiracy to falsely charge this plaintiff with crime and by false and perjured testimony to procure the arrest and incarceration of this plaintiff and by reason of same to procure the property and children of this plaintiff.[15]

Ellen responded with equally ugly charges against Red in her petition, and the donnybrook was on. In preparation for trial, Red's attorneys took the written deposition of Mrs. Cordie Jones, age twenty-six, of Knox City, who testified that she had observed Ellen and Sil Morton's carryings-on during the past year in Knox City. She testified that she had a conversation with Ellen in the latter part of 1915 (shortly before Red killed Morton) and that Ellen told her that Red had made threats to kill Sil Morton. According to Cordie Jones's testimony, Ellen then made this reply to Red Mitchell: "Darn you, I will shoot you if you do [kill Morton]." Ellen, she testified, admitted to her that Morton had been coming to her house in Knox City around midnight every night and staying until one or two o'clock in the morning and that Ellen told her that "she never loved Red Mitchell a day in his life" and that instead she loved Sil

Morton "with all my heart and always will and I know Sil loves me."[16]

The citizens of Knox and King counties—two small, sparsely populated frontier communities where everybody knew everything about everybody else's business—began to take sides in the drama of good versus evil, or at least perceived good and evil. If the divorce brawl itself was not bad enough, other complications, aggravating circumstances, and outside parties with axes to grind surfaced to throw even more kindling on the fire. Red and Ellen each had no-account, trouble-making brothers who showed up, and both were armed to the teeth.

When George Douglas heard that Red Mitchell was charging his sister with being a lewd woman—and worse—he came roaring down from his home in Tennessee to enter the fray. Enraged, he publicly avowed that "No S.O.B. will live to testify [to the allegations that Red Mitchell was making against his sister]." Douglas was described by county attorney John Bunyon Rhea as "a man in his late fifties of medium build and with nothing striking about his appearance."[17]

Meanwhile, William Mitchell (known as "Bill" or "Will"), brother to Red Mitchell arrived next. He was a hardcase who hung out in the bars and pool halls along Ohio Street in Wichita Falls, Texas—the rough, seedy part of that town. Over the preceding few years he had earned notoriety as the survivor of several saloon knife fights. There was little resemblance between Will and his brother; Red Mitchell was almost a giant, while Will was short. Will also had a crippled leg and wore an iron brace that caused a pronounced limp. For good measure, Will brought a few of his lowlife buddies from Wichita Falls with him to add bile to the witch's brew then a-bubblin'.[18]

Since Ellen filed her divorce first, their first public skirmish took place at Guthrie in King County. A preliminary hearing was held on Ellen's petition in September 1916. Armed partisans from both camps confronted each other at the courthouse. In pleadings later filed by George Douglas, he told the court that on that occasion Will Mitchell informed his witness, J. H. Lyon, that "strangers were in the county and to tell [George Douglas] that he better look out and be careful and keep his hands off of the divorce business." Douglas also alleged that one of Ellen's witnesses, Mrs. Ross Davis, would testify that when she, George Douglas, and Ellen Mitchell attempted to leave the hotel in Guthrie and enter the courthouse for the preliminary hearing they were prevented from doing so by the defendant, J. J. Mitchell; his brother, Will Mitchell; Frank Irving; "and some strangers who were in the courtyard." Douglas alleged that when they got within about one hundred fifty yards of the courthouse, they saw the Mitchell partisans "hurriedly" go to their automobiles "and there got some long guns and held them in their hands." Douglas also stated in his pleadings that Red Mitchell had communicated death threats against him.[19] In this supercharged atmosphere, the King County District Court found a temporary solution by sending the case to Knox County on a change of venue, thus allowing both divorce cases to be consolidated there.

Ellen Mitchell and brother George Douglas were apparently not the only ones who felt threatened by the opposing camp, for on September 1, 1916, Red Mitchell sat down and, in his own handwriting and without benefit of legal counsel, rewrote his will and cut Ellen out of his legacy. He left all his estate to his three children. Most interesting, however, was the prophetic preface of the will. It began: "I, J. J. Mitchell, realizing that life is uncertain and my life is sought in order that my children may be robed [*sic*] . . ."[20]

Since in that multi-county rural district, the district court convened only twice a year in each county, the resulting delay of several months (after the King County District Court transferred the divorce case back to Knox County in September 1916) exacerbated the heated passions of the parties, as well as the partisans.

The boiler pressure climbed. Perhaps the final stick of kindling thrown onto the blaze, the one that blew the lid off the boiler, was the serving upon Ellen of a notice to take the written deposition of one Tom Fine, who apparently had been another occupant of the Mitchell Hotel during 1915. The questions to be propounded to Mr. Fine were similar to those embarrassing questions formerly put to Mrs. Cordie Jones and presumably would have elicited similar responses. An additional question was whether he had witnessed Ellen and Sil "drinking whiskey together." Mr. Fine would be asked if he had ever received any letters from Ellen concerning this matter, and, if so, he was to attach the letters to his answers. Finally, did Ellen ever tell him she and Sil Morton planned to run off together?[21] This notice to take the deposition of

Thomas Fine was served on Ellen on December 22, 1916. It stated that Brookerson, Red's attorney, intended to take the deposition five days thereafter. And that blew the top right off!

According to county attorney Rhea's account, on Christmas Eve George Douglas (who later gave his own very different account) sought a confrontation with Red Mitchell at Mitchell's King County ranch. However, Mitchell had gone to Knox City. There were few automobiles at that time, but Douglas made a quick deal with the local mail carrier, Will Winter, to drive him the thirty-five miles back to Knox City for twenty dollars. Winter owned a Ford touring car, and he buttoned up the side curtains to at least partially deflect the stiff norther blowing that Christmas Eve night. Winter noticed that Douglas was armed with both a rifle and a shotgun. When they arrived at Knox City, Douglas directed Winter to park in front of the Frizzel Drug Store, a well-lighted area. Winter went into the drug store to buy cigars for Douglas—or so he later testified. Not long thereafter, Red Mitchell came walking down the street with a friend identified as "Shorty." As they approached Winter's automobile, in which Douglas was still seated, Shorty was between the car and Red Mitchell. However, since Red towered head and shoulders above Shorty, this fact did not pose a problem for Douglas. As the unsuspecting Mitchell passed within ten feet of Douglas, a single shot from Douglas's rifle passed over Shorty and hit Mitchell in the back of his head, neatly cutting the band of his ten-gallon Stetson hat and killing him instantly. Douglas would later testify to a very different version of what happened, although he did not deny killing Mitchell.

Douglas then sprang out of the car carrying his rifle and a pistol. Startled Christmas shoppers scattered in every direction. L. C. Everett, the city marshal of Knox City and deputy city marshal Joel Reed, happened to be two or three blocks from the scene and, hearing the shot, decided to investigate. Seeing people running away from the Frizzel Drug Store, Everett and Reed started running toward that spot. However, Marshal Everett was as elderly as he was portly, and Reed outran him to the scene. Douglas was still pacing about, agitated with a pistol in his right hand and the rifle in his left. He looked up and saw Reed coming at him—armed. Douglas then shot Reed dead. It was at about that time Everett arrived on the scene. Douglas wheeled around, and in one sweeping motion with his rifle knocked the pistol from Everett's hand and fled into the darkness.

Once again, county attorney Rhea and Sheriff Britton were summoned from Benjamin to rush to a Knox City murder scene. They arrived about an hour after the shooting. Britton insisted on starting a search for Douglas; Rhea was understandably reluctant. As Rhea related the tale:

> I thought such action would be useless, and, furthermore, in view of what had just happened, should we chance upon him he probably would shoot it out. But the sheriff was adamant that it was his duty to go after Douglas at once. So, after picking up a deputy, we took off for the western part of the city since witnesses said that Douglas was going in that direction when last seen. We combed the railroad yards, although I was secretly hoping we would not find him. After a fruitless search we finally returned to Benjamin.
>
> In a couple of days I received a telephone call from J. M. Hawkins, a lawyer in Paducah, who said he understood that Douglas would probably be arrested soon and he wanted to know whether I would agree to bail. I consulted with the sheriff, who agreed, suggesting that Douglas be located and arrested. I called Hawkins and told him that though this might be a non-bailable case, a judge upon proper hearing would probably grant bail. I told him to bring his man in and we would accept a $10,000.00 bond. Later that day Hawkins called back and suggested that if the sheriff went alone and unarmed to a certain abandoned ranch house in King County west of Benjamin, Douglas would surrender there. The sheriff did as he was directed and was back in Benjamin with Douglas early the next morning where Douglas' lawyer and bondsman were waiting. In a few minutes they were out of town.[22]

Four grand jury indictments were promptly handed down: two murder indictments against George Douglas for the murders of J. J. Mitchell and deputy city marshal Joel Reed and two identical murder indictments against the wheelman, Will Winter, who, under the state's theory, was an accomplice to both murders.[23]

An interesting tactical issue was presented to both the prosecution and defense: what advantage would be gained by prosecuting which defendant first and for which murder? Obviously, both cases against Douglas were stronger than either of the cases against Winter, who was, at best, an unarmed wheelman accomplice. So the prosecution wanted to try Douglas first, while the defense wanted Winter tried first. Douglas's attorneys moved to continue the case until after Winter was tried, feeling that he probably would be acquitted, and then he would be free to testify as a defense witness when Douglas's cases were called. Not to mention the great tactical advantage for the defense if it could go into the Douglas trial with a prior victory under its belt.

The judge, however, denied the continuance, and forced Douglas to trial first. The question then became whether to try Douglas first for the murder of Red Mitchell or for the murder of deputy city marshal Joel Reed. The prosecution's theory was that George Douglas was guilty of a "cold-blooded ambush" when he killed Sheriff Mitchell. The defensive theory centered on self-defense: that just before the shooting, Mitchell recognized Douglas in Winter's car and had tried to draw his pistol on Douglas. However, the physical evidence, the fatal bullet wound in the back of Red Mitchell's head, was obviously more consistent with the state's "ambush theory." At first glance, it might appear that the cold-blooded, calculated ambush killing of a sheriff would be more likely to inflame a jury and thus result in a conviction.

On the other hand, Red Mitchell was himself under indictment for murder (for killing Sid Morton), and he, his brother, and their entourage had made dire threats against Douglas, including threatening to kill him if he didn't stay out of his sister's divorce. Plus, in that more chivalrous day, Red Mitchell had publicly alleged some terribly scandalous things about his own wife and the mother of his children. Under those circumstances, the prosecution considered it better, tactically, to try Douglas first for killing an innocent law enforcement officer who was only performing his duty when he was shot down by Douglas.

But there was a problem in the Reed murder trial that was not present in the Red Mitchell murder case. Actually, there were two weak spots in the Reed murder case, and the defense would not hesitate to exploit them. First, at the time he was killed, Reed had only recently been hired as deputy city marshal; he was not a native of the area; and he was not wearing a uniform. Few folks thereabout knew him or realized he was a police officer. Second, he ran up to Douglas with a pistol in his hand. This allowed Douglas to make the credible claim that he didn't know Reed and that he had no idea that he was an officer. He simply saw Reed running toward him with a pistol, and so, logically assuming that he was a Mitchell partisan intending retaliation, Douglas shot Reed in self-defense.

In the end, the court ordered the trial of George Douglas for the murder of Knox City deputy marshal Joel Reed to proceed first.

The trial was before district judge Jo A. P. Dickson of Seymour, an able and colorful jurist. District attorney Ollin Newton headed up the prosecution and was assisted by J. R. Stubblefield, a noted criminal lawyer from Ranger, who had been hired by the Reed family. Also assisting the state was county attorney John Bunyon Rhea.

The Douglas defense fielded an all-star team, headed by J. F. Cunningham of Abilene, a powerful criminal trial lawyer whom we met previously in the chapter about Thomas J. Fulcher's murder trial. He was assisted by J. M. Hawkins of Paducah and the ubiquitous D. J. Brookerson. Brookerson was not only an able trial lawyer, but he also knew just about everybody in Knox County, which, as we have observed, proved invaluable when selecting juries. Ironically, until Red Mitchell was killed by Douglas, Brookerson had been representing Mitchell in his pending murder case. In this case he was representing his deceased client's killer. In early Texas jurisprudence, client loyalty died with the client.

At the time of the trial, Douglas was free on bail, and he, his sister, Ellen Mitchell, and their party (including the defense lawyers) stayed at the local hotel in Benjamin. In response to the inflamed passions of both factions, the officers escorted Douglas to and from a packed courthouse every day and searched everyone entering the courtroom except court officials and the attorneys.

Douglas told the jury that he hired Will Winter on the evening of December 24, 1916, not for the purpose of taking him to Knox City to confront Red Mitchell, but for the purpose of taking him to Stamford, Texas, to meet lawyer Charles Coombes with the intent of employing him to represent his sister Ellen in the divorce case. Douglas did produce a letter written to him by Coombes, dated earlier that month, stating that he would be pleased to consult with Douglas concerning possible representation of his sister. However, the letter did not set any specific date for an appointment. It might also have seemed peculiar to the jury that Douglas selected this particular time—late Christmas Eve night— to travel over to Stamford and consult with Coombes on legal business.

Douglas told the jury all about the Mitchell mob's threats to kill him on sight, which explained the reason why he armed himself wherever he went and explained why he was armed with a pistol, a shotgun, and a rifle en route to consult with an attorney. He said he directed Winter to stop at the Frizzel Drug Store as they passed through Knox City en route to Stamford in order to buy some cigars. He remained in the parked automobile, he said, while Winter went inside. At this point, he contended that Red Mitchell recognized him and testified that Mitchell, as anticipated, had attempted to pull his pistol. That, he continued, was when he shot Mitchell in self-defense. Then the hapless Deputy City Marshal Reed rushed up, armed with a pistol, and he mistook Reed for a Mitchell partisan, so he shot Reed, also in self-defense.[24]

Douglas testified that after the shootings he told Winter to get out of harm's way and that he, Douglas, then fled the scene on foot. (The prosecution always contended that Winter not only knew well the true purpose of the trip was to kill Mitchell but also that he helped Douglas escape.)

On March 20, 1917, ten days after it began, the trial of George Douglas ended in a hung jury—eight to four for acquittal.[25] Judge Dickson declared a mistrial. But the proceedings for that day were far from over. Jurors, witnesses, spectators, attorneys, and court officials milled around in the courtroom while the attorneys and the court considered various motions. Douglas and his attorneys again presented a motion to continue the Douglas case until after Will Winter was tried, asserting that Douglas was suffering from Bright's disease and was too ill to stand trial in the near future. George Douglas signed that motion for continuance just after the mistrial.

It was the last thing he ever did.

While the lawyers and the court were discussing this and other motions, Will Mitchell entered the crowded courtroom. County attorney John Bunyon Rhea had seen Will come in and was apprehensive. Still, he had seen the officers search Will, and after a few moments Rhea forgot about him. Unfortunately, however, the officers hadn't done a very good job of searching Mitchell and had failed to detect the .32 caliber pistol secreted under his broad-brimmed western-style hat.

A low railing separated the trial area from the spectator's portion of the courtroom, and Douglas and his defense attorneys were seated at the counsel table with their backs to the spectator area. Sheriff Britton was also inside the railing serving as the bailiff. Two other deputies were present. Will Mitchell stealthily worked his way through the crowd until he got to the railing immediately behind George Douglas. Three shots suddenly rang out, creating absolute chaos! Spectators made a mad stampede for the two exits. Will Mitchell's first shot hit Douglas in the back between his shoulder blades and severed the main artery to the heart, killing him almost instantly. Sheriff Britton grabbed Mitchell's arm sending his next two shots wild, but not harmless. One hit defense attorney J. F. Cunningham in the thigh, and the third shot hit a witness, Henry Delk of Paducah, in the stomach.

At that point Sheriff Britton managed to knock the pistol out of Will Mitchell's hand, but that didn't end the crisis. Sheriff Britton was inside the railing struggling with Will Mitchell, who was on the outside of the railing, and when the pistol was dislodged from Mitchell's hand it fell outside the railing. Mitchell was desperately trying to free himself from the sheriff's grip and regain control of his pistol. But Will Mitchell and the sheriff weren't the *only* ones who were trying to get their hands on that pistol. Ellen Mitchell, sister of the just-murdered George Douglas, saw what was happening and charged upstream through the fleeing crowd in an attempt to grab the pistol and, no doubt, use it to kill Will Mitchell. Sheriff Britton yelled out, "For God's sake, somebody get that gun!"

County attorney John Bunyon Rhea finally grasped what was happening, leaped over the railing and scooped up the pistol just barely ahead of Ellen Mitchell, who collided with him. Rhea commented, "She was not a small woman, and her 175 pounds made quite an impression on my 165 pounds." Rhea continued:

I tried to lead her from the courtroom but she insisted upon going back to where her brother was. I had briefly seen him gurgle once and partially straighten up, only to fall forward on the table. I told

Mrs. Mitchell that neither she nor anyone else could do Douglas any good. Convinced that he was dead, she allowed me and a court bailiff to lift Douglas from his chair, lay him on the long lawyer's table and place a law book under his head. . . . Ellen Mitchell told me she didn't know why she didn't have her pistol with her that day and that this was the first time she had been in the courtroom during the trial without it.[26]

Sheriff Britton later told Rhea that the very day George Douglas was shot, Douglas begged the sheriff to allow him to take his gun into the courtroom. The sheriff refused and assured him that he would be duly protected. Douglas then told the sheriff that he would never come out of the court room alive. Rhea reflected, "Whether he had a simple premonition or a baleful glance from Will Mitchell, I don't know. This thought has always haunted me."[27]

Both of the wounded survived. After the dust settled, defense lawyer Cunningham yelled for a rancher friend, Gene Mayfield of Aspermont, to get the car so he could leave. The rancher asked whether he meant his car or Cunningham's. The exasperated defense attorney shouted, "It don't make a damned bit of difference . . . let's just get out of this damned town." With only a first aid dressing on his wound, he was driven to Munday, where he caught the Wichita Valley train to Abilene. But it wasn't that simple—or painless. Twice along the road to Munday their car veered into deep sand and got stuck. The wounded lawyer was thus obliged to get out and help push. When he finally got to Abilene, Cunningham told the story to a newspaper reporter and then went into a tirade about the incompetence of Benjamin law enforcement—comments that made Sheriff Britton's blood boil. From his bed that night, Cunningham told the *Abilene Daily Reporter*:

> The sheriff and two deputies were standing nearby, but never attempted to shoot Mitchell. . . . I have more feeling against the officers who let Mitchell come armed into the courtroom where he could kill Douglas and shoot us all, than I have against Mitchell.

However, Cunningham then retreated somewhat when he added this comment, "Sheriff Britton, however, is a fine and good man."[28]

From 1888 to 1890 J. F. Cunningham Jr. of Abilene, Texas, at only twenty-eight, served as the first district attorney of the multi-county 39th Judicial District, which included most of West Texas. He didn't run for reelection because he was more inclined to practice on the other side of the docket; from then until his death in 1933, Cunningham earned a reputation as the preeminent lion of the criminal defense bar in that area.
(Courtesy of the Southwest Collection/Special Collections Library, Texas Tech University, Lubbock, Texas, Southwest Collection Photographs, No. 135 E-1 #8.)

Cunningham told a reporter that he was shocked that in these "civilized" times (1917), a man with such contempt for the law would boldly come in the courtroom and, in the presence of the judge and officers of the court, proceed to shoot three unarmed men. Referring to his earlier and wilder days when he was district attorney of the 39th Judicial District (1888–1890), he remarked:

There was never a moment in those days [when] litigants, lawyers and witnesses were secure in their lives while in district court.[29]

The courtroom finally cleared, leaving only county attorney Rhea and the recently departed George Douglas. George's spirit may have departed, but his corpse still lay on the counsel table with his head still resting on a law book. As there was no funeral parlor in Benjamin, Ellen Mitchell arranged for an undertaker from the nearby town of Crowell to come and prepare her brother's body for shipment back to Tennessee. The undertakers came by train from Crowell to Benjamin, riding on the little regional railway with a wonderfully grand name: "the Kansas City, Mexico, and Orient Railroad." John

Bunyon Rhea recounted the macabre finale of that day's Knox County courtroom drama:

> After about an hour, a couple of undertakers arrived, and immediately set about their work. I went out to try to relax and had dinner at the hotel. After dinner, I went out to see the girl I was soon to marry [Mora Moore]. Naturally, time passed rapidly and pleasantly and soon I had shaken off the depression of the last few hours, so I was feeling pretty good when I returned to my sleeping quarters in the courthouse about eleven o'clock that night.
>
> The undertakers seemed about to complete their task, and after a few exchanges of small talk I went into the jury room and locked the door. But sleep didn't come. From outside my door I could hear the men bustling about, and in about thirty minutes I could hear them lumbering down the steep stairs with their burden.
>
> At the foot of the stairs I could hear them grumbling about something. Then the slow and laborious climb back up the stairs. I got up and went back into the courtroom to see what the problem was. The undertakers explained that their work had to be partially done over. Stitches had not held, releasing embalming fluid that had flooded the casket. They worked rapidly and again gathered up their instruments and tools and prepared to leave.
>
> Suddenly I realized what was about to take place. It was after midnight and they had missed the train [back to Crowell]. There would not be another until the next afternoon and George was to be with me the remainder of the night. They said he would be all right "Well," I replied, "I won't be all right."
>
> I could almost hear them chuckling, as they bade me goodnight and swept downstairs into the outer darkness. There was George and I, just the two of us, in the cavernous courtroom, lighted only by a few dim bulbs. Everywhere I turned shadows and eerie figures danced before my eyes. The events of the day marched through my mind. In my imagination I could see a previous county attorney [D. J. Brookerson] who had likewise slept in this courtroom, being set upon by a madman, slashed by a dagger and only saved by his own terror-stricken strength in casting his assailant to the floor below, breaking

his back. I rushed into the jury room where I was temporarily sleeping, locked the door, sank into bed, where hours later I fell into a
troubled sleep.[30]

The very next day, county attorney John Bunyon Rhea resigned his
position and enlisted in the U.S. Army for service in World War I. He
figured that facing the German army in the front line trenches of
France would be a damn sight safer than hanging around the Knox
County Courthouse.[31]

Immediately after the shooting, the sheriff upbraided Will for having broken his promise to let the law take its course. Will, in a matter-of-
fact way, said it was evident that the case was going to be postponed with
the resultant continuation of the cat-and-mouse game between him and
Douglas, and he was relieved to have it over with.

The day after Will Mitchell killed George Douglas, a Knox County
grand jury returned three indictments against Will Mitchell for the
murder of George Douglas and for assault with intent to murder Jim
Cunningham and Henry Delk.[32] The Knox County District Court lost no
time in changing venue from Knox County to adjacent Baylor County to
the east.[33] It was obvious that lynch-mob fever was rising, for the court
went further than merely changing venue: it directed that Will Mitchell
be removed to the Baylor County jail for "safekeeping on account of the
jail in Knox County, Texas, not being safe for the keeping of the prisoner."

But, if the prosecution thought they had a slam-dunk, they were
soon disabused of that notion. On August 4, 1917 (while a Knox County
jury was trying Will Winter), a Baylor County jury in Seymour tried
Will Mitchell for slaying George Douglas, who had killed Will's brother,
Red Mitchell. The result was a hung jury and a mistrial. All twelve
voted "guilty," but they were hung on punishment at eight for life, four
for death.[34]

In Knox County, meanwhile, on August 22, 1917, D. J. Brookerson had
little difficulty in persuading a jury to find his client, Will Winter, not
guilty of being George Douglas's accomplice in the alleged murder of
Brookerson's former client Sheriff Mitchell. That accomplished, Brookerson encountered little resistance the same day in persuading the court

to dismiss the second indictment against Winter for being Douglas's accomplice in the alleged murder of Deputy City Marshal Reed.[35]

Back on the Baylor County front, however, Will Mitchell was still a very long way from walking away from the courthouse as a free man. The first Baylor County jury had agreed unanimously that he was guilty of murdering Deputy City Marshal Reed, and four of them wanted to hang him. The long shadow of the hangman cast by the first trial must have been sobering for the defense.

It certainly caused a change in their strategy. Perhaps "incompetence" might provide an escape hatch. First, Will Mitchell's lawyers managed to persuade the judge to set a $7,500 bond, and Will was freed on bail pending retrial. Shortly thereafter, Will was observed marching up and down the streets of Seymour, a .45 pistol in hand, banging away at invisible targets. When collared by the law, he explained that he was on a crusade against grasshoppers. A few other wild stunts laid the foundation for a lunacy trial.[36]

Although the grasshopper-shooting episode smelled like a stunt contrived to bootstrap an incompetency or insanity plea,[37] it should be mentioned that Will did have a history of episodes of bizarre behavior leading to violence. Will was born in 1871 and grew up on a farm near Sparta, Tennessee. In 1896 his spells of weird behavior alarmed neighbors, and officers were dispatched to haul Will before the local county court to investigate his sanity. Will objected to the invite, and that led to an altercation during which Will was shot twice. Upon his recovery, he was found by the court to be a "dangerous lunatic," and on November 29, 1897, was shipped off to a Tennessee mental institution. Will insisted on taking his pet possum with him, a companion he absolutely refused to release from his grasp.[38] Three months later, Will and the possum were discharged—"marked improved," the doctor noted.[39] It was not entirely clear whether that remark referred to Will or the possum, since several months later Will got really weird again.

At a protracted revival in a country church near Sparta, Will came down with a serious case of religion. One of the flock, Mrs. George Steakley, Will's niece, who later moved to Paducah, Texas, testified that Will "took quite a keen interest in religion." Got so interested in fact that, as she recollected it, "his forwardness interfered with the meeting."

Near the close of one sermon, Will brought the proceedings to an abrupt halt when he stood up, denounced the preacher as a hypocrite, and then proceeded to give him a pretty fair cussing. Not satisfied with that, Will went on to announce the founding of his own ministry, mounted the pulpit, and took up the sermon where the bewildered preacher had left off.[40]

Soon afterward, the church mysteriously burned down. Though Will was not charged with arson, he was nevertheless the prime suspect. Once again Will's erratic antics proved to be a bit much for the neighbors, and on April 23, 1899, they had Will shipped off to the funny farm for a second visit. This time the asylum kept him four months before marking him "restored" and setting him free. The hospital records noted that Will was twenty-eight years old, single, and a laborer. His diagnosis was "chronic mania; he is also marked as syphilitic."[41]

After his release on August 16, 1899, Will was never institutionalized again—at least not in mental facilities. Will migrated west and settled in Wichita Falls, Texas. Wichita County justice of the peace W. J. Howard (a former Wichita County sheriff) testified as a character witness for Will and told the jury that he believed Will's reputation as a peaceable and law-abiding citizen was good, at least until he went on a drinking spree. On cross-examination, the ex-sheriff did have to admit, however, that Will had seen the inside of the Wichita County jail several times over the years, usually the result of complaints about the destruction of barroom furniture and fixtures occurring in the course of political debates between Will and other bar patrons. (Will, the ex-sheriff explained, "takes great interest in elections.") He also recalled that Will was pretty handy with a knife and had once done some extensive carving on a constable. Other than that, the ex-sheriff thought that Will was a pretty good citizen.[42]

Playing the insanity card for all it was worth, Mitchell's attorneys contended that Will was "temporarily insane" at the time he killed George Douglas, a condition from which, according to his lawyers, he had "temporarily" recovered, but had now, alas, once again slipped down the insanity slope—perhaps permanently this time. A jury trial had to be called to determine whether Will Mitchell was presently competent. If found incompetent, then the state could not put Will on trial until, and unless, he regained his mental competency. If found to be competent in the "lunacy trial," then a second jury would be called to determine his guilt or innocence for the killing. Will could then raise the defense of insanity at the time of the crime.[43] On January 19, 1918, Will went through a second jury trial in Baylor County to determine his mental competency. Result: a hung jury. On July 15, 1918, the case was called for a third jury trial to determine the competency issue. This time the jury did not hang. They found Will mentally competent, thus allowing the prosecution to go forward on the merits, which it did on July 19, 1918. Will's attorneys contended that he was not guilty by reason of insanity at the time of the crime. Result: another hung jury, another mistrial. The district judge threw up his hands, and on February 3, 1919, he changed the venue again, stating there was so much notoriety after four trials that it was impossible for the state or defense to obtain a fair jury in Baylor County. This time the venue was changed to the Wilbarger County District Court in Vernon—and there it died of unknown causes.

The case was set for trial in Vernon on February 23, 1920, and the state and defense both subpoenaed scores of witnesses. One state witness was the widow Ellen Douglas Mitchell. For some reason that does not appear in the record; the trial was not held on that date. The only other record of this prosecution is a cryptic notation contained in the Wilbarger County District Court minutes where, on September 6, 1920, the district judge stated that the case of *The State v. Will Mitchell* for the murder of George Douglas was "called and dismissed"[44]—with no explanation given.

What happened to Ellen Douglas Mitchell, the mail-order bride who started this orgy of revenge? Red Mitchell's homemade will, leaving his estate to his three minor children, had been duly probated shortly after his death. His five-thousand-acre ranch in King County was sold by his executors to Burk Burnett at a private sale, part for four dollars an acre and the rest for seven dollars an acre.[45] Since Red Mitchell bought a part of this ranch before his marriage to Ellen, those lands were his separate property under Texas law, and all the proceeds from the sale of this part of the ranch went, in equal shares, to his three minor children. However, the part of his ranch acquired after his marriage to Ellen was their community property, and Ellen owned a half interest in it. Therefore, regardless of any provision in Red's will, half of the proceeds from the sale of the community land went directly to Ellen.

The kicker, however, was that after Red's death, Ellen lost no time in qualifying in the court of King County as the guardian of their three minor children. As such, she obtained not only sole custody of the three children but also the right to receive, as guardian of the children's estate, all the proceeds from the sale of Red's land and livestock. The net result was that *all* of Red's estate ended up in Ellen's hands.

Another very interesting entry is found in the minutes of the King County Probate Court dated May 5, 1919. In her children's guardianship proceeding, Ellen reported to the court that her name was now Mrs. Ellen Barkley as she had "intermarried with J. C. Barkley" and that she was now a permanent resident of the city of Fort Worth in Tarrant County, Texas. Therefore, she petitioned the King County Probate Court to change the venue of the guardianship case to the Tarrant County Probate Court. Her motion was granted.[46] This occurred less than two and a half years after Red was killed and more than a year before the murder case against her brother's killer, Will Mitchell, was dismissed by the district court in Vernon.

Justice may be satisfying; revenge may be sweet—but rarely is either very profitable. The mail-order bride must have so concluded, for after the smoke cleared from the courtroom shootout in which her brother was killed, she apparently let the family feud rest in peace and went on to more lucrative pursuits.

Off the Record

So why was the Will Mitchell murder case dismissed when there were plenty of credible eyewitnesses? John Bunyon Rhea, in his memoirs, speculated that because of World War I witnesses had become unavailable and the state was forced to dismiss the case. Rhea's speculation doesn't seem plausible, however. First, the Knox County courtroom was crowded with eyewitnesses who saw Mitchell shoot Douglas. Secondly, although World War I had ended nearly two years before the murder case against Mitchell was dismissed in September 1920, it seems unlikely that there was a lack of witnesses because only the previous February, when the case had been first scheduled for trial in Vernon, the state had subpoenaed a total of ninety-eight witnesses.

Why do juries sometimes fail to convict defendants such as Will Mitchell or George Douglas even though the prosecution's case is over-powering and the defendant has no apparent viable, legal defense? The operative word in the preceding sentence is *legal*—that is, a defense that is supported by the facts in evidence measured against the law as set out in the court's instructions. In the Will Mitchell murder case, the com-munity, as reflected by the pool of potential jurors summoned, had no uniformly strong bias either for or against the killer or the victim. But there *were* strong and widespread biases in the community, both for and against the defendant and the victim, and therein lay the prosecution's problem.

Although the victim, George Douglas, was undoubtedly a sorry spec-imen of humanity, he was only one sorry in a wad of sorries populating this case. His killer, Will Mitchell, was as sorry, or probably sorrier, than he. Undoubtedly, a sizable portion of the public probably viewed Red Mitchell as an outlaw sheriff who was himself a murderer, who sur-rounded himself with a gang of bullies, and who, in an age inclined toward a more chivalrous view of womankind, publicly accused his wife and the mother of his children of unspeakable misconduct. Moreover, Douglas was perceived by a good portion of the public as having bravely stood up to the Mitchell gang (even in the face of death threats) and defended the honor and life of his besmirched sister. The bottom line was that it would have been practically impossible to find twelve jurors in any county within 150 miles of Knox County who had a slate-clean mind going into the trial. One pro-Mitchell skewed juror would have meant an impossible conviction, regardless of the evidence.

Consider also these factors: (a) the prosecution had already been through four jury trials and come up with an empty sack; (b) every time a retrial is called the defense has another chance to pick at the state's witnesses on cross-examination and hopefully develop discrepancies in their testimony, plus the memory of the state's witnesses begins to fade and some witnesses may die or disappear; (c) as time goes by, the prosecution becomes burdened with more recent and pressing cases; (d) the victim's outcry and the public's outcry for justice diminishes; and (e) state prosecutors are political animals. Like any other elected officials who want to get re-elected, they are sensitive to public opinion. In the Mitchell case, the victim's family was neither prominent, wealthy, influential, nor bloodthirsty. Along that same line, another political factor was in play here. As long as prosecution was kept in the 50th Judicial District (which included King, Knox, and Baylor counties), the elected district judge and the elected district attorney of that district were accountable for the outcome of that prosecution. But when the venue was finally changed to Wilbarger County, the case fell into different hands. Wilbarger County was a part of the 46th Judicial District, so a different district judge and a different district attorney became responsible for the fate of the case. Neither of these two elected officials were accountable to the voters of the 50th Judicial District, where the killings had occurred. At the same time, the district judge and the district attorney of the 50th Judicial District were off the hook with their constituents. Whatever happened in the case from that point forward could not be laid at their doorsteps.

Given all of the above, it sounds very much as if everyone involved just got tired of this jinxed and emotionally divisive prosecution and quietly scuttled it.[47]

Another early-day stumbling block on the way to justice can be found in the story of these cases. In Will Mitchell's first jury trial, although all of the jurors agreed that Will was guilty, the jury hung up on punishment, thus necessitating a new trial. Modern laws have created a better system. Nowadays Texas law provides for a "bifurcated," or two-part, criminal trial. The first part focuses on the guilt-innocence issue and the second on the punishment issue if the defendant is found guilty. This change prevents an unnecessary and illogical retrial on the guilt-innocence issue in cases where the jury finds that the defendant is guilty but subsequently deadlocks on punishment. As such, the first trial is not a complete waste of judicial time, effort, and taxpayer expense. Unlike the first Will Mitchell trial, today the guilty verdict would stand. In noncapital cases, the case would be retried by another jury only on the issue of punishment. In capital cases, such as this one, if the jury deadlocks on punishment, the court is required to hand down a life sentence in lieu of the only other alternative: death.

Since such violence as chronicled in the Will Mitchell case could take place within a courthouse, the reader can easily see that the times were indeed violent. They got away with murder in this and many of the other murder trials recounted in this book in large part because the society as a whole was more accepting of that violence.

STRYCHNINE IN THE BRIDE'S FLOUR

Illicit Sex and the Unwritten Law

THE BRIDE'S MOTHER TRIED FOR KILLING SENATOR BELL

L ATE ONE summer night on a lonely country road near the tiny Texas town of Crowell, an event occurred that, at the time, no one, not even the two participants, would have considered important. But it turned out to be an incident of life-and-death magnitude not only for themselves but also for their two families and their community, and the incident resulted in the death of a popular and powerful state senator. His untimely death in turn altered the course of state action—the impact of which probably affected and continues to affect the lives of many more.

Fred Bell and his girlfriend, Suetta Gafford, both seventeen years old, were the children of two prominent pioneer families. On that fateful evening Fred and Suetta drove out on a country dirt road to court, or as it was termed in those days, to "spark." The sparks got out of control, and Suetta soon discovered that she was pregnant, which, in those strict, puritanical times, presented a family crisis of enormous proportions. A short time later, on December 8, 1918, Fred and Suetta drove over to Vernon, a nearby town, and tried to get a marriage license, but they were turned down because they didn't have parental consent. The distraught teenagers returned to Crowell and painfully admitted the truth to their parents. For the Gaffords only one option existed. Family honor must be salvaged by making an honest woman out of their daughter. Fred Bell's father agreed. Although Fred initially agreed to the marriage and drove Suetta to Vernon for that purpose, he was less than enthusiastic about the prospect of becoming a husband. He apparently came down with an aggravated case of cold feet and balked. Nevertheless, the next day, under pressure from both families, a marriage license was obtained from the Foard County clerk, and then, in the Gafford home, the Methodist minister was summoned to perform the marriage ceremony.[1]

Unfortunately, however, the shotgun wedding did not solve the problem as the family elders had hoped. Fred Bell soon moved out of the young couple's home and back to the family farm. He confided to his high school buddy Baxter Johnson (who would later become a cattle baron) that he might have had to marry Suetta, but he certainly didn't have to live with her. Parental pressures most likely coerced Fred to change his mind and move back in with Suetta, but that didn't last very long either.

We do not have a record of Suetta's feelings about the matter except that which we may deduce from what happened next. Whatever feelings of shame, guilt, anxiety, and despondency she may have had, she did not have to endure them for long. Only two months after the marriage, and before she gave birth to the baby, Suetta died.[2]

The Gaffords were a popular Foard County family. Suetta's father, James A. (Jim) Gafford, born December 3, 1873, in Hopkins County, Texas, was a respected cattleman and land trader. His wife, Myrtle McKown Gafford, was born August 31, 1882, in Rockdale, Texas. Jim and Myrtle married in Quanah, Texas, on January 12, 1901. Their first child, Suetta Gafford, was born October 20, 1901. The next year, a son, Gordon, was born to the union, followed several years thereafter by a second daughter, Jim Lois Gafford.[3]

The Bell family was also popular and well respected. Every one who remembers them remarks that the Bell menfolk were all strikingly handsome. The remaining pictures of Fred Bell's father, W. S. (Steve)

Prominent rancher James A. Gafford died on July 2, 1919, from a gunshot wound suffered in the June 21, 1919, Bell-Gafford feud shootout. He was the husband of Myrtle Gafford, who was later tried for (and acquitted of) the killing of senator Steve Bell. The feud began when his daughter, Suetta Gafford, died. The Gafford family believed she was killed by strychnine poisoning at the hands of her husband, Fred Bell.
(Photo circa 1909, courtesy of Robert Kincaid.)

Bell attest to that fact. Good looks, however, were far from Steve Bell's only asset. He was also blessed with a pleasing personality and a generous helping of common sense and business acumen. Born on March 18, 1869, in Clay County, North Carolina, Steve, together with his father, Robert Russell Bell, his mother, Lucinda Hampton Bell, and four other siblings migrated to Texas in 1884. Once grown, Steve married another North Carolina native, Julia Emma Haren, who was recalled by old-timers as an elegant woman. The couple had six children, five of whom survived childhood, including Fred Bell, who was born on January 23, 1901. The others were Everett, Ralph, William S. Jr., Ora Lee, and Daisey (who died shortly after birth).[4]

The Bells settled in Foard County near Crowell some thirty miles south of the Oklahoma border on the eastern cusp of the Texas Panhandle. By 1914, Steve Bell had accomplished much. He first came to the fore as a breeder of championship hogs, for which he became acclaimed over a multi-state area. (The Texas legislature, in 1917, passed a resolution commending Steve Bell on his consistent record as the best hog breeder in Texas.)[5] Through his economic endeavors, Bell acquired title to about 2,700 acres of productive farm land. He also became a successful banker.[6]

Senator W. S. (Steve) Bell was killed in the June 21, 1919, Bell-Gafford family shootout in downtown Crowell, Texas. A popular and powerful state senator, Bell championed the cause of a new state university for West Texas—a dream later realized after his death when Texas Tech University was founded in 1923.
(From the *Dallas Morning News*, June 23, 1919.)

In 1914 Steve Bell ran for, and was elected, representative of the 103rd District of the Texas house of representatives; he was re-elected to that post in 1916. In 1918 Steve upped the ante by throwing his hat into the ring for a seat in the Texas senate, intending to represent the largest district in the state, the mammoth 29th Senatorial District, which sprawled across forty-nine West Texas counties.[7] He won that hotly contested race. The same qualities of rich native intelligence, an unfailing sense of fairness, and down-to-earth affability that had played so well with his constituents in the hinterlands gained Steve Bell respect among his legislative peers in Austin. Commenting on his legislative record, the August 31, 1917, edition of the *Foard County News* observed:

> He has the reputation of never flinching from a question that requires careful thought and deliberate judgment, and he cannot be turned from a course he believes to be right.[8]

During his freshman year in the Texas senate, he was appointed to the influential Senate Financial Affairs Committee.[9]

At the same time Steve Bell, ever alert to new financial opportunities, had been one of the first in the state to open a silent movie theater, or picture show, as it was then called. At first, Steve Bell and his brother, J. W. Bell, operated their picture show out of the old opera house. In 1917 the Bell brothers constructed a large outdoor facility they called the Air-dome. It was located just across the street and north of the Foard County Courthouse in Crowell and had a seating capacity of one thousand. It was the forerunner of the drive-in movies of later years. Patrons entered on foot, sat on wooden benches, and waited for twilight so they could then observe the images flashed across the screen.[10] The June 1, 1917, edition of the *Foard County News* marveled at the new facility and its advanced technology:

> A 1917 Simplex, motor drive picture machine, the very best on the market, was ordered Tuesday from Kansas City. Also a Goldleaf cur-tain was ordered from Altus. As soon as the curtain and machine arrive, the Airdome will be opened. . . . The opera house will be left as is so in case of rain the picture show can be had as usual.[11]

It would seem that affable, popular, fair-minded Steve Bell would be one of the least likely of all people to become embroiled in, and the vic-tim of, a bitter interfamily feud—especially one pitting them against the Gafford family. Until the events of this story occurred, the Bells and the Gaffords had been close friends, and Steve Bell and Jim Gafford were brothers in the local Masonic Lodge. Their wives were both respected matrons active in community affairs. And, when it became known that Suetta was pregnant, Senator Bell had not hesitated to urge his son Fred to "do the right thing" and marry her.[12]

Nevertheless, the ensuing feud and its aftermath ripped apart the social fabric of the entire community. To this day, descendants of both the Bell and Gafford families make their homes in the Crowell commu-nity, and while feudal tensions will most likely never again reach the 1919 flash-point, old-timers still warn strangers not to press the matter too far with either camp.

The feud had its beginnings with the impregnation of Suetta by Fred Bell. Fred's subsequent reluctance to take his role as husband and expec-tant father seriously exacerbated the incipient animosity of the

Gaffords. And animosity turned to pure rancor when Fred's statement to the effect that he had no intention of living with Suetta reached Gafford ears. But it was Suetta's death—or, to be more precise, the cause of her death—that fanned the flames of bitterness into a revenge-driven inferno.

On February 10, 1919, Suetta suddenly and mysteriously died. Despite apparent good health, she became sick and died within the space of a day.[13] There were no wounds or other visible evidence of violence on her body. Over the coming months and years, the cause of her death would be the subject of much debate, rumors, and whispered speculations. However, no one, and especially no one in the medical community, wanted to go on record and express an opinion. Dr. J. M. Hill was on duty when Suetta was rushed to the Crowell hospital, and he was the physician who signed her death certificate. When he came to the "Cause of Death" blank, Dr. Hill neatly side-stepped the issue, simply noting, "Dead on Arrival."[14]

While others may have been inclined to skirt the issue, the Gafford family entertained no doubt at all about one thing: Fred Bell was responsible for their daughter's death just as if he'd shot her through the heart with a 30/30 rifle. They suspected that Fred had poisoned Suetta and decided to send off a sample of Suetta's baking flour for analysis.

Things got very ugly very fast after that. Chance meetings between members of the two families were more than strained. Violence smoldered just below the surface, and, depending upon whom you believed, death threats were exchanged by members of each of the families. In any event, it seems obvious in retrospect that the vein-popping hatred of the Gaffords toward Fred Bell would not simply cool and recede unavenged.

It all came to a head one balmy summer evening more than four months after Suetta's death. Shortly before 11:00 Saturday evening, June 21, 1919, in downtown Crowell, right in front of Senator Bell's Airdome theater, spectators aplenty witnessed the mayhem—shouting, clubbing, and shooting. The Saturday night silent movie, ironically entitled *Terror on the Range,* had just concluded, and movie-goers, including Senator Bell, his wife, and his sons Fred and Everett Bell, spilled out of the theater and into the street. There the Bells were confronted by the Gaffords—Jim, Myrtle, and their sixteen-year-old son, Gordon.

Terror on the Range was the last picture show for Senator Bell and Jim Gafford.

It was far from clear exactly who did what, when, and to whom when the wild free-for-all involving four Bells and three Gaffords broke out that fateful night.[15] One resurfacing, but unsubstantiated, community rumor has it that a third party, not a member of either family, produced a rifle and shot into the melee, hitting Lord knows whom, if anyone.

It was clear, however, that Senator Bell, his son, Everett, and Jim Gafford all sustained gunshot wounds. Although the wounds Everett Bell and Jim Gafford suffered appeared not to be serious, Senator Bell's wounds actually were. He died later that night. Everett Bell soon made a full and uneventful recovery. Jim Gafford, however, was not so fortunate. He died eleven days later (July 2, 1919) from blood poisoning caused by the gunshot wound.

After his death, the *Fort Worth Star-Telegram* eulogized Senator Bell as follows:

> He led in almost every line of endeavor . . . as a banker, wheat grower, hog raiser and even in other lines, he was an active and untiring leader. . . . He was not a brilliant and highly educated man; he was not an eloquent orator. He was simply a straightforward honest man of the people, with unusually good judgment and a great store of common sense. People knew always where to place him, and he was recognized very quickly in the Legislature as a man to tie to. Without any of the usual advantage of a public man, he became one of the most influential legislators simply because he was trusted by all factions. He was a real man in all that word can be made to mean.[16]

Senator Bell's great popularity was attested by the enormous turnout for his funeral. And, instead of the usual custom of driving the body the two or three miles south of town for burial after the funeral service, the pallbearers walked all the way carrying Senator Bell's body, and every one else who was able so followed on foot to the cemetery.

After the funerals of Senator Bell and Jim Gafford, the Foard County grand jury considered the mayhem that had shattered the tranquility of this small town on the night of June, 21, 1919. It returned an indictment against Myrtle Gafford for the murder of Senator Bell by shooting him with a pistol. The grand jury also indicted Myrtle for assault with intent to murder Fred Bell and for assault with intent to murder Everett Bell. Inflamed passions on the part of just about every citizen in Foard County resulted in the district judge changing the venue of all three cases. They were transferred twenty miles north to Quanah, the county seat of Hardeman County.[17]

Predictably, on March 16, 1920, some nine months after the killings, when the murder trial of Myrtle Gafford commenced, the Quanah courthouse was packed—primarily with Foard County spectators supporting both the Bells and the Gaffords.[18] The smouldering hostility was so palpable that district judge J. A. Nabors ordered sheriff's deputies to search all parties and spectators for weapons.[19] Outside the packed courtroom, as many as 135 witnesses jammed the halls. Tensions erupted into action once during the trial when an automobile backfired just outside the courtroom. Mistaking it for a gunshot, the spectators stampeded, and many rushed to the windows.

An impressive array of counsel represented both the state and the defendant. The Bell family hired former district attorney W. D. Berry of Vernon to act as lead counsel for the state, assisting district attorney James V. Leak. The Bells also hired Robert Cole of Crowell and C. M. Hankins of Quanah to assist the prosecution. The Gaffords responded by hiring the redoubtable A. J. Fires of Childress as lead counsel for the defense. To assist Fires they also hired C. E. Shepherd of Sipe Springs and W. T. Perkins of Quanah.

Prosecutor Berry announced that the state would seek the death penalty, and then he read the murder indictment while A. J. Fires and his client stood and listened respectfully at the defense table. When asked, in a hushed courtroom, Myrtle Gafford quietly but firmly answered, "not guilty." And the trial began.

A number of key facts presented at the trial were undisputed. The fracas began just before 11:00 p.m. when the picture show ended and all the patrons (most of the prominent people of the town) were exiting the Airdome.[20] Senator Bell, his wife, and his sons Everett and Fred Bell were about to get into the Bells' automobile in front of the theater when the Gaffords—Jim, Myrtle, and Gordon—drove up in their automobile. Either Myrtle alone or all three of the Gaffords then confronted the Bells. Myrtle Gafford advanced toward Fred Bell and fired two shots at him, but she missed. Fred took off running and got out of harm's way by hiding behind the theater building. Everett Bell, in an effort to neutralize Myrtle, grabbed her and pinned her arms to her body. Meanwhile, Senator Bell, also in an effort to subdue Myrtle Gafford, grabbed a shotgun from his car and, using it as a club, whammed Myrtle over the head with the butt, cutting a large gash in her head and knocking her to the street. Both during and after the fight, shots rang out. Everett Bell was wounded in the fleshy part of one leg by a pistol bullet, and Jim Gafford was wounded in the hip or groin also by a pistol bullet. Senator Bell sustained two pistol wounds and several shotgun pellet wounds and died later that night. As noted previously, Jim Gafford's wound did prove fatal some eleven days later.

As to the weapons involved, it was undisputed that Everett Bell and Fred Bell were unarmed, although Myrtle Gafford would later testify that she thought Fred Bell was armed. Senator Bell did have a shotgun—one retrieved from his car. The officers who examined the weapons afterward testified that Senator Bell's shotgun was not loaded.[21] It was also undisputed that both Myrtle and Jim Gafford were armed with pistols and that Myrtle's pistol was of a smaller caliber than Jim's. Senator Bell suffered two fatal pistol shot wounds: one in the jaw, which lodged in the spinal column, and one in the chest. The jaw wound was inflicted by a smaller caliber pistol than the one that caused the chest wound.[22] Incomplete news accounts of the trial leave some question as to whether Gordon Gafford was armed and, if so, with what? However, he was with his parents during the confrontation, and there is a strong implication that he was armed with a shotgun. Dr. Hill, in describing the event testified that "shotguns [plural] figured in the shooting."[23] Describing the wounds sustained by Senator Bell, Dr. Hill testified that "Senator Bell went down *with contents of a shotgun* and two bullets of different calibers."[24] If shotguns were in play, and none of the Bells were armed except Senator Bell wielding an unloaded shotgun, and if, as was undisputed, both Jim and Myrtle Gafford were firing pistols, then, by process of elimination, Gordon was left with the loaded shotgun that apparently peppered Senator Bell, although not fatally. Gordon, together with Myrtle and Jim (before he died), were all arrested for the murder of Senator Bell. Gordon was never indicted, though it was (likely) only because he was a juvenile at the time. Another startling deduction: if, as it appears from all accounts of the melee, Jim Gafford was fatally wounded by a pistol shot, and only Jim and Myrtle Gafford were firing pistols during the melee, then it appears Myrtle must have accidentally shot and killed her husband.

Also undisputed was the testimony of the chemist who tested the contents of the sack of flour found in Suetta's kitchen the day after her death. He swore he found traces of strychnine in that flour.[25]

The state's case was simple, straightforward, and supported by several of the many moviegoers who were leaving the theater. The Gaffords stalked and "waylaid" the Bells in a premeditated and coordinated attack, knowing that the Bells would be coming out of the theater when the show was over and would probably not be armed.[26] The Bells were, in fact, unarmed, but when they saw what was happening, Everett yelled for Fred to run while he and Senator Bell put up what resistance they could to protect him. Several eyewitnesses said they heard someone (apparently one of the Bells) yell as the Gaffords were advancing, "Here they come!" Then they saw Myrtle Gafford "run toward" Fred Bell, yelling his name. She then fired two misdirected shots at her fleeing son-in-law.[27] The fight commenced, and Senator Bell, Everett Bell, and Jim Gafford were all shot.

Under the state's theory of the case, it really didn't matter which of the Gaffords fired the fatal shot or shots, killing Steve Bell. Under the "law of parties," all three were equally liable since they were united in a concerted attack. Under that law, it didn't matter that Senator Bell was not the real target of their attack. Although Fred Bell was their primary—and probably only—target of vengeance, it didn't matter, because no matter who got killed in their rampage, it was murder, just as if they'd succeeded in killing Fred.

On the face of it, the state's case appeared to be more than just compelling—presuming, of course, the jury considered only the relevant facts and the applicable law. To the average courtroom railbird, the defense's mountain must have seemed almost insurmountable, but this defendant was in the sure and skillful hands of A. J. Fires. No one could read a jury better than A. J. Fires, nor was anyone better attuned to the times and the pulse of the plebeians from whom the jury pool was derived. Defending those accused of murder was his specialty, and during his long career in the trenches of the criminal courts, he won acquittals for 119 of the 123 murder-indicted defendants he represented.[28] If you were accused of murder and A. J. Fires took your case, he practically lived with you until it was over—you weren't just a client, you were family. Of course, after it was all said and done, you were, for sure, a much poorer relative. Fires's dedication to justice only kicked in after a healthy fee had been collected. If you were the prosecutor, well . . . just expect a "no-holds-barred" battle when you faced off against the old gray fox of the defense bar—they didn't teach much high-falutin' "ethics" where A.J. went to law school. Whatever it took to win, that was A.J.'s motto. Behind his back, contemporary lawyers in the area often remarked—sometimes with a chuckle but more often with a grumble—that old Amos Fires might not actually commit murder to get his client acquitted—but that he'd probably damn sure consider it![29]

When his turn at bat came up, Fires presented a masterfully crafted and multi-layered defense for Myrtle Gafford. Although he unveiled a feint in the direction of "legal" defense, anyone who had ever crossed paths with A. J. Fires could have predicted that the law and the facts would play a poor second fiddle to an emotional plea carefully constructed to appeal to the prevailing Victorian mores of the day.

When illicit sexual capers led to killings, one "extra-legal" defense was the weapon of choice for most defense lawyers. In the corridors of hundreds of county courthouses across the South, as well as from Texas westward to the Pacific, defense lawyers of the time discussed "the unwritten law" defense.[30] Typically, however, that was a man's defense. In countless books and articles, scholars and law professors explained how trial lawyers had skillfully employed the unwritten law's "honor" defense to exonerate male defendants who had killed or maimed to avenge an insult to their honor or to redress a wrong perpetrated against their womenfolk. But in this case, A. J. Fires was determined to put a skirt on that defense and make it dance for Myrtle Gafford. Fires also intended to play the gender card for all it was worth in yet another way, one that played to the popular stereotype of the refined Southern lady. Everyone knew that women were the weaker sex; that they had to be protected by the menfolk in their family; that they were much more moral, sensitive, and compassionate than any man could ever aspire to be; and that no real lady (at least not one in her right mind) was capable of calculated evil, lascivious conduct, or violent acts. It followed, therefore, that if a lady did commit some violent act, then she must have been in a state of hysteria or temporary insanity obviously triggered by the outrageous doings of a lusty libertine scoundrel. Someone like Fred Bell, for instance.

In sum, Fires's underlying trial strategy was astutely designed to take full advantage of both the inbred cultural values and the gender stereotypes prevalent in the society of that time and place.[31]

The actual legal defense also played into Fires's hand. The fracas featured six players doing various things at the same time, and the drama played out in front of a number of eyewitnesses, thus ensuring that the many eyewitness accounts of exactly who did what, when, how, and to whom would differ greatly. This arrangement offered Fires the opportunity to interview numerous eyewitnesses and then pick and choose those whose stories most nearly fit his defensive theory—or ones that cast doubt upon the state's witnesses.

Of course, the state could also pick and choose from the pool of eyewitnesses. Still, on balance, this was an advantage to the defense because the state had the burden of proving its case beyond a reasonable doubt. It needed to produce, as best it could, an undisputed, clear-cut, and persuasive case to meet its heavy burden of proof.

The defense, on the other hand, typically thrives on the ambiguous as well as the inconsistent and the contradictory. Inconsistent and contradictory eyewitness testimony (regardless of however minute or immaterial the inconsistency may be), inconsistent and contradictory versions of "what really happened," and inconsistent and contradictory defensive legal theories all add to the defensive stance. And it matters not how preposterous some of these inconsistencies may seem to neutral observers—just sling as much mud as possible on the mental walls of twelve jurors and hope that something sticks in at least one juror's mind. Prosecutors constantly strive to clear the water; defense lawyers typically strive to muddy the water.

Also in Fires's favor was the fact that Myrtle Gafford had been clubbed over the head and addled during the fracas, thus permitting considerable latitude in her selective recollection of certain events when convenient for the defense, and forgetting other things when not so convenient.

When it was time for Myrtle Gafford's star performance, A. J. Fires had her primed and ready. Before that, however, Fires had skillfully set the stage for Myrtle's appearance. A news reporter noted that "the way for Mrs. Gafford's testimony was carefully prepared."[32] Myrtle's version of the encounter went like this: the Gaffords had no preconceived plan to attack the Bells that night. They went to the theater to pick up her sister, Mattie McKown. When the car stopped, Myrtle alone got out and started toward the theater. She then saw the Bells. She saw Fred Bell glaring at her. She had previously heard that Fred Bell was "carrying a gun for them." Therefore she became alarmed when Fred "threw his hand toward his pocket," causing her to think he was probably going for a pistol. She then exclaimed, "Don't shoot, Fred"—an exclamation that no other witness seemed to have heard. Nevertheless, Myrtle continued, fearing for her life, she drew her pistol and opened up on Fred, firing once or twice, but with no effect. Then Everett Bell grabbed her and pinned her arms to her sides. According to Myrtle, when Everett grabbed her it caused her to fire another round accidentally, and that bullet might have hit Senator Bell or Everett. Or maybe, seeing Senator Bell approaching her with a shotgun and fearing for her life, she shot him in self-defense. At any rate, that was when Senator Bell clubbed her over the head with the shotgun butt and addled her. She went down, but as she did, and still fearing for her life, she yelled to her husband, "Shoot! Shoot! Shoot!" It was only at *that* point, she said, that Jim Gafford got out of their car and came to her rescue. (She didn't mention son Gordon's whereabouts or actions while all this was going on.) She believed that her husband then fired the shots that killed Senator Bell.

Myrtle Gafford's alternative legal defenses may be over-simplified and summarized as follows:

- I didn't shoot Senator Bell—my husband shot and killed him, and it was not pursuant to any premeditated plan by the Gaffords, so I am not accountable for Jim Gafford's acts; *or*

- If I did shoot and kill Senator Bell, then it was an accident—a wild shot fired accidentally when Everett Bell grabbed me; *or*
- If I did shoot and kill Senator Bell, and it wasn't an accident, then I did it in self-defense; *or*
- If I did shoot and kill Senator Bell, and it wasn't self-defense or an accident, then I killed him while under the influence of a sudden passion arising from adequate cause, and so therefore at most it would only be manslaughter and not premeditated murder. (Of course, after Fires got through massaging this "sudden passion arising from adequate cause" in front of the jury, he transformed it from a mitigation ground [read manslaughter] into a total exoneration [read not guilty] defense.); *or*
- If I did shoot Senator Bell, I only shot him once in the jaw, and that wasn't a mortal wound, so I could only be guilty of some lesser offense—such as assault.

Basically, however, all of these legal defenses simply provided a convenient peg upon which the jury could hang the desired emotion-driven verdict.

Fires then employed another tried and true tactic beloved by all criminal defense lawyers: he put somebody else on trial in order to divert the jury's attention away from the sins of the defendant and away from the sad plight of the innocent victim. He put Fred Bell on trial. And when it came to trying Fred Bell, Fires had plenty of ammunition.

The state, of course, vigorously protested the introduction of any testimony concerning Fred Bell's misdeeds or any of the other sordid background facts (including Suetta's mysterious death) that had occurred prior to the shootout. After all, what relevance did all that have to the narrow issue of whether or not Myrtle Gafford (and/or Jim Gafford in concert with Myrtle) intentionally shot and killed Senator Bell that night in front of the Airdome? Nevertheless, the trial judge overruled the state's objections and allowed it on the grounds that the statements were relevant to Myrtle Gafford's state of mind at the time of the killing. Her state of mind was relevant, in turn, because if the jury believed that she killed Senator Bell but also believed that at the time she pulled the trigger she was consumed by a sudden passion (or rage) to the extent that it rendered Myrtle's mind "incapable of cool reflection" and that this sudden passion or rage arose from an "adequate cause," then Myrtle could be found guilty of the lesser offense of manslaughter instead of first degree murder. Therefore, the judge admitted all of this emotionally charged background material.

From a strictly legal standpoint, however, no matter how justly enraged Myrtle Gafford might have felt at the time of the shooting, it still would not serve as a legal ground for the jury to exonerate her—it would only have reduced the degree of the crime. Nevertheless, as A. J. Fires knew well from long experience, if a jury could be sufficiently inflamed, it rarely paid much attention to such picky judicial distinctions.

And so Fires was ready to get to the heart of his defense and play his hole card, one he knew would resonate well with the jury, one that would inflame and enrage them—Fred Bell had seduced, impregnated, and thus "ruined" the virginal Suetta, and then, instead of "doing the right thing," he had publicly thumbed his nose at Suetta and the entire Gafford family, resulting not only in the shaming of them all but also in Suetta's death. Even by today's more tolerant and sexually permissive standards, Fred Bell's arrogant, insensitive, and irresponsible behavior would ignite flames of rage and notions of retribution in most folks. But in that small-town, Victorian society, it was absolutely intolerable and inexcusable, and more than enough to drive any mother over the top, even a southern-bred, refined lady.

Fires called to the stand E. H. Golez, a chemist from Austin, who testified that he had tested the flour found in an open sack in Suetta's kitchen at the time she died and that he detected traces of strychnine in the bride's flour. However, he also testified that he had later examined the contents of Suetta's stomach and could find no traces of strychnine. He then ventured what would seem to be a rather unlikely opinion. Perhaps, he said, "acute indigestion might have caused her death.[33] Fires then tried, unsuccessfully, to introduce testimony that Fred and Suetta's dog had eaten some of Suetta's leftover biscuits and had died the same day as Suetta and that Fred and their hired hand had *not* eaten any of the bride's biscuits that fateful day.

The defense also produced testimony from a three-member board of local doctors (Drs. J. M. Hill, Hinds Clark, and R. L. Kincaid) who had been appointed by the court to exhume Suetta's body and do a post-mortem examination. They found Suetta had been pregnant for several months at the time of her death. (With a nod to the Victorian standards of the day, the *Fort Worth Star Telegram* story eschewed the use of the naughty *P*-word, opting instead to tell its readers that the doctors found that Suetta "would soon have become a mother.") The doctors also reported that they had found marked discoloration around Suetta's throat, although they didn't give an opinion as to whether or not this was caused by strangulation.[34] Fires, of course, argued that that was exactly what it meant, but on cross-examination by the state, it was pointed out that the discoloration might have been due to the fact that the postmortem had been performed several months after her death.[35] Curiously, the doctors were not asked to give an opinion as to the exact cause of her death. We might wonder why they bothered with a post-mortem at all if not to ascertain the cause of death? One theory, whispered in the community, was that the real cause of death was blood poisoning due to a botched abortion attempt.[36] In a time when dainty Victorian sensibilities on the subject of sex were such that the *P*-word was too crude to be mentioned in mixed company, then no doubt a botched abortion would have been completely out of bounds. We may conjecture that the local doctors' diffidence to express such an opinion might also have been due to their sensitivity toward the feelings of the already shamed and bereaved Gafford family. Plus, the doctors may have prudently concluded that such a disclosure would have served only to further inflame the passions of the opposing factions.

That A. J. Fires had carefully prepared his client for her appearance before the jury is apparent from the *Wichita Daily Times* account, appearing in its March 18, 1920, edition:

> The defendant is a rather small, slightly built woman, still young in years, but with her features strongly marked with the effects of the tragedies she has gone through, an effect which was rather heightened by the severe dress of deep black which she wore during the trial. On the witness stand she made a rather good impression, expressing herself well and telling her story in a rather straightfor-

ward way—except in the telling of the details of the forced marriage of Fred Bell with her dead daughter, and of the latter's sudden death soon before she was to be become a mother, when, losing the composure she had maintained throughout the trial, she was clearly affected, at the time almost breaking down and being compelled to pause in her story in order to regain sufficient composure to proceed.[37]

Fires then called twenty-five character witnesses for Myrtle Gafford who attested to her good character and high standing in the community. She was known as a woman of high character, a church worker, a Sunday school teacher, and a prominent club woman. [38]

Fred Bell was called by the prosecution as a rebuttal witness, and his testimony went like this: He and Suetta had been childhood sweethearts; they had a happy marriage and shared "mutual love." On the day of her death, he had, in fact, eaten her biscuits. When she became ill he did everything he could to save her and called two doctors. Myrtle Gafford fired two shots at him when he came out of the theater. He was unarmed. He ran behind the theater and hid. Fred also denied that he had ever made any threats to harm any of the Gaffords, but Jim Gafford had insulted and threatened him shortly after Suetta's death.[39]

During the final arguments, District Attorney Leak contended that Senator Bell had suffered two mortal wounds, both from pistol shots but by pistols of different calibers. The smaller caliber pistol was fired by Myrtle Gafford, and Senator Bell's jaw wound (the slug lodged in his spinal column) must have been made by Myrtle's pistol. He also called attention to the fact that Senator Bell's shotgun was not loaded. He told the jury that whatever Fred Bell might have done, Senator Bell had never harmed or threatened the Gaffords, had instead counseled Fred to "do the right thing" and marry Suetta and thus make the best of a bad situation for the benefit of both families. In fact, the only thing Senator Bell could be accused of was trying to protect his son, who was under a deadly and unprovoked attack.[40]

Nevertheless, the outcome was not much in doubt. The jury was out only about thirty minutes before finding Myrtle Gafford not guilty. In the March 25, 1920, edition of the *Quanah Tribune-Chief*, the editor, in the style of the day (and inadvertently commenting upon the effectiveness of Fires's gender-based strategy), concluded his account of the trial with this comment:

> This verdict was a foregone conclusion, popular sentiment being strong for the accused woman, and it would have been hard to find a *man* who would have voted for her conviction.[41]

The prosecution then promptly—and wisely—dismissed all other pending indictments against Myrtle Gafford.

First Epilogue

Unfortunately, Myrtle Gafford did not have the opportunity to enjoy life for very long after her vindication. Slightly more than three years later, on September 15, 1923, she died of natural causes in Clovis, New Mexico—just a few days after her forty-first birthday.

Fred Bell, although handsome like his father, did not inherit his father's character, common sense, or business acumen. According to a couple of long-time Crowellites, who wish to remain anonymous, Fred never amounted to much. He soon managed to squander his share of his father's estate and thereafter earned his living as a day laborer. Although, to the best of his ability, he tried not to let common labor interfere with his enjoyment of spirits. He married again and fathered a son, but he was soon divorced. His ex-wife changed her name and the surname of her child to something other than Bell.[42]

The only person present at the June 21, 1919, shootout still living as of August 2001 was the youngest child of Jim and Myrtle Gafford, Jim Lois Gafford Johnson, then eighty-five years old and living in Amarillo. When interviewed for this story (in the presence of her daughter, Mrs. Carolyn Price), it became apparent that the passage of many years had neither dimmed Mrs. Johnson's mind nor assuaged the poignant and painful memory of that long-ago tragedy.[43] Although she was with her mother, father, sixteen-year-old brother, and aunt (Myrtle Gafford's sister, Mattie Page McKown) at the scene of the shootout that night outside the Airdome, she points out that she was only three and a half years

old at the time, and thus her direct recollection of the event is very frag-
mented. However, from what she did remember of that night along
with Gafford family lore she heard thereafter, she was able to shed considerable light on the tragedy.

She recalls Senator Bell and Mrs. Bell as being "nice and well-
respected citizens," and that Senator Bell insisted that Fred do the right
thing and marry Suetta. She lays the blame for the whole disaster on
Fred Bell's doorstep. (Jim Lois recalls that Fred was "pretty rough" and
that her daddy didn't want Suetta to date him.) Fred was determined
that he didn't want to be married to Suetta. And, according to Jim Lois,
the Gaffords were convinced that Fred killed Suetta by poisoning her
flour. She recalls that the day before Suetta died, the new bride invited
her mother (Myrtle) over to her home for a noon meal. Myrtle and Jim
Lois went over for the meal. She was thrilled to death to cook dinner for
us, Jim Lois recalled. She hadn't cooked too much because she hadn't
been married very long.

She recalls that neither husband Fred nor her father, Jim Gafford,
took the noon meal with them. As to the poisoned biscuits (or whatever
Suetta cooked using that flour), Jim Lois continued: "I guess we [Myrtle
and Jim Lois] didn't eat what she [Suetta] ate, or she might have eaten it
for breakfast, and it caught up with her. Anyway, she was sick by night
and dead by morning. Somebody sent the flour to Austin to be analyzed,
and it came back that it had strychnine in it, and that only created a war
in our families."

As to why the cause of death blank was not completed on Suetta's
death certificate by Dr. J. M. Hill, Jim Lois explained, "I think the doctors were afraid to make a report on it because there wasn't much to be
done about it until she [Myrtle Gafford] was arrested."

After Suetta's death, but before the shootout some four months later,
Jim Lois recalls that there were a lot of threats from each family.

This is what Jim Lois tells of the shootout: She, her father, Jim, her
mother, Myrtle, and her aunt, Mattie McKown, went that Saturday
night to the Airdome picture show. They didn't go to see the show but
were there when it let out. She thinks they went to pick up her brother,
Gordon. She and her aunt were inside their car parked outside the theater when the shooting started. She doesn't think that Fred Bell had any-

thing to do with firing any shots, and she doesn't know who fired the first shots. However, she doesn't think it was her mother who fired the first or, for that matter, any shots "because I don't think she even knew how . . . to shoot a gun." Jim Lois theorizes that it was probably her brother, Gordon, who fired the shot or shots that killed Senator Bell.

> I think my mother had gone to get my brother out of the movie. And my mother took the blame for the shooting, because my brother was sixteen, and she was afraid they would accuse him and get an indictment on him, and take him to court. Whatever happened, my mother kind of took the blame for it and went to court.[44]

The question occurs, of course, since husband Jim was dead, why was it necessary for Myrtle to step up and take any blame for Gordon? On the other hand, if Jim Lois's recollection is accurate, and she and her Aunt Mattie were in the Gafford car when it pulled up in front of the Airdome, it would not seem probable that the Gaffords were spoiling for a fight with the Bells. If the Gaffords had plotted an attack on the Bells, it hardly seems likely that they would have brought along their three-year-old daughter. Jim Lois's contention that her mother did not fire *any* shots, however, contradicts Myrtle's own testimony and the testimony of other disinterested eyewitnesses to the effect that she did fire the first shots.

Jim Lois recalls that for years after the tragedy, people in the community were afraid to talk about it. There was just too much friction, too much hate. And they didn't talk if they didn't have to. She recalls that the Gaffords would never thereafter speak the name of Fred Bell even among family. "My mother was the kind of person who just tried to love everybody, and not say anything unkind," she concluded.

Today, one of the Bell family descendants (and a cousin to Fred Bell) is the county judge of Foard County, and has been for many years. Judge Charlie Bell is nothing if not affable, straightforward, and candid. In a recent conversation, Judge Bell said he reckoned enough time had elapsed to allow the bad blood to settle, and so he was willing to recount some of the family tales about the feud and the shootout that had been passed down to him.[45] (Judge Bell, of course, was not present during the shooting—in fact, he had not been born then.) He said that for a long time after the shootout, Everett and Fred had gotten into fistfights with some of the Gaffords.

In addition to what came out at the trial, Judge Bell said that neither Fred nor Everett were armed at the shootout, and that the only weapon the Bells had was the shotgun that Senator Bell got out of his car. Jim Gafford, he pointed out, was not wounded by a shotgun but by a pistol slug, so Jim Gafford's wound must have been inflicted by one of the Gaffords.

I asked him directly, "Do you think Fred poisoned Suetta with that strychnine?" Charlie replied, "No, I really don't think he did—although he was capable of it!" To underscore that last remark, he recalled one of Fred's subsequent misadventures. Once a guy who had been in a crap game with Fred and his drinking buddies (and was apparently a winner) was discovered the next day drowned in a nearby pond. When an inquest was held to determine the cause of this suspicious death, and Fred was called as a witness, he denied there had even been a crap game. He said they had all just gone out for a midnight swim, and after a while noticed that the deceased had disappeared. Another credible source recalls that in the 1950s a similar incident occurred involving Fred Bell as a princi- pal. After an all-night poker game in the Lancier building in Crowell, the structure burned to the ground, and the body of a local painter was discovered in the charred ruins. It was later learned that the painter had been the big winner in the poker game. However, no investigation was pursued, and no autopsy performed on the painter's body.[46]

Judge Bell recalled another anecdote illustrating Fred Bell's rough and crusty character. When Fred was an old man, Charlie and a friend decided to seine a local stock pond for fish. They knew Fred had a large seine and went to borrow it. When they got there, Charlie noticed that Fred was acting crazy—staggering around and slurring his words.

   Charlie: Fred, what the hell's the matter with you?
   Fred: Hell, I've had a stroke.
   Charlie: Well, get in the car, I'll take you to the hospital.
   Fred: Hell no—ain't going to no hospital. Besides I had it two weeks
     ago.[47]

Second Epilogue

Toward the end of my conversation with Judge Bell we were discussing Senator Bell's popularity and his formidable clout in Austin at the time of his death. Judge Bell, as an afterthought, then added a stunning comment. "By the way," he said, "you know that if Steve Bell hadn't been killed that night, Texas Tech University would now be located in Quanah, don't you?"

Although that chance observation was indeed a stunner, additional research tends to support the proposition that Judge Bell's remark was not nearly as far-fetched as it first sounded.[48]

The struggle for the establishment of a major state-funded college to be located somewhere in West Texas began in earnest around 1915. Senator Bell, whose district covered a huge chunk of West Texas, was a leading champion of the effort. His district included all of the Panhandle (including Amarillo), down south to cover much of the South Plains (including Lubbock), and east to cover much of the Rolling Plains (including Wichita Falls, Jacksboro, and Graham).

Although Bell resided in Foard County, he realized that its county seat, Crowell, was too small for consideration. The closest town large enough for consideration was Quanah, about twenty miles north of Crowell, and that's where, according to Judge Bell, the senator wanted the new school to be located. Lubbock, with a population of 7,000 when the college site was finally selected in 1923, was only slightly larger than Quanah, which had about 5,000 people. In fact, Hardeman County (population 12,487) was larger in the 1920 census than Lubbock County (population 11,096). However, while all this political jousting was going on, the Gaffords permanently removed Senator Bell from the political arena.

The governor, W. P. Hobby, lost no time in calling a special election to fill the vacancy in the 29th Senatorial District.[49] On July 14, 1919, the voters elected W. H. Bledsoe of Lubbock to be their new senator. Bledsoe was also a popular and powerful leader, having served in the Texas House before this election. Senator Bledsoe then picked up the torch and continued the struggle to land a major state university for West Texas.

On February 10, 1923, governor Patt Neff signed Senate Bill 103 (sponsored by none other than senator W. H. Bledsoe), which created Texas Technological College. The only remaining issue was where the school was to be located.[50] Many towns put in their bid. Lubbock and Quanah were major contenders along with Amarillo, Abilene, San Angelo, Brownwood, Plainview, Sweetwater, Lampasas, Vernon, Midland, Snyder, Big Spring, and others. Although Senator Bledsoe represented Quanah, Amarillo, Plainview, and other contenders located within his district, he was understandably dedicated to locating Texas Tech in his hometown of Lubbock.

According to a 1998 article in the *Lubbock Avalanche-Journal* written by Matthew Henry, state leaders at the time gave much of the credit for Lubbock's victory to Senator Bledsoe. In fact, T. Whitfield Davidson, Neff's lieutenant governor, said, "Senator Bledsoe was one of the most powerful figures in the State Senate. . . . Those familiar with the situation felt that the location of the school at Lubbock was to a large measure due to its being the home of Senator Bledsoe, the author of the bill creating Texas Tech."[51]

Yet one wonders "what if" Senator Bell had lived to carry the torch. Even if he had not been successful in locating the school in Quanah, without Bledsoe's influence, it might well have been located at a site other than Lubbock, which was, after all, considerably west of the geographical center of the area to be served by the college. Both Abilene and Sweetwater, for instance, made strong bids for the college, and both are located much nearer the geographical center.

Off the Record

This fascinating case raises more questions than it answers. The state announced at the outset that it would seek the death penalty. Was it justified in this case? Was it a wise decision from a purely tactical standpoint?

The debate over whether the death penalty should ever be imposed —and if so, under what circumstances and with what safeguards—has raged for years and will, no doubt, continue for many years to come. It is interesting to note that under present Texas law the Myrtle Gafford case would not qualify as a death penalty case. Today, a murder has to have been committed under special circumstances to bring it within the capital murder statute. The circumstances include the intentional killing of a policeman during the performance of his duty, killing a guard while trying to escape prison, murder for hire, murder during the commission of a felony such as burglary or kidnapping, multiple murders during one criminal episode, murder of a child under six years of age, and others. During Myrtle Gafford's time, however, the death penalty was an option in any Texas murder prosecution. Yet one thing remains the same today as it was in 1920: if a case qualifies as a capital murder offense, then it is within the sole discretion of the prosecuting district attorney to decide whether or not to seek the death penalty—an awesome and chilling responsibility.

Even though the victim in the Myrtle Gafford case was an extremely popular man and a powerful political leader, considering the circumstances of this case, it should have been clear to the prosecutor that the possibility of the jury inflicting the ultimate penalty upon Myrtle Gafford was remote. After all, in the opinions of most Texans of the day, Fred Bell had ruined Suetta and then publicly rejected her (thereby humiliating not only her but the entire Gafford family). Plus, he may have even killed her. Furthermore, Myrtle had been a model citizen before these events, and the prospect of her posing any future threat to society seemed nil. On top of all that, Myrtle Gafford had lost her husband. Plus, taking Myrtle's life would have orphaned two innocent Gafford children. Under all those circumstances, wasn't it unwise, tactically, for the state to insist that Myrtle Gafford be hanged? Wasn't that very likely to have been perceived by a jury as "overzealous" prosecution at best and "blood-thirsty" at worst? Wasn't that likely to have seriously diminished the prosecution's credibility in the eyes of the jury?

Would it have made any difference in this case if the defendant had been a man instead of a woman? Would the all-male jury have been as eager to acquit if Jim Gafford had been on trial—presuming that he had escaped the fray unscathed and presuming further that the evidence clearly indicated that Senator Bell had been killed by a single bullet and that bullet had been fired by Jim Gafford? Did gender matter? If so, how much? As noted earlier, the local editor's take on the verdict reveals that gender mattered—and mattered a lot.

Challenging questions could also be posed as to the efficacy of the criminal justice system itself as well as those who, in this case, were operating it. Did the system fail the Bells? The Gaffords? The public? If law enforcement officers hadn't been so squeamish and had pursued the cause of Suetta's death and the possible culpability of Fred Bell, wouldn't that have likely diffused the mounting tensions regardless of whether the investigation ultimately exonerated or inculpated Fred? (This presumes, of course, that had the evidence inculpated Fred, a vigorous prosecution would have followed.)

What about the Bells? Everett Bell was wounded and his father killed in an unprovoked attack. Yet no one was made to pay. And what about Senator Bell's widow? Was any consideration given to her plight, her feelings, her loss, her need for closure? It appears that the victims' rights and interests were virtually ignored.

When the criminal justice system ignores (or appears to be incapable of dealing with) real or perceived grievances, doesn't that simply encourage the aggrieved to take the law into his or her own hands—as exemplified in this case? And if in the eyes of the public the criminal justice system appears to be unable to address and vindicate a citizen's grievances (as it would appear to have been the case here), then doesn't that encourage future lawlessness when someone else is victimized?

It could certainly be argued that, in the Myrtle Gafford case, sympathy trumped justice; that emotion completely routed reason; argued that, balancing reason and emotion, the jury should have taken into account not only the Gaffords' tragedy but also the interests and rights of the Bells as well as the interests and rights of the public. Had the jury done so, shouldn't it at least have found Myrtle Gafford guilty of manslaughter and imposed the minimum sentence? All of which raises a broader issue: what role should reason play and what role should emotion play in a jury's verdict? People are, after all, emotional animals, which is not only an incurable condition but also a good one, providing that emotions can be measured and restrained by reason. After all, emotions are the distilled product of a panoply of life experiences that are invaluable (times twelve) to a jury whose task is to interpret and evaluate evidence—much of which is conflicting. (Plus, sympathy for deserving parties is certainly not out of order.) May not the problem be defined as follows: how to allow both reason and emotions to play their proper roles, meanwhile safeguarding against runaway emotional verdicts.

And, if so, how in the real world can we hope to achieve that idealistic balancing act?

... AND THE PERPETRATOR
WALKED

A Sampler of Misfires, Mistrials, and Manipulations

NO HOLDS BARRED IN THE EARLY COURTS

The Time Temple Houston Shot a Jury out of the Box

IN A previous chapter we witnessed the courtroom mastery of the eloquent, eccentric, and charismatic Temple Houston, youngest son of Texas hero Sam Houston. Temple was as innovative as he was eloquent. He always had a trick up his sleeve or a rabbit in his hat to combine with an unerring sense of theatrical timing and effect.

Once during an 1893 Oklahoma Territory murder trial at Enid, he succeeded in freeing his client by using a strategy never before imagined or implemented by any other defense lawyer. And no one has had the temerity to attempt it since. Temple was representing a lowly cowboy who had been indicted for fatally shooting a respected rancher—worse yet, he was also accused of stealing the rancher's horse. The rancher was reputed to be a deadly gunman while the cowboy was just that—a cowboy. But witnesses called by the prosecutor claimed the cowboy shot his antagonist without giving the rancher a chance to draw. Houston had no witnesses to contradict the prosecution's testimony, and the prosecutor railed at the jury that horse stealing could not be countenanced in a civilized society. When you stacked murder on top of that . . . well, a noose was much too good for the culprit.

But there was even worse news for the defense. Much to his dismay, during the course of the trial Houston learned that the prosecutor had managed to liberally sprinkle the jury with close friends of the deceased rancher. It appeared to be a hopeless case—except for the fact that the defendant was represented by Temple Houston.

When the territory concluded its opening argument, Temple took the stage. Only thirty-three years of age, he was a commanding six-foot, two-inch figure, and he was already known to carry a pearl-handled Colt revolver. In court or out of court, he always packed "Old Betsy."

Despite the fact that witnesses told the jury the defendant had drawn on and shot the victim without giving him a chance to draw, Houston argued self-defense. He portrayed his client as a simple cowboy accosted by a skilled shootist and deadly adversary. Houston contended that the defendant's only chance to escape with his life was to draw first. He said:

> He [the defendant] could no more have stood up to his malefactor
> than the spark from a lowly firefly could outshine the noonday sun—
> could no more have outshot him than the stubborn, plodding jackass
> could outrun the fleetest race horse.

As he addressed the jury, Houston lowered his voice and crept closer and closer to the jurors. Their attention was riveted on him. They all leaned toward him, nerves taut. Then Houston tossed his long hair and roared:

> This malefactor was so adept with a six-shooter that he could place a
> gun in the hands of an inexperienced man, then draw and fire his
> own weapon before the victim could pull the trigger—like this!

Whereupon Houston whipped out "Old Betsy" from under his frock coat, pointed it directly at the jury, and began firing away—emptying the six-shooter! The terrified jurors bolted from the jury box and joined the spectators in a mad dash for the nearest exit. The judge dove under the bench.

When the dust cleared and some semblance of order was restored, Houston, with an air of wide-eyed innocence, explained to the infuriated judge that he was only firing blanks in an effort to dramatize his self-defense argument. When the jurors (who were not in the least amused by Houston's stunt) were finally rounded up and returned to the box, it didn't take them long to find Houston's client guilty of murder, a verdict that Houston expected. Undeterred, however, Houston moved for mistrial. The judge had to grant it. Houston called the court's attention to the fact that when the jury was impaneled, the trial judge had ordered it sequestered for the rest of the trial. He specifically instructed the jurors to remain together, and under no circumstances were they to mingle with any other persons. As Houston then pointed out, the judge had just witnessed the entire jury violate its duty by jumping out of the jury box and mingling with a courtroom full of spectators. Upon retrial of the case, Houston was able to select a jury that was much more congenial to his client, and thus he obtained the desired result.[1]

In this case we see several reasons why they got away with murder in those free-wheeling times when strict adherence to rules of trial procedural and courtroom decorum were never too high on the frontier lawyer's priority list. Often inexperienced and untrained trial judges were frequently unable to reign in rambunctious trial lawyers.

More Than One Way to Skin a Cat—Or to Win a Murder Trial

Very few corrals or fences existed in 1880s West Texas cow country. Roundups were open range affairs where a few cowboys gathered and surrounded cattle out on the prairie while others rode in to cut out certain critters to brand or send to market.

One hot, dusty afternoon in July 1889 a range roundup was in progress several miles south of Paducah, in northwest Texas. Cattle baron J. J. McAdams got into a squabble with his brother over which animals should be cut out of the herd. "Sam, if you cut out another one of those goddamned Easley cattle out of the herd, I'm gonna kill you," J.J. shouted. Of course Sam went right back into the herd and cut out another one of the Easley cattle, whereupon J.J., right before the eyes of a bevy of startled cowhands, abruptly terminated the dispute by draw-

Cattle baron J. J. McAdams, shown with his wife, Dora, shot and killed his brother,
Sam McAdams, during an open range cattle roundup in King County, Texas, on July
25, 1889. He hired the best trial lawyers in West Texas—Temple Houston
and A. J. Fires—to save him from the gallows.
(Courtesy of the family of Carmen T. Bennett.)

ing his '73 Winchester rifle and shooting brother Sam right off his
horse. (Sam, by the way, was not armed when he was aburptly
unhorsed.) In fairness to J.J., it should be mentioned that several years
earlier, Sam, during another family fuss, unlimbered his own Winchester and shot J.J. in the leg. The incident left J.J. with a pronounced hitch
in his get-along for the rest of his life.[2] (According to family legend, J.J.
cured his wound by packing it with fresh cow manure.)

Although the shooting occurred in Cottle County in West Texas, Sam
didn't die there. They took him back to the family home in Gainesville
in Cooke County, north of Dallas, where he died thirty-eight days later
on September 2, 1889. Therefore, under Texas law J.J. was subject to
prosecution in either Cottle County, where the mortal wound was
inflicted, or in Cooke County, where Sam subsequently expired. The latter venue was disadvantageous to J.J. because the McAdams family was

A. J. Fires, an early-day bulldog of a
defense lawyer, lost only 4 of the 123
murder cases he defended. He often
worked with Temple Houston. Whatever Fires may have lacked in Hous-
tonian eloquence, he made up for in
tenacity, toughness, and total dedication to his client.
(Courtesy of the A. J. Fires family and
the Panhandle-Plains Historical
Museum, Canyon, Texas.)

prominent there, and they all wanted J.J. hanged . . . high. Cottle
County, on the other hand, was a very favorable venue because J.J. and
his best friend, rancher W. Q. (Bill) Richards, owned (or at least laid
Winchester claim to) most of the county.

A Cooke County murder indictment was promptly returned,[3] and
prosecutors there were salivating in anticipation of getting their hand-
cuffs on J. J. McAdams. Besides the unfavorable atmosphere in Cooke
County, there was no shortage of eyewitnesses who saw J.J. shoot the
unarmed Sam out of his saddle. J.J. found himself in one hell of a bind,
and he was in dire need of a great trial lawyer. He hired two: the consummate courthouse magician, Temple Houston,[4] and his frequent associate, the redoubtable A. J. Fires.[5]

They both agreed that the best way to rescue J.J. from peril was to
beat Cooke County to the draw and have the case tried in the client's
home county. The problem was that Cottle County was still an unorganized frontier county. Cases arising there had to be tried in another organized county to which the unorganized county was attached for judicial
purposes—Childress County, in this instance.

No legal action had been taken against J. J. McAdams in the Childress-Cottle County area. Meanwhile, Cooke County prosecutors pressed, without success, for the arrest of J.J. to answer their indictment. They even sent an arrest warrant to the sheriff of neighboring Hardeman County demanding that he arrest J.J. and hold him without bail. However, sheriff D. P. Gibson returned the warrant unserved with this notation, "not executed after diligent search in Cottle County and the whereabouts of J. J. McAdams cannot be found." The good sheriff's detecting abilities might well have been called into question, because had Sheriff Gibson stopped the first citizen coming down the street, the passerby could, no doubt, have directed him to the whereabouts of J. J. McAdams.

But the Cooke County authorities did not give up. On January 22, 1890, another arrest warrant was sent to the Childress County sheriff. The Cooke County prosecutor had a little better luck this time, but not much. They did succeed in getting J.J. arrested by the Childress County sheriff, but he refused to allow the Cooke County authorities to remove J.J. from his custody. Gibson claimed that he was holding McAdams in Childress by authority of a "prior writ" out of the Childress County District Court—a lie cut from whole cloth, because no indictment had been returned against J. J. McAdams in Childress County. However, the Childress County judiciary, dragged off high center by the pressure from Cooke County, finally got around to returning an indictment against J.J. on February 5, 1890—some fourteen days after the Childress sheriff claimed he was holding J.J. under a "prior writ" and seven months after the shooting itself.[6] It would have been difficult to fault even the most dull-witted courthouse railbird for suspecting that Temple Houston and A. J. Fires were somehow behind the judicial chicanery and feigned ineptitude of local law enforcement officials. Nevertheless, Houston and Fires saw the handwriting on the wall: sooner or later Cooke County would force the prosecution of J.J. in that unfavorable venue unless something was done. But it was also evident that Childress County wanted no part of the high profile murder case lodged against one of the area's most prominent citizens. Therefore, only eight days later, on February 13, 1890, the Childress County district judge, on his own motion, pitched this hot potato to Wilbarger County (sixty miles to the east) on a change of venue.[7]

There it sat for another two months until yet another arrest warrant from Cooke County arrived on April 19, 1890. The warrant finally galvanized the Wilbarger judiciary into action, and J.J. was arraigned and put to trial in Vernon, Texas, on April 21, 1890. On April 23, 1890, while the trial was in progress, still another Cooke County arrest warrant arrived.

Since Wilbarger County was not far from J.J.'s home turf, and since, in the sparsely populated frontier, nearly everyone knew at least their more prominent neighbors, Houston and Fires probably thought they could count on a fairly sympathetic jury. They probably thought they could finesse the Wilbarger County jury even though their tried and true "self-defense" plea was mighty thin in this case. The best they could come up with was the rather lame testimony of one of the roundup hands, A. G. Carruth. Carruth had seen J.J. shoot Sam out of the saddle. He said he had assisted in carrying Sam "from the scene of the shooting to a place around 600 yards away, and that the manifestations and appearances of the deceased at said time indicated that he had on his person a pistol or other deadly weapon."[8] He had not, however, actually seen a pistol or other deadly weapon in Sam's possession or on his body. This testimony must have sounded a tad strange to the jury considering Carruth had dragged Sam about six hundred yards to a shelter and then presumably ministered to his needs. In addition, Carruth did not hear Sam make any threats prior to the shooting against his brother J. J. McAdams.

Although self-defense was an almost a sure-fire defense for most murder cases on the frontier,[9] in this instance—even for the likes of Houston and Fires—self-defense would prove to be a steep hill to climb. The missing complement to their self-defense plea was the "the-sorry-S.O.B.-needed-a-damned-good-killing-anyhow" element. After all, Sam was J.J.'s brother, and, undisputedly, it was J.J. who threw down the gauntlet and provoked the fatal confrontation. In addition, at the time of the shooting, Sam was engaged in an endeavor of honest labor. It must also have been apparent to the jury that, Carruth's vague and tepid testimony to the contrary notwithstanding, Sam really wasn't armed at the time. Furthermore, there was no shortage of eyewitnesses to the killing, and none of them saw a "pistol or other deadly weapon" in Sam's possession or witnessed him making any suspicious "manifestations or appearances" prior to being shot.

For those, and perhaps other reasons not appearing in the record, Houston and Fires were not able to work their usual magic and persuade the Wilbarger County jury to clear J.J. But the jury didn't convict him either. After wrestling with the case for seven days, it became apparent that the jury was hopelessly deadlocked, and the judge declared a mistrial.

Houston and Fires had thus dodged the bullet, but their plight—and the fate of their client—seemed very bleak. They had taken their best shot with what they must have considered a jury pool tilted at least slightly in their favor, and missed. They knew it was unlikely they would fare any better before another Wilbarger County jury, and, in light of what had just happened, the outcome of a new trial in Vernon might be much worse. Even worse, the Cooke County prosecutors came at them again—more determined than ever.

But first things first. Houston and Fires persuaded the Wilbarger County district judge to set bail so that J.J. could be released pending a retrial. No sooner was he released, however, than the Wilbarger County sheriff arrested J.J. on the Cooke County warrant. Houston and Fires responded by immediately filing a habeas corpus petition challenging the legality of his arrest. In an action that may be characterized most charitably as one of questionable legality, the judge granted the defense petition finding that the Wilbarger County District Court had "sole and exclusive jurisdiction" of the murder case against J. J. McAdams and thus the Cooke County arrest warrant was "in contravention of the previously acquired jurisdiction of this court and is illegal." J. J. McAdams was again released.

The defense triumph was temporary. On June 2, 1890, Cooke County issued yet another warrant for J.J.'s arrest. For the time being Houston and Fires persuaded law officers to simply ignore it, but it was clear that one way or another—one place or another—J.J. would have to answer for the killing of Sam.

If only they could have the trial in Cottle County. The more they thought about it, the clearer it became: that was the only way they were ever going to clear J. J. McAdams. Well then, Houston and Fires reasoned, let's just get busy and get defendant-friendly Cottle County

W. Q. "Bill" Richards was a cattle baron
and owner of the sprawling Moon
Ranch in Cottle County, Texas. He was
also a lifelong friend of J. J. McAdams.
He and his horses were instrumental in
officially organizing Cottle County in
1891 so that his friend's murder trial
could be held in a favorable
environment.
(Courtesy of the family of
Carmen T. Bennett.)

organized so it could beat Cooke and Wilbarger counties to the prosecutorial punch and host J. J. McAdam's murder trial. However, J.J.'s lawyers
immediately ran into still another seemingly insurmountable obstacle.
State law required that at least 150 residents of an unorganized county
had to sign a petition requesting an election on the issue of whether or
not the county should be organized.[10] Yet, when Houston and Fires
began casting about for signatures, they couldn't find 150 people who
called Cottle County home.[11]

But not to worry. Legend has it that Houston, Fires, and McAdams
completed the petition by filling in the blanks with the names of other
bona fide Cottle County residents. Turned out that J.J. and his friend Bill
Richards had a lot of horses, all of whom had names, and all of whom
were residents of Cottle County.[12] What is not recorded is how J.J. and
Richards trained those horses to sign their names to the petition. Nevertheless, it was accepted; the election was called; and Cottle County was
formally organized.

Elation quickly turned into dismay when a surveyor laid out the official boundary lines for Cottle County and thus discovered that the shoot-

ing had not occurred in Cottle County after all—it had occurred in King County, just south of the Cottle County line.[13] Frustration struck again—King County was not an organized county. However, some of the residents were already in the process of attempting to organize it.

Not surprisingly, proponents of the organization of King County were encountering the same problem their counterparts in Cottle County had faced: a lack of bona fide human residents. Even when they signed up a few traveling salesmen and several transients, they still didn't have their petition completed. They finally succeeded—although later, after the county was organized, it was revealed that petitioner "Sam Householder" was actually "Sam," the pet dog at the Q. B. Ranch headquarters and that "John B. Jackass" really was a jackass, a donkey who peacefully grazed the pastures of the 8 Ranch, who, when it suited his fancy, answered to the name, "John B."[14] But by the time these shenanigans were discovered it was too late—King County was officially organized.

Meanwhile, Houston and Fires, by various tactics to be admired more for their imaginative originality than for their strict adherence to legal procedures, were desperately engaged in beating off repeated attempts by Cooke County officials to capture J.J. and haul him off to Gainesville. In the end they succeeded in holding the fort and hiding J.J. in the remote cedar breaks of Cottle County until King County was organized. Governor Stephen Hogg then appointed a new and inexperienced district judge and a new and inexperienced district attorney. One is tempted to speculate that neither was much of a match for J. J. McAdams's two lions of the defense bar. The two wily veterans, by methods and means upon which we can only speculate (some of which may have even been legal), managed to persuade King County's new and inexperienced prosecutor and its new and inexperienced district judge to immediately call a grand jury and indict their client for the murder of Sam and, on the very same day and before the ink had dried on the King County indictment, they further persuaded those same officials to change the venue back to Cottle County. Thus, it came to pass that the murder case of *The State of Texas v. J. J. McAdams* had the unique distinction of having been filed as Cause No. 1 on the dockets of two Texas counties. Finally, anchored in the safe harbor of Cottle

County, Houston and Fires saw to it that the case was immediately called for trial. With that accomplished, well . . . it was all over but the shoutin'. A few judicial eyeblinks later, J.J. departed the brand new Cottle County Courthouse unencumbered by any bothersome legal restraints—and left the seething Cooke County prosecutors gnashing their teeth.

As demonstrated by the foregoing story, veteran criminal defense lawyers were not in the least hesitant to take full advantage of the failings of the infant legal and political systems of the day as well as the inexperience or ineptitude of neophyte judges, prosecutors, and political officials. Many acquittals were thus obtained by shameless and cavalier manipulations of all of the above.

Making an Honest Woman out of Minnie Stacey

Not all of Temple Houston's cases involved defendants accused of murder. In fact, his most celebrated performance, demonstrating his mastery in blending eloquence, earthiness, and imaginative resourcefulness, was showcased in the defense of a prostitute.

One fine spring morning in May 1899, Temple and a fellow barrister, while awaiting the opening of court in Woodward, Oklahoma Territory, retreated to a local saloon to fortify themselves for whatever courtroom combat lay ahead. When they finally arrived at court, the judge was arraigning Minnie Stacey for prostitution. Minnie, it seems, had been targeted by the more self-righteous brethren of the community who were bound and determined to run her out of town. She told the court that she did not have a lawyer to represent her and that she had no funds with which to hire a lawyer. Her plight aroused Temple's sympathy for the underdog, and he volunteered to represent her without fee.

The court gave Houston no time for preparation; the case was called for trial immediately. The prosecution presented its case and rested. Houston did not cross-examine any of the territory's witnesses and neither did he offer any evidence upon Minnie's behalf, choosing instead to rely solely upon his closing argument before the jury. And what an extemporaneous, spellbinding oration it was! It may have been the very best, and it certainly was one of the most often quoted jury arguments in

U.S. legal history.[15] He advanced so close to the jury (all male in those days) that he could have reached out and touched the men on the front row, and in a low, clear voice, he spoke to their consciences. His argument, in part, was this:

Gentlemen, you heard with what cold cruelty the prosecution referred to the sins of this woman, as if her condition were of her own preference. The evidence has painted you a picture of her life and surroundings. Do you think they were of her choosing?

Do you think that she willingly embraced a life so revolting and terrible? Oh, no! Gentlemen, one of our own sex was the author of her ruin, more to blame than she. Then let us judge her gently. What more pathetic a creature than the spectacle she presents? An immortal soul in ruin. . . .

You know the story of the prodigal son. He was one of us—like her destroyers. But for the prodigal daughter, there is no return. Were she, on her torn and bleeding feet, to drag herself back home, she, the fallen and the lost, what would be her welcome? Oh, consider this when you come to decide her guilt. . . . They wish to fine this woman and make her leave. They wish to wring from the wages of her shame the price of this meditated injustice; to take from her the little money she might have. . . .

If the prosecutors of this woman, whom you are trying, had brought her before the Savior, they would have accepted his challenge, and each one gathered a rock and stoned her in the twinkling of an eye.[16]

No, gentlemen, do as your Master did twice, under the very circumstances that surround you. Tell her to go in peace.

Thus Minnie Stacey, the disgraced prostitute, as did nearly all of Temple Houston's clients, went on her way in peace. In fact, Minnie moved from Woodward to Canadian, Texas, joined the Methodist church, took in washing for a living, and remained a dedicated Christian for the rest of her life.[17]

Temple Houston died an untimely death in 1905 of a brain hemorrhage at his home in Woodward. He was only forty-five years old. Fittingly, among the many tributes paid to Temple Houston upon his passing, the most touching came from Minnie Stacey who credited Temple with changing her life. Minnie sent her condolences to the family . . . along with a garland of wild prairie flowers—a tribute that Temple Houston would have, undoubtedly, treasured beyond all others.[18]

The Wailing Chorus of W. B. Plemons

Another courtroom gladiator encountered in earlier tales is Judge W. B. Plemons of Amarillo. In his heyday as a criminal defense lawyer, he was almost unbeatable. Although not as eloquent as Temple Houston perhaps, Plemons was, nevertheless, a powerhouse in the courtroom who simply refused to be derailed, denied, or defeated. Keen of wit, with a withering satire and overwhelming invective, he flayed his opponents and reveled in their discomfort.[19] Blatant melodrama, more likely nowadays to induce laughter rather than tears, played well to juries in those early days, and the great trial lawyers such as Plemons knew how to squeeze every tear out of it, as is demonstrated by the following story.

In 1896 Plemons defended a father, an old German immigrant named Swin Crump, as well as his two grown sons, Billy and Albert, all of whom were indicted for stealing cattle. (Crump operated a butcher shop in Amarillo.) The case was transferred on a change of venue from Amarillo to Clarendon. The old man's wife and mother to the two grown boys was also the mother of three younger children, and, when the trial was called, they all sat in the front row of the spectator section, directly behind Plemons and the defendants. However, since the family was not known in the Clarendon area, Plemons saw an opportunity to beef up the emotional appeal. So, before he left Amarillo, he borrowed three more small children and added them to the brood. Now momma was surrounded by six little tykes, and Plemons had them all primed to cry (on cue) at appropriate times—which they proceeded to do often and profusely during the trial. He had assured momma that if she and all the kids didn't crank it up to the maximum, her husband and sons would go to the pen "as sure as God made little green apples." However, toward the end of the trial, when Plemons gave her the cue once again, there was no tearful response forthcoming. He turned and glared at her, whereupon the old lady blurted out, "I'm all dried up. I can't cry no more if the whole damned family goes to the pen!" After the laughter subsided, Plemons managed somehow to adroitly reprime the waterworks and thus wash clean the sins of Crump and sons.[20]

Racism—Lynching, Burning, and Denial

You have to look hard and search diligently, and even then you will come up with very few particulars about this tragic story. The local history books barely acknowledge it, and even today the few folks in Seymour, Texas, who have ever heard about it would just as soon forget it.

In most tales of crimes and the trials of criminals, there are at least a few humorous incidents or anecdotes—but not in this one. On August 8, 1916, Stephen Brown, a black man and a prisoner of Baylor County sheriff W. L. Ellis, succeeded in overpowering and then murdering the sheriff. He escaped, but a posse ran him down and captured him the same day, and then they brought him back to the courthouse square in Baylor County.

The only eyewitness to give an account of what happened next was William F. Ballard, the district clerk of King County, Texas, some eighty miles or so to the west of Seymour. Ballard, together with King County sheriff Garrison Moore, happened to be staying overnight at the Washington Hotel in Seymour while en route to Fort Worth on a business trip.

He knew nothing of the previous happenings. However, when he and the sheriff left the hotel that evening, they found themselves surrounded by an angry mob. Ballard gave this account:

> The posse had him in the little square near the jail in the center of Seymour. As we watched, they hung him with a rope, making a terrible racket as he was choked to death. It was a pretty grim sight. But that wasn't enough for them. They then gathered a lot of wood, put it under the Negro man, and set fire to it. He was literally burned to a crisp as he hung there, although he was already dead from the rope. The men from Seymour, along with the deputies, had taken the law into their hands that day . . . and it was a very ugly scene.[21]

The mob's rage, however, was still not assuaged. The next morning a group of men went up and down the streets of Seymour rounding up all of the black men and women and loading them into a boxcar for deportation out of town. That would put an end to the town's racial problem once and for all—or so they thought.

On that day Jessie Celia Blanks was an eight-year-old girl who lived with her father, John Dennis Blanks, and mother, Frannie Ellis Blanks, at the corner of Arkansas and Nevada streets in Seymour. John Dennis Blanks was, at that time, the town's volunteer fire chief, and he and his brother, Joe, owned a barbershop. They employed a black man as the shop's "shoe-shine boy." He and his wife lived in a small house owned by the Blanks located just behind the family home. His wife served as the Blanks's maid.

The events of August 9, 1916, are etched indelibly in the memory of that eight-year-old child. In the year 2005, eighty-nine years after that traumatic day, ninety-seven-year-old Jessie Celia Blanks Powell (she married Eugene Rowland Powell) vividly recalls standing with her mother in their backyard watching the mob coming down the street toward them, determined to seize, drag off, and deport the black couple.

"I still remember those faces of hate," she says. "I had an early lesson in mob psychology." But her mother was not intimidated. Jessie Celia tells what happened next:

> My mother grabbed a gun to defend our Negroes and positioned herself right behind the fence that separated our front and back yards. As one man advanced toward her, she screamed, "The first one of you who jumps over that fence will be shot full of holes."

The mobster and his companions had second thoughts. They beat a prudent retreat and went on down the street. However, before the rampage ended that day, one of the mob threw a rock that hit a black baby in the head, killing it. Jessie Celia believes that their maid and shoe-shine man were the only blacks left in Seymour by nightfall.[22]

No one, of course, even harbored the vaguest notion of prosecuting the mob for the murders of two defenseless blacks.

Sex and the Unwritten Law Further Explored

Until 1973 it was legal in the State of Texas for one man to kill another if the former caught the latter in the act of committing adultery with the killer's wife.[23] Needless to add, shooting rights were not granted (at least not by written law) to wives when the situation was reversed.[24] Written law to the contrary, Fort Worth attorney Walter Scott once managed to get a wife acquitted even though the evidence was clear that the woman had, with premeditation, killed her husband's paramour. She was only "protecting her home," he explained to a turn-of-the-century jury, and then, making an irresistible plea, he rose to theatrical heights when he re-enacted the poor woman bravely defending her home. Scott (still pretending to be the defendant) gathered the couple's several (imaginary) children about him, and in a doleful tenor, treated the jury to a heart-rending version of "Home Sweet Home."[25]

Although the pre-1973 Texas law granted husbands certain shooting rights, the scope of that written law was fairly limited. The "unwritten law," however, as commonly understood by most early-day Texas juries, was much broader. Under that folk law, not only was the cuckold granted unlimited shooting rights, but those rights were also extended to just about anyone else in his family. Shooting rights were also acceptable for a "wronged woman" (the wife of an adulterous husband or the innocent maiden) and her family. Not only that, but, as we shall see in the John Beal Sneed murder cases, everyone else in a lecherous male's family was also considered fair game. Most times, defense lawyers attempted to disguise and euphemize their "unwritten law" appeals while ostensibly relying upon some legal defense, usually self-defense. But not always, as is demonstrated in the account of Colonel John Hallum's trial.

One day in 1896, Colonel John Hallum, a sixty-three-year-old Confederate Civil War veteran, did his dead-level best to kill an unarmed Baptist preacher. Hallum shot the preacher four times at a busy train station in Texarkana, Texas, in front of God only knows how many witnesses, and then left him there for dead. But the preacher, Reverend Forbes, with or without divine assistance, simply refused to expire. So they tried John Hallum for "attempted murder."[26]

Hallum and his wife had been faithful members of Forbes's flock.

Colonel John Hallum and his soon to be unfaithful wife.
(From a pamphlet written by Colonel Hallum, the Phoenix Press,
Muskogee, Oklahoma, 1911.)

However, while Hallum was on a prolonged business trip out of state, the Reverend Forbes, by all accounts, seems to have taken a special interest in Mrs. Hallum that went considerably beyond the needs of her spiritual welfare. When John Hallum, a born and bred Southerner, got wind of this, he immediately umbraged up and got out his old Civil War pistol.

At the outset of the prosecution, Colonel Hallum was unable to secure the services of a local lawyer, because of the great public outcry against Hallum's violent and deadly attack upon an unarmed servant of the Lord. Fortunately, Colonel Hallum was a self-educated lawyer and undertook to defend himself in this very hostile environment.

Initially, at least, it seemed that the old saw about the lawyer who represents himself has a fool for a client was about to be validated. In spades. Hallum let the prosecution have a free hand in parading a string of witnesses to the stand and permitting them to testify at will. He didn't bother with much cross-examination. In fact, when his turn at bat came, he frankly admitted that he had shot the preacher four times (missed him once), and intended with all five shots to kill Forbes. His only regret was that he hadn't succeeded. His was no mealymouth, weak-kneed, "self-defense" charade nor any other contrived "written law" defense. He rested his defense four-square on "the unwritten law." Take it or leave it. The Reverend Forbes, he told the jury, was a "knavish, psalm-singing hypocrite." And then, with world-class candor that— agree with the content or not—must be admired, he laid it all on the line.

> I would have shot the base-born libertine [Reverend Forbes] if the angels of heaven had been guarding him when I got within gunshot of him, and I would have camped on his trail a thousand years, if . . . it had required that time to come up with him. And let me say further that I shot him with all the coolness and premeditated deliberation that it is possible for a rational mind to conceive . . . I would repeat the same remedy a thousand times in defiance of all the penal statutes of the world. There are some things in which I fix my own standards, and this is one of them. The remedy I applied is certainly more effectual than sacramental wine or catnip tea.

Then Colonel Hallum got down to the business of educating the jury on the dictates of, the history of, and the supremacy of "the unwritten law." That education took hours and hours, but Hallum was up to the task.

First he traced the rise and fall of almost every tribe of mankind from the dawning of recorded time to the present, attributing the fall of each to the failure of men to protect the sanctity of their homes and the chastity of their women. Then, he quoted (rather selectively) from the bards—Shakespeare on down. He really got hot when he hit the Bible. Again, his citations of biblical passages seem to have been rather selective. For example, his many references to the Ten Commandments seemed to be weighted strongly in favor of that part about not committing adultery, while, frankly, Colonel Hallum's righteous indignation tapered off noticeably when he got to that part about not killing other folks.

Finally, bringing it all up to the present (1897), he decried modernism and its resulting decline of morality.

> Society itself is on trial, at a critical period when virtue and morality is [sic] on a fearful downward trend, without any apparent

protest against the advance of the social revolution which threatens so much to the sanctity of the home and the state itself. We are yet fighting the battle of civilization; my struggles today may be yours tomorrow. . . .

. . . the puny statute of man repealing an ordinance of God for the government of the world [is not a] primal sanction . . .

Gentlemen, this case is governed by the higher law, you will render a verdict of not guilty.

John Hallum's exhaustive discourse on the unwritten law—"*lex non scripta*" as he so classically phrased it—carried the day. The jury found him not guilty of attempted murder.

However, the jurors didn't let him off completely. Tossing at least a morsel in the direction of the written laws of Texas, they found Colonel Hallum guilty of a misdemeanor, assault, and fined him fifty dollars.

In 1912, "the unwritten law" was invoked in a much bloodier and a much more complex case.[27] Albert Boyce Jr., son of a prominent Panhandle rancher, began an affair with Lena Snyder Sneed, the wife of an Amarillo wheeler-dealer named John Beal Sneed. When the enraged John Beal Sneed found out about the affair, he promptly had his wife committed to a Fort Worth mental institution. (After all, John Beal Sneed reasoned, any wife of his who would run around on him *had* to be insane.) However, the amorous Al Boyce was not to be denied. He snatched Lena from the institution, and they "eloped"—all the way to Canada—before John Beal Sneed and the Burns Detective Agency finally ran them to ground.

When Al Boyce eventually returned from Canada, John Beal Sneed ambushed and killed him on the streets of Amarillo. However, before that, the vindictive John Beal Sneed had already shot and killed Al Boyce's father as he sat, unarmed, in the lobby of a Fort Worth hotel—the latter's primary sin being his attempt to obtain a dismissal of questionable kidnapping charges filed against his son by John Beal Sneed.

In four subsequent murder trials—two in Fort Worth and, on changes of venue, one in Memphis, Texas, and one in Vernon, Texas—both John Beal Sneed and his henchman were acquitted by juries. They escaped prosecution not only for the killing of Al Boyce, the lover, but also the lover's father, Colonel Boyce. Although the defense made a few feeble nods in the direction of "self-defense" in both cases, it was clear that the real defense was "the unwritten law," which Sneed's attorneys euphemistically referred to by using the code phrase "protecting the home." The turn-of-the-century juries thus, relying on the "unwritten law," "protected" John Beal Sneed's home, not only from the lecherous Al Boyce, but also from his dastardly sixty-four-year-old father, Albert Boyce Sr.

One of John Beal Sneed's lawyers, W. P. McLean, explained it to the jury this way:

> Were the penitentiaries made for such men as Beal? If they were, then I want to go to the penitentiary and associate with the home protectors. . . . Whenever a home is despoiled, gentlemen, I say there ought to be a killing.

His partner, Walter Scott, chimed in:

> The best shots ever fired in Texas were the shots that took Al Boyce's life, and I hope every home destroyer in the land meets the same fate.

The defense excused Lena from any complicity in the matter, explaining (by experts of questionable expertise) that due solely to the wiles and blandishments of the lecherous Al Boyce, Lena had become "morally insane." It was thus left to the selfless and long-suffering John Beal Sneed to swallow his pride and rescue her.

In his final argument, Sneed's lawyer commended John Beal Sneed for "saving" Lena from herself and Al Boyce. Had Sneed let her go, the defense lawyer assured the jury, it would have been but a short time before Lena would end up "in the red light district of some big city, flitting about dark corners as a shadow, then gone." (Assuming, of course, that Al Boyce would have encouraged and approved of Lena's "flitting about.")

Another of Sneed's lawyers, Cone Johnson, in his jury oration even compared John Beal Sneed to Jesus Christ: "Beal Sneed is the only man

I have ever heard of since the days of Christ that [*sic*] has stood by his wife under all circumstances."

Still, the competing pre–World War I social values and attitudes of Texans toward sex and the law could not have come into a clearer focus than in the following exchange of views between the prosecution and the defense in their final jury arguments.

Jordan Cummings for the state: Regard for human life is the highest and the ultimate test of a country's civilization.

W. P. McLean for the defense: Human life is not the highest consideration of our law, being less regarded by the law than domestic relations. . . . Every time there is a home broken up, there ought to be a killing of all who assisted in it.

The jury had little difficulty agreeing with McLean.

Sometimes Juries Do the Damndest Things

Even veteran trial lawyers and judges are often surprised by jury verdicts—and even more surprised when they learn how and why the jurors reached their results. Every trial lawyer, at one time or another, has departed the courthouse shaking his head in despair after hearing jurors give the most outlandish and illogical reasons for their decision. Juries, particularly in frontier times, often generously leavened their judicial deliberations with purely pragmatic considerations that had absolutely nothing to do with the law or the evidence.[28]

A fellow by the name of Jack Ryan was on one early-day jury that tried a murder case in Tascosa. Jack was a popular saloonkeeper, and his saloon was also headquarters of the "Knights of the Pasteboard." While Jack rarely partook of the drinks he dispensed, he dearly loved a good high-stakes poker game. In fact, he was an obsessive, and apparently successful, gambler. Given such an occupation and disposition, one would ordinarily think that Jack would be a defendant-leaning juror—liberal-minded and not inclined to judge his fellow man too harshly. However, in this case, Jack found himself deadlocked with the other eleven jurors, all of whom voted for an acquittal. Strong-willed as ever, Jack obstinately held his ground for conviction. Known as a "stout-hearted debater," Jack was usually set in concrete when he made up his mind. However, in those early days, the secrecy of a jury's deliberations was not enforced with the zeal common in today's practice, and somehow it leaked out that Jack was causing a deadlock in the jury by holding out for a conviction. A friend of the beleaguered defendant heard of the situation through the community grapevine and took matters into his own hands. Somehow he sneaked into the courtroom unobserved, and, standing on a chair, he looked into the jury room through a transom above the door. He caught Jack's eye and motioned him over. He whispered to Jack that there was the finest poker game he ever saw going on in Jack's saloon. "The stakes are high, the sky's the limit and the boys are well fixed," he reported.

Jack immediately reconsidered his position and told the other jurors this:

> Now boys, we have fought over this long enough. We ought to bring in a verdict and be done with it. I believe you are wrong, but as there are eleven against me, I do not think I should hold out and be too stubborn. Now, if you boys won't come over, I will have to go with you and agree to a verdict of not guilty.

Soon thereafter Jack was thus able to return to his saloon and engage in his lucrative obsession.

In yet another case, a proven horse thief regained his freedom by virtue of the questionable logic of one juror:

> I have no doubt he is guilty, but if you turn him loose he will leave the country and this is the best thing that can be done.

He was acquitted, and he did leave the country, and so a degree of "regional justice" was thus achieved—at least the horse-thieving problem was shifted to a distant place.

Then on yet another jury sat John Morrell, a bootmaker with a decidedly pragmatic turn of mind. The jury began deliberating the defendant's fate. Some were inclined toward a guilty verdict, while others leaned toward an acquittal. Morrell, however, carried the day for the defendant when he told his fellows the following:

Why the son-of-a-gun is guilty all right, but we must turn him loose. He owes me for a pair of boots, and if we convict him I'll never get my money.

Sometimes Appellate Courts Do the Damndest Things

Even into the 1940s the Texas Court of Criminal Appeals occasionally lapsed into the nit-picking absurdity of earlier times in reversing murder convictions. A seventy-year-old woman, Fannie McHenry, was driving her car near Chickasha, Oklahoma, en route to Dallas when she stopped and picked up a seventeen-year-old hitchhiker named Buster Northern. She requested that he help by taking turns driving her car.

When they got to Dallas, Buster decided he enjoyed driving so much that he would just keep the car for himself. When Mrs. McHenry objected, he kicked the legs out from under her and proceeded to stomp her to death. A few days later the police arrested Buster, who was still driving Mrs. McHenry's car. He confessed to stealing the car and stomping Mrs. McHenry to death. After the jury heard the facts and Buster's confession, it didn't take it long to find him guilty and sentence him to death. But the appellate court rode to the rescue of Buster Northern. The indictment under which he was convicted had charged Buster with killing Mrs. McHenry "with malice aforethought . . . by then and there kicking and stomping" her to death. Not good enough, held the Court of Criminal Appeals. Three key words were omitted: "with his feet."

To his credit, one judge dissented, wondering aloud how, pray tell, could Buster have "kicked and stomped" Mrs. McHenry to death *other than* by doing so "with his feet"? Well, the majority sniffed, if you start allowing an indictment to be completed by inferences, just where will it all end? Result: the court overturned Buster's conviction and ordered the prosecution dismissed.[29]

The Court of Criminal Appeals was only following its prior decisions.

In 1945 that court reversed another murder conviction on account of a faulty indictment. A fellow named Gragg who had been indicted (and convicted) for "then and there drowning" his wife was let off the hook. The sloppy prosecutor forgot to add "in water."[30] Earlier still (1894), the court set one Mr. Jackson free after a jury had convicted him of murder under an indictment alleging that he had "unlawfully and with malice aforethought killed one Sam Crow by shooting the said Sam Crow." The prosecutor forgot to add "with a gun."[31]

More than three decades after the Buster Northern debacle, the Texas Court of Criminal Appeals was petitioned to take the Northern doctrine yet one step further. With his feet, Mr. Vaughan had kicked and stomped Mrs. Vaughan to death. The careful prosecutor (doubtless heeding the lesson of the Northern case) obtained an indictment charging the defendant with kicking and stomping his wife to death "with his feet."

"Not good enough," cried the defendant on appeal. The indictment, he asserted, was fatally defective because it failed to allege that the defendant kicked and stomped his wife to death "with shoes on his feet!" "Enough already!" cried an obviously embarrassed court. Noting the public outrage triggered by its 1947 Northern decision, the court in 1980 declined to tread further down that path, and, for good measure, it nixed the noxious Northern doctrine and kicked it right out of Texas jurisprudence.[32]

In all fairness, however, it should be noted that the Texas court wasn't the only one to insist upon slavish adherence to old common law rules of pleading and procedure. Courts in other jurisdictions, particularly in the nineteenth century, insisted that all the technicalities of the common law be rigidly observed. One Mississippi jurist of that period recalled how he had quashed eighty indictments at one time over one such technicality.[33]

Lawyer for Hire: Have Evidence—Will Travel

If you're going to be tried for murder, it sure helps a lot to hire a lawyer who can not only provide expertise in the courtroom but also furnish evidence and testimony proving your innocence.

In several previous tales we have encountered the unrelenting A. J.

Fires, a frequent cohort of Temple Houston in the defense of criminal cases. Members of the bar still pass along tales of Fires's audacious stunts both inside and outside the courtroom. The following tale was told by retired district judge John T. Forbis of Childress, who, as a young lawyer, became well acquainted with Fires.[34] Once during A. J. Fires's salad days, a local farmer burst into Fires's office in a state of panic. He blurted out a tale of killing a neighbor with whom he had been feuding for several years. The two had chanced to meet on a country road somewhere near Childress—tempers flared, and matters went from bad to worse, culminating in Fires's client-to-be grabbing his 12-gauge shotgun and blasting his antagonist into kingdom come. The victim had been unarmed. Fires's client-to-be left the victim lying beside the road and immediately rushed to town to consult with Fires. He told Fires there were no witnesses to the incident except himself and the victim, and he didn't think the body had been discovered.

After digesting all this, Fires immediately loaded up his new client and tore out for the crime scene. Sure enough, there was the body. No one had discovered it. While examining the area, A.J. noticed a broken wagon wheel spoke about the size of a small baseball bat down the road some distance. He called his client to bring his shotgun. Then he had the client shoot the wagon spoke from about the same distance he had been from the victim when he fatally wounded him. Then he seized the wagon spoke (now sprinkled with several shotgun pellets) and threw it down beside the body, whereupon A.J. and client departed in haste. The client was then directed by A.J. to immediately rush into the sheriff's office (by himself, of course, and *not* in the company of his lawyer) and breathlessly report the killing, adding that he had no choice but to shoot the fellow since he was coming at him with a club, threatening to beat his brains out. "Then," Fires directed his client, "shut up, and I'll take it from there." Sure enough, when the sheriff arrived on the scene and conducted his investigation, he discovered the body and the wagon spoke club lying beside it—both liberally punctured by the same-size shotgun pellets, all of which neatly corroborated Fires's client's recently inspired version of the fatal confrontation.

A.J. then encountered little difficulty making the self-defense plea stand up in court.

AFTERWORD

TALES OF SENSATIONAL frontier killings still fascinate in this very different and modern world, and tales of the ensuing murder trials are typically an intriguing mix of riveting drama and pure farce featuring the outrageous tactics of early-day lawyers—bombastic oratory skills and calculated, melodramatic stunts. Plus, almost inevitably, the trials took unexpected twists and turns. But beyond the entertainment, an analysis of the murder cases helps us better understand the problems our nascent criminal justice system encountered while struggling to establish order in a wild land and to bring the concept of justice under the rule of law to fruition. As we have seen, the progress made toward achieving that goal was painful and halting, but it was finally achieved—if not perfectly.

Perhaps, however, there are additional lessons to be learned from an examination of these murder trials. Each trial gives us a sense of the times and of the people of those times; each trial is, in effect, a freeze-frame shot of our forebears and their world. When pieced together, a mosaic emerges that accurately depicts us the way we were back then. To understand what we are, we have to understand what we were. Criminal trials—and murder trials in particular—provide an excellent, ready-made laboratory in which to place the society of that time under a microscope and study its central themes and underlying cultural values. As one historian commented, "Lawyers functioning as attorneys for real clients with real problems provide the best evidence of behavior and the historical realities for the participants."[1]

Consider the various aspects of those criminal trials.

What cases did the prosecutors elect to prosecute (and with how much vigor), and which cases did they choose to ignore or downgrade?

Scholars from diverse disciplines may well employ the murder-trial laboratory, including the news accounts of the proceedings, to great benefit to view the late-nineteenth-century and early-twentieth-century Texas society through the prism of their own respective fields—and, in doing so, make numerous cogent observations and deductions. Yet one salient, overriding impression comes into clearer focus with each murder trial under investigation: the feeling in the minds of all classes, from childhood up, that homicide is one of the probable contingencies of ordinary social life.[2] While Texans of the time took property crimes seriously—especially the theft of livestock—the casual acceptance of violence accounts in large part for the woefully low conviction rates when it came to crimes of violence.

But why were Texans so tolerant of violence? And why did the frontier mentality that condoned acts of violence continue so long—well after the physical frontier had moved on? Two reasons immediately come to mind. First, because of the sizeable migration of settlers from the Old South, the cultural values of that region were exported to Texas (as well as other western states), including the South's Victorian "Code of Honor," which posited that the preservation of one's honor was more important than life itself—yours or anybody else's. A high level of violence was thus ensured by this bloody thirst for retribution. Novelist Robert Penn Warren, who grew up in the Old South (Kentucky) in the early twentieth century, wrote of those times:

> There was a world of violence that I grew up in. You accepted violence as a component of life. . . . You heard about violence, and you saw terrible fights . . . not the violence of robbery, you see; it was another kind of violence in the air: the violence of anger, what sociologists call status homicide . . . there was some threat of being trapped into this whether you wanted to or not.[3]

Still, there appears to be more to it than simply the importation of some of the Old South's cultural values. Another contributing factor—and this one is peculiar to the State of Texas—was the state's long history of bloodshed beginning when the first immigrants flocked into the Mexican province west of the Sabine River in the late eighteenth century and continuing until well after the turn of the twentieth century. Texas became an independent nation in 1836 after defeating the Mexican army under General Santa Anna, but that came only after bloody massacres at the Alamo and Goliad. Even then, however, Texas was not at peace. Not by a long shot. The Indian wars heated up and continued until the mid-1870s when Colonel Ranald McKenzie and the U.S. Army defeated Chief Quanah Parker and the Comanche in the Texas Panhandle—three decades after Texas was admitted to the Union in 1845. In the meantime the Civil War broke out, and, taking advantage of the loss of manpower on the Texas frontier, Indians escalated their raids and pushed the frontier back a hundred miles or so.[4] After the numbing effect of the horrific slaughter of more than half a million Americans during the Civil War, a second war was spawned in its aftermath: the war of the Reconstruction era. Violence broke out not only between Texans and their Reconstruction masters (the embittered Texans called them "carpetbaggers" and "scalawags") but also between Texans themselves. A sizeable minority of Texans were Union sympathizers, and during and after the war, old grudges festered and erupted into terrible savagery in that lawless vacuum. For example, in October 1862 in the north Texas village of Gainesville, Confederate supporters discovered the existence of a "Peace Party" composed of Union-minded men. Many were arrested and tried before a kangaroo court resulting in "the Great Hanging in Gainesville." Forty-one Texans were hanged on the same day.[5] After the Civil War, a number of the kangaroo court members were tried, but no convictions were returned.

Meanwhile, outlaws took full advantage of the social disorganization and the lack of meaningful law enforcement. Cattle rustling was so rampant that it threatened the economic viability of even larger ranches. The late nineteenth century was also a time of numerous fights over land or water rights, fence-cuttings, and an inordinate number of bitter family feuds.

Such outlawry and killings in a society where no organized law enforcement or court system was in place inevitably resulted in the formation of vigilante groups, which, in turn, resulted in even more violence and bloodshed. Texas had the dubious distinction of fostering sixty-two vigilante movements before the end of the nineteenth century—considerably more than any other state.[6]

To add more to the bloodshed, conflicts continued along the Rio Grande border, pitting Mexicans and Hispanic Texans against Anglo-Texans. Even as late as 1915 the border was home to big trouble. In that year, ethnic Mexicans implemented their "Plan de San Diego." The plan called for the slaughter of all white American males over the age of sixteen and the overthrow of United States rule in Texas and other Southwest border states. Predictably, once the killing started, it was countered by local posses, Texas Rangers, and thousands of federal soldiers dispatched to quell the violence. Just as predictably, it then degenerated into a prolonged episode of savage racial violence.[7]

Thousands of violent encounters occurred in Texas during the turbulent nineteenth century and the early years of the twentieth century, and most of them were incited by either the Civil War and its aftermath or by bitter hatred between the races. Even though each incident was different in event, actors, and causation, each still contributed to the collective psyche of the people. Having inherited the Old South's violence-prone folkways and values to begin with, and then having survived more than a century of wholesale bloodshed, is it any wonder that most Texans had become anesthetized to murder and mayhem in their everyday lives, had come to accept it all as the norm?

Eventually, however, while the Texas soil may have been rocky and thin, and the climate harsh, still, by dent of the sacrifice and toil of the many—mostly unheralded champions of an ideal—the fragile plant of justice under duly enacted law finally took root and matured. Judge *Blackstone* finally ousted Judges *Lynch* and *Winchester*.

It would be wonderful (wonderfully naive, that is) to believe that the battle for the supremacy of the rule of law and the attainment of justice under that law has been won once and for all. However, just as the battle for freedom and democracy—against tyrants and terrorists—demands eternal vigilance and sacrifice, so also does the battle for law and justice.

Obvious miscarriages of justice still occur in our courts, as well-publicized modern cases attest. In California, a mountain of scientific evidence adduced at the trial of O. J. Simpson, a black man, proved beyond any reasonable doubt that he was guilty of the vicious murder of two white people. In another California case, a video tape made by an unbiased spectator, proved beyond a reasonable doubt that several white policemen severely beat Rodney King, a black man, after he was already under arrest and subdued. But, a predominately black jury acquitted Simpson, and a predominately white jury acquitted the policemen who beat Rodney King. In both cases, racism, emotion, and bias trumped overwhelming evidence and the law, enabling guilty defendants to get away with their crimes.[8] As demonstrated by stories within this book, the miscarriage of justice, now as then, seriously undermines the public's confidence in the criminal law system and cynically skews the beliefs and attitudes of those from whom future jury pools will be summoned.

"Jury nullification," a common result of the lack of public confidence in the criminal justice system comes in two different varieties. The jury, in acquitting a guilty defendant, either ignores the evidence or the law—or both. In the O. J. Simpson and Rodney King cases, the jury ignored the evidence. Other juries nullified cases and acquitted defendants because the jurors disagreed with the law(s) applicable to the case. In Michigan Dr. Jack Kervorkian, an advocate of assisted suicide, was twice acquitted of murder even though evidence showed beyond any reasonable doubt that he killed (by assisted suicide) several people, in clear violation of Michigan's homicide laws.

Jury nullification has been, in recent years, advocated by a fairly vocal minority. Volumes could be written on that subject, and it is beyond the scope of this afterword to discuss it in detail. Suffice it to say that jury nullification is, I contend, a very slippery slope down which we don't want to slide, for it will only lead back to the rule of man as opposed to the rule of law.

When any jury is seated, it is required to take an oath that it will render a "true verdict based on the law and the evidence." Is it then okay for a juror (who, after all has just become an officer of the court) to violate his or her oath because of a personal bias for or against the defendant or for or against the applicable law? If so, I suppose judges, prosecutors, and policemen should be equally free to violate their oaths when they have strong emotional feelings about a case or a defendant. I am sure the policemen who beat Rodney King mercilessly were understandably angered by his prior conduct. So is it okay that they, giving vent to their emotions, violated their oaths to uphold the law and to protect and defend the rights of all citizens, good or bad?

And, as to those who disagree with the applicable criminal statute in a criminal case, is it okay that they simply undertake to unilaterally repeal that statute by their verdict? Aren't laws supposed to apply to every one and be enacted—or repealed—only by consent of a majority of the governed? And, if a citizen is opposed to any law on the books, isn't the proper democratic way to apply political pressure upon the legislature to repeal or amend the offending statute? Is it a part of our democratic system that we, as individuals, can pick and choose which laws we will honor?

Former U.S. Supreme Court justice Felix Frankfurter put it this way:

> If one man can be allowed to determine for himself what is law, every man can. That means first chaos, then tyranny. Legal process is an essential part of the democratic process.[9]

Jury nullification, despite any self-righteous window-dressing that may be put upon it, is nothing more or less than a step backward toward the law of the jungle.

Since imperfect humans devise and operate criminal justice systems, none will ever be perfect—none will ever result in perfect justice in every instance. The best we can hope for is an approximation of justice in most cases. Despite its all too frequent misfires and failures, the American system of criminal justice must nevertheless be preserved and improved upon as time goes by. That, as observed, takes eternal vigilance, dedication, and sacrifice by an informed public.

The problem is not so much with the system itself as with the human frailties of those who operate the system and who fail to perform their assigned duties faithfully and honestly, from the cop on the beat to the prosecutor to the defense attorney to the presiding judge and, finally, to informed and unbiased jurors who render true verdicts based on the evidence and the law.

NOTES

Foreword

1. John Phillip Reid, *Policing the Elephant: Crime, Punishment, and Social Behavior on the Overland Trail* (San Marino, Calif.: The Huntington Library, 1997).

2. John W. Davis Jr., *A Vast Amount of Trouble: A History of the Spring Creek Raid* (Niwot: University Press of Colorado, 1994).

3. Jill Mocho, *Murder and Justice in Frontier New Mexico, 1821–1846* (Albuquerque: University of New Mexico Press, 1997).

4. Clare V. McKanna Jr., *The Trial of "Indian Joe": Race and Justice in the Nineteenth-Century West* (Lincoln: University of Nebraska Press, 2004).

5. Clare V. McKanna Jr., *White Justice in Arizona: Apache Murder Trials in the Nineteenth Century* (Lubbock: Texas Tech University Press, 2005).

6. Sidney L. Harring, *Crow Dog's Case: American Indian Sovereignty, Tribal Law, and United States Law in the Nineteenth Century* (Cambridge: Cambridge University Press, 1994).

7. John W. Davis Jr., *Goodbye, Judge Lynch: The End of a Lawless Era in Wyoming's Big Horn Basin* (Norman: University of Oklahoma Press, 2005).

8. Frederick Allen, *A Decent Orderly Lynching: The Montana Vigilantes* (Norman: University of Oklahoma Press, 2005).

Prologue

1. Corwin W. Johnson, "Texas' Uncommon Laws," *UT Law: The Magazine of the University of Texas School of Law* 2, no. 2 (Summer 2003): 64.

NOTES

The Coming of the Law

1. Charles E. Coombes, *The Prairie Dog Lawyer* (Dallas: University Press of Dallas, 1945), viii.

2. Wayne Gard, *Frontier Justice* (Norman: University of Oklahoma Press, 1949), 254–258.

3. Coombes, *The Prairie Dog Lawyer*, 31–35.

4. Ellis Douthit, "Some Experiences of a West Texas Lawyer," *West Texas Historical Association Year Book* 18 (1942): 42–46; Gordon Morris Bakken, *Practicing Law in Frontier California* (Lincoln: University of Nebraska Press, 1991), 1–17.

5. Daniel H. Calhoun, *Professional Lives in America* (Cambridge: Harvard University Press, 1965), 60–61; Everett Dick, *The Dixie Frontier: A Social History* (Norman: University of Oklahoma Press, 1993), 230.

6. *The Childress County [Texas] News*, July 14, 1938 (recollections of Judge A. J. Fires).

7. Bakken, *Practicing Law in Frontier California*, 1–17; *The Childress County News*, July 14, 1938 (recollections of Judge A. J. Fires).

8. Problems gathering evidence in criminal cases and problems encountered subsequently in the trial of criminal cases when sagebrush courts had little guidance in the way of rules of evidence or court procedures plagued all advocates of law and order in all parts of the western frontier. For instance, emigrants on the Overland Trail en route to Oregon or California in the mid-nineteenth century had no law enforcement officials on board. The emigrants simply went about gathering evidence themselves as best they could. When it came to trials by ad hoc people's courts selected by popular consent, they attempted to emulate remembered rules of evidence and court procedure from back home in the East. Witnesses, however, were allowed to testify freely and tell their tales unfettered by those irksome objections such as "hearsay" or "irrelevant" or "unsubstantiated opinion" or "speculative." Defensive pleas for delays were seldom granted. Despite it all, professor John Phillip Reid in his work *Policing the Elephant: Crime, Punishment, and Social Behavior on the Overland Trail* (San Marino: Huntington Library Press, 1997), 96–97, 117–119, 128–132, 148–150, and 158, found that the emigrants' amateur efforts were anchored in a spirit of fairness and were, for the most part, surprisingly successful.

9. Judge R.W. Hall, "The Prairie Dog Lawyers," *The Texas Law Review* 48 (1929): 265–271.

10. J. F. Cunningham, "Experiences of a Pioneer District Attorney," *West Texas Historical Association Year Book* 8 (1923): 134–135.

11. John Anthony Moretta, *William Pitt Ballinger: Texas Lawyer, Southern Statesman, 1825–1888* (Austin: Texas State Historical Association, 2000), 96–98, 186–190. The problems and progress encountered by the practicing bar in both

rural and settled areas of California in the last half of the nineteenth century in regard to obtaining adequate law library facilities and upgrading the legal education program are well described in Bakken, *Practicing Law in Frontier California,* 26–32.

12. Allen G. Hatley, *Bringing the Law to Texas: Crime and Violence in Nineteenth-Century Texas* (LaGrange, Tex.: Centex Press, 2002), 22; Bakken, *Practicing Law in Frontier California,* 111–112; C. L. Sonnichsen, *I'll Die before I'll Run: The Story of the Great Feuds of Texas* (Lincoln: University of Nebraska Press, 1951), 319.

13. *Abilene [Texas] Daily Reporter,* March 21, 1917.

14. J. Evetts Haley, *Charles Goodnight: Cowman and Plainsman* (Norman: University of Oklahoma Press, 1949), 376.

15. Bill O'Neal, *Cattlemen vs. Sheepherders* (Austin: Eakin Press, 1989), 15–32. See also John W. Davis, *A Vast Amount of Trouble: A History of the Spring Creek Raid* (Niwot: University Press of Colorado, 1993); John W. Davis, *Goodbye, Judge Lynch: The End of a Lawless Era in Wyoming's Big Horn Basin* (Norman: University of Oklahoma Press, 2005).

16. Gard, *Frontier Justice,* 58–59; Robert M. Utley, *Billy the Kid: A Short and Violent Life* (Lincoln: University of Nebraska Press, 1989).

17. Bill O'Neal, *The Johnson County War* (Austin: Eakin Press, 2004). Insofar as cattlemen versus sheepherder wars are concerned, the Texas Panhandle seemed to have been relatively peaceable when compared to other frontier areas. See Frederick W. Rathjen, *The Texas Panhandle Frontier* (Lubbock: Texas Tech University Press, 1973), 190.

18. Ty Cashion, *A Texas Frontier: The Clear Fork Country and Fort Griffin, 1849–1997* (Norman: University of Oklahoma Press, 1996), 216–230; Robert K. DeArment, *Bravo of the Brazos: John Larn of Fort Griffin, Texas* (Norman: University of Oklahoma Press, 2000).

19. William Rathmell and Robert K. DeArment, eds. *Life of the Marlows: A True Story of Frontier Life of Early Days* (Denton: University of North Texas Press, 2004); Glenn Shirley, *The Fighting Marlows: Men Who Wouldn't Be Lynched* (Fort Worth: Texas Christian University Press, 1994).

20. See, for example, Charles H. Harris III and Louis R. Sadler, *The Texas Rangers and the Mexican Revolution: The Bloodiest Decade, 1910–1920* (Albuquerque: University of New Mexico Press, 2004).

21. Cashion, *A Texas Frontier,* 236–261.

22. W. C. Holden, "Law and Lawlessness on the Texas Frontier, 1875–1890," *Southwestern Historical Quarterly* 44, no. 2 (October 1940): 203. Holden, perhaps overdramatizing a bit, nevertheless makes the following insightful comment:

> It is in a measure strange that in a land where murder was common and not seriously regarded, where horse thievery was recurrent and considered the most

heinous of crimes, a thing to be ruthlessly stamped out without recourse to law, where prostitution was condoned, where drunkenness was taken for granted, where fighting was a pastime, where men bounced chairs over each other's heads in court without incurring "contempt," where a judge's ability to maintain order in court depended upon his own dominating personality and perhaps a couple of six-shooters lying on the bench in front of him—it is strange and somewhat contradictory that in such a land people trusted each other, never locked the doors of their houses, loaned one to the other of their time and substance without stint, and considered each other's "word as good as his bond."

23. *The Childress County News,* July 14, 1938 (recollections of Judge A. J. Fires).

24. Edward L. Ayers, *Vengeance and Justice: Crime and Punishment in 19th-Century South* (New York: Oxford University Press, 1984), 18–19. See also crime statistics collected by Clare V. McKanna Jr., *Homicide, Race, and Justice in the American West, 1880–1920* (Tucson: University of Arizona Press, 1997), 18–27.

25. Commandment Number One of the sacred "Code of the Old West Gunfighter" (according to Hollywood) dictated that the fast-draw hero must never, never slap leather until *after* the villain had gone for his gun. Poppycock, as numerous noted western historians have observed: "Only an idiot would allow a murderous opponent the opportunity to draw first," Johnny D. Boggs, *Great Murder Trials of the Old West* (Plano: Republic of Texas Press, 2003), viii; "Frontiersmen were not cowards, but neither were they fools," Frank Richard Prassel, *The Great American Outlaw: A Legacy of Fact and Fiction* (Norman: University of Oklahoma Press, 1993), 159; "The gunfight was a fact; the fast draw, a fantasy," Joseph G. Rosa, *The Gunfighter: Man or Myth?* (Norman: University of Oklahoma Press, 1969), 198–200. See also Leon C. Metz, *Pat Garrett: The Story of a Western Lawman* (Norman: University of Oklahoma Press, 1974).

26. Compare the findings and conclusions of McKanna, *Homicide, Race and Justice in the American West,* with that of W. Eugene Hollon, *Frontier Violence: Another Look* (New York: Oxford University Press, 1974).

27. Eugene Hollon asserts that the degree of lawlessness was greater in Texas than other western states and that the duration of the lawless period was much longer. Hollon, *Frontier Violence,* 36.

28. For instance, the history of violence that occurred in the area of interest in this book is completely different from other parts of Texas. For the most part, the area of concern in this book escaped the terrible family feuds that afflicted east and south Texas. Sonnichsen, *I'll Die before I'll Run.* And, again, for the most part it escaped the awful bloodshed that erupted in central and east Texas as a result of the Civil War and the vengeful and chaotic Reconstruction era. David Pickering and Judy Falls, *Brush Men and Vigilantes: Civil War Dissent in Texas* (College Station: Texas A&M University Press, 2000); James M. Smallwood, Barry A. Crouch,

and Larry Peacock, *Murder and Mayhem: The War of Reconstruction in Texas* (College Station: Texas A&M University Press, 2003); Richard B. McCaslin, *Tainted Breeze: The Great Hanging at Gainesville, Texas, 1862* (Baton Rouge: Louisiana State University Press, 1994). The area was also mercifully spared the racially inspired violence that plagued the Rio Grande country in south Texas for so many years. Benjamin Heber Johnson, *Revolution in Texas: How a Forgotten Rebellion and Its Bloody Suppression Turned Mexicans into Americans* (New Haven: Yale University Press, 2003); Charles H. Harris III and Louis R. Sadler, *The Texas Rangers and the Mexican Revolution: The Bloodiest Decade, 1910–1920* (Albuquerque: University of New Mexico Press, 2004). For an interesting and insightful work that explores the early lawless period and vigilante activity in a portion of our area of concern (that being the Ft. Griffin and the Albany, Texas, country along the Clear Fork of the Brazos), see Cashion, *A Texas Frontier.* Also see Robert K. DeArment, *Bravo of the Brazos: John Larn of Fort Griffin, Texas* (Norman: University of Oklahoma Press, 2000).

29. Joe B. Frantz, in Hugh Davis Graham and Ted Robert Gurr, eds., *The History of Violence in America: Historical and Comparative Perspectives* (New York: Frederick A. Praeger, Publishers, 1969), 127–154.

30. Ayers, *Vengeance and Justice,* 270. See also Sonnichsen, *I'll Die Before I'll Run,* 8–9, 317.

31. Hollon, *Frontier Violence,* 180; Ayers, *Vengeance and Justice,* 247–250: Dick, *The Dixie Frontier,* 226.

32. Ayers, *Vengeance and Justice,* 12. See also Sonnichsen, *I'll Die Before I'll Run,* 8–9.

33. Ayers, *Vengeance and Justice,* 12. See also Douthit, "Some Experiences of a West Texas Lawyer," 34.

34. Ayers, *Vengeance and Justice,* 17–18.

35. Gard, *Frontier Justice,* 190, 192, 202; Hollon, *Frontier Violence,* 167; Holden, "Law and Lawlessness on the Texas Frontier," 203.

36. Cashion, *A Texas Frontier,* 217, quoting frontier editor, "Captain" George W. Roberson, *The Jacksboro [Texas] Frontier Echo,* April 28, 1876.

37. Holden, "Law and Lawlessness on the Texas Frontier," 196–197.

38. Darwin Payne, *As Old As Dallas Itself—A History of the Lawyers of Dallas, the Dallas Bar Associations, and the City They Helped Build* (Dallas: Three Forks Press, 1999), 12. Payne, carrying forward remembrances from frontier lawyer John Jay Good (1827–1882) as related by Berry B. Cobb, *A History of Dallas Lawyers, 1840–1890* (Dallas: The Bar Association of Dallas, 1934), gave this colorful insight into early-day frontier law practice:

> When the time for holding the courts arrived, it was not unusual to see a dozen or
> more lawyers and the judge mount their horses, with saddle-bags, blankets, and

tie ropes; and thus equipped, start on their journey around the district, which then embraced many counties, comprising a large scope of country . . . they would camp out at a place near water. They would build a fire, make coffee, and have their snack meals. After eating and drinking they would sit around the campfire, tell jokes and stories, sing a song, and finally roll themselves into their blankets with their saddle for a pillow . . .

39. Dick, *The Dixie Frontier*, 229–234.

40. Richard Maxwell Brown, *No Duty to Retreat: Violence and Values in American History and Society* (New York: Oxford University Press, 1991), preface.

41. See trial court's 1912 instructions to the jury on the law of self-defense and the "no duty to retreat" doctrine as given in *State v. S. B. Burnett*, Cause No. 1100, Baylor County District Court in Seymour, Texas.

42. Quoted in Mark DeWolfe Howe, ed., *Holmes-Laski Letters: The Correspondence of Mr. Justice Holmes and Harold J. Laski, 1916–1935*, 2 vols. (Cambridge: Harvard University Press, 1953), I: 335–336.

43. *Brown v. United States*, 256 U.S. 335 (1921).

44. Interview of James H. East by J. Evetts Haley, September 27, 1927, Haley History Center, Midland, Texas.

45. Brown, *No Duty to Retreat*, 28.

46. Sections 9.31 and 9.32, *Texas Penal Code*.

47. Dick, *The Dixie Frontier*, 229–234; Hatley, *Bringing the Law to Texas*, 22; Ayers, *Vengeance and Justice*, 18.

48. *Wichita [Texas] Daily Times*, July 11, 1913.

49. Paul Kens, "Don't Mess Around in Texas: Adultery and Justifiable Homicide in the Lone Star State," in Gordon Morris Bakken, ed., *Law in the Western United States* (Norman: University of Oklahoma Press, 2000), 114–117.

50. Article 1220 of the *Texas Penal Code of 1925* provided:

. . . a homicide is justifiable when committed by the husband upon a person of any one taken in adultery with his wife; provided the killing takes place before the parties to the act of adultery have separated.

This statute appears to first have been enacted in 1857 as Article 562 and brought forward in succeeding *Texas Penal Codes* as Article 567 (1879), Article 672 (1895), Article 1102 (1911) and finally Article 1220 (1925).

51. See *Jones v. State*, 26 S.W. 1082 (Tex.Ct.Crim.App., 1894), quoting and explaining subdivision 4 of Article 567 of the *Texas Penal Code*.

52. Richard F. Hamm, *Murder, Honor, and Law* (Charlottesville: University of Virginia Press, 2003); Ayers, *Vengeance and Justice*.

53. *Fort Worth Star-Telegram*, February 22, 23, and 24, 1912.

54. King County [Texas] Historical Society, *King County: Windmills and Barbed Wire* (Quanah, Texas; Nortex Press, 1976), 16.

55. Race and criminal justice in the West has an emerging historiography. See for example, McKanna, *Homicide, Race, and Justice in the American West*, 155–163. McKanna, in a statistical study of violence perpetrated against minorities in three frontier counties (against blacks in Douglas County, Nebraska; Hispanics in Las Animas County, Colorado; and Apaches in Gila County, Arizona), finds that racial animosity resulted in much violence and that frontier law did little to punish offenders.

56. *Dallas Morning News*, February 27 and 28, 1896; *Dallas Semi-Weekly News*, February 28, 1896; and *Wichita Daily Times*, July 7, 1951.

57. Texas appellate courts weren't the only ones given to splitting legal hairs. Courts of that day in other states also frustrated prosecutors by rigidly observing all the technicalities of the common law. See Ayers, *Vengeance and Justice*, 32.

58. *Middleton v. State*, 25 S.W. 2d 614 (Tex.Ct.Crim.App, 1930).

59. *Dallas Morning News*, February 28, 1896.

60. Thomas F. Turner, "Prairie Dog Lawyers," *Panhandle-Plains Historical Review* 2 (1929): 121–122.

61. Sergeant W. J .L. Sullivan, *Twelve Years in the Saddle for Law and Order on the Frontiers of Texas* (originally published by W. John L. Sullivan, 1909. Reprint, Lincoln: University of Nebraska Press, 2001), 227–229.

62. Gard, *Frontier Justice*, v.

63. Coombes, *The Prairie Dog Lawyer*, ix (quoting Judge R.W. Hall, chief justice of the Court of Civil Appeals at Amarillo.)

64. Darwin Payne, *As Old as Dallas Itself*, 18–19.

65. At a banquet of the Texas Bar Association at Amarillo in 1929, Judge R.W. Hall, chief justice of the Court of Civil Appeals at Amarillo, made a humorous address entitled "The Prairie Dog Lawyer," which was printed in the *Texas Law Review* in October 1929: R.W. Hall, "Prairie Dog Lawyer," *Tex.L.Rev.* 48 (1929): 265–271. He said this about the origination of the nickname:

> As applied to those of our profession who came to the wide-open spaces of North-west Texas when they were peopled with prairie dogs, coyotes, jack-rabbits, bad men and worse women, the phrase "Prairie Dog Lawyer" was not intended in any sense to be laudatory or eulogistic. As then used and intended, it was a nick-name, and worse, for it was often applied as an epithet. While it originated in a spirit of ridicule, many of those who were so classified made it famous and respected . . . and who have made such names honorable and have . . . glorified them by deeds of heroism and sacrifice . . . they were not all perfect, but they were strong, rugged characters, true to their clients and their profession; their sterling qualities, their loyalty to each other and the eternal principles of justice, is a rich heritage.

66. Coombes, *The Prairie Dog Lawyer*, ix (quoting Judge R.W. Hall).

67. Turner, "Prairie Dog Lawyers," 104–106.

68. Ibid.

69. Calhoun, *Professional Lives in America*, 60–61; Cunningham, "Experiences of a Pioneer District Attorney," 127.

70. Coombes, *The Prairie Dog Lawyer*, xiii–xiv; Turner; "The Prairie Dog Lawyers," 108.

The Unlikely Saviors of Thomas J. Fulcher

1. Eleanor Mitchell Traweek, *Of Such As These: A History of Motley County and Its Families* (Wichita Falls: Nortex Publications, Inc. 1973), 23.

2. What follows in the text recounting the crimes of Thomas J. Fulcher and his two murder trials, including witness testimony, unless specifically noted otherwise, has been compiled from the following sources: court records and trial testimony in *State v. Thomas J. Fulcher*, Cause No. 50 in the District Court of Crosby County, Texas, and *State v. Thomas J. Fulcher*, Cause No. 12, in the District Court of Motley County, Texas; appellate court opinions in *Thomas J. Fulcher v. State*, 13 S. W. 750 (Tex.Ct.Crim.App., 1890) and *Thomas J. Fulcher v. State*, 33 Tex.Crim.Reports 22 (Tex.Ct.Crim.App., 1893); J. F. Cunningham, "Experiences of a Pioneer District Attorney," *West Texas Historical Association Year Book* 8 (1932): 128; and Charles E. Coombes, *The Prairie Dog Lawyer* (Dallas: University Press in Dallas, 1945), 21–30.

3. Coombes, *The Prairie Dog Lawyer*, 24.

4. Ibid.

5. Marisue Burleson Potts, *Motley County Roundup: A Centennial History*, 2nd ed. (Floydada, Tex.: Marisue Potts, 1991), 45; *State v. Joe P. Beckham*, Cause No. 35 in the District Court of Motley County, Texas (for the murder of Jeff Boone).

6. *State v. Thomas J. Fulcher*, Cause No. 22, District Court of Crosby County, Texas. See also letter dated April 29, 1889, from Ball and Burney, Attorneys at Law, Colorado, Texas to H. H. Campbell, Matador Ranch, Matador, Texas, Matador Land and Cattle Co. Files, Headquarters Correspondence, 1883–1889, H. H. Campbell, 1888–1889, Folder No. 3, Box 13, Southwest Collections/Special Collections Library, Texas Tech University, Lubbock, Texas. An interesting aside, the exact defects leading to the dismissal of the first indictment cannot be determined.

7. *State v. Thomas J. Fulcher*, Cause No. 50, District Court of Crosby County, Texas, indictment returned May 22, 1889.

8. J. F. Cunningham, "Experiences of a Pioneer District Attorney," 130. Judge Cockrell's favorite biblical passage was taken from the Old Testament where it described the Children of Israel's desperate flight from Egypt to the Promised Land, facilitated by divine intervention—namely, the parting of the Red Sea. Cockrell cited this passage so much in his sermons that the lawyers in his entourage

(having nothing much else to do during their evenings in those tiny frontier villages), often amused themselves by listening to Cockrell's nightly sermons and wagering on whether or not Cockrell would, during that particular sermon, allude to the divine parting of the Red Sea.

9. Coombes, *The Prairie Dog Lawyer*, 27, 254.

10. Coombes, *The Prairie Dog Lawyer*, 203–205.

11. Since the foregoing text was written, the U.S. Supreme Court has handed down a decision that appears to limit the "excited utterance" and "dying declaration" exceptions to the hearsay evidence rule. When the "excited utterance" or "dying declaration" is made to police officers during the course of an official investigation or interrogation, it will, apparently, no longer be admissible. *Crawford v. Washington*, 124 S.Ct. 1354, 158 L.Ed.2d 177, 2004 WL 413301 (2004).

12. *Thomas J. Fulcher v. State*, 13 S. W. 750, 751 (Tex.Ct.Crim.App., 1890)

13. Ibid.

14. *Miranda v. Arizona*, 384 U.S. 436, 86 S.Ct. 1602, 16 L.Ed.2d 694 (U.S.Sup.Ct., 1966).

15. See Leonard W. Levy, *Origins of the Fifth Amendment* (London: Oxford University Press, 1968).

16. *Matador Tribune*, August 25, 1960; Harry H. Campbell, *The Early History of Motley County*, 2nd ed. (Wichita Falls: Nortex Offset Publications, Inc., 1971), 51–53.

17. Coombes, *The Prairie Dog Lawyer*, 6.

18. *State v. Thomas J. Fulcher*, Cause No. 12, District Court of Motley County, Texas, indictment returned March 28, 1893.

19. Coombes, *The Prairie Dog Lawyer*, 6, 254.

20. A brief biography of Charles Coombes is recounted in Josephine Hooper Campbell, *Knox County History* (Haskell, Tex.: The Haskell Free Press, 1966), 57.

21. Coombes, *The Prairie Dog Lawyer*, 206.

22. Coombes, *The Prairie Dog Lawyer*, 27.

23. Ibid.

24. Coombes, *The Prairie Dog Lawyer*, 6–7.

25. Coombes, *The Prairie Dog Lawyer*, 27–28.

26. *Thomas J. Fulcher v. State*, 13 S. W. 750, 751 (Tex.Crim.Ct.App., 1890).

27. Coombes, *The Prairie Dog Lawyer*, 21.

28. Coombes, *The Prairie Dog Lawyer*, 28.

29. Coombes, *The Prairie Dog Lawyer*, 29.

30. *Thomas J. Fulcher v. State*, 33 Tex.Crim.Reports 22 (Tex.Ct.Crim.App., 1893).

31. Coombes, *The Prairie Dog Lawyer*, 29–30.

32. *Thomas J. Fulcher v. Minnie E. Fulcher*, Cause No. 23, District Court of Motley County, Texas.

33. *State v. Thomas J. Fulcher*, Cause No. 51, County Court of Motley County, Texas.

34. *State v. Thomas J. Fulcher*, Cause No. 32, District Court of Motley County, Texas, indictment returned August 14, 1895, for Assault with Intent to Murder Jim Turner.

35. Minutes of the District Court of Motley County, Texas, Vol. 1, pg. 171 in Cause No. 32 cited above.

36. Coombes, *The Prairie Dog Lawyer*, 30.

The 1896 Wichita Falls Bank Robbery

1. *Dallas Morning News*, February 28, 1896; *Wichita Daily Times*, June 10, 1951.

2. *Wichita Daily Times*, June 10, 1951.

3. *Wichita Daily Times*, April 9, 1908.

4. *Wichita Daily Times*, July 1, 1951.

5. *Fort Worth Gazette*, March 3, 1896.

6. *Wichita Daily Times*, April 9, 1908.

7. The story of Lewis and Crawford's ill-fated Wichita Falls bank robbery, their doomed escape attempt, and their lynching have been compiled from the following sources: *Ft. Worth Gazette*, February 26, 27, 28, March 3, and April 29, 1896; *Dallas Morning News*, February 27, 28, and May 9, 1896; *Dallas Semi-Weekly News*, February 28 and March 3, 1896; *Wichita Daily Times*, April 9, 1908, March 21, 1920, March 5, 1950, June 10, June 17, June 24, and July 1, 1951; *Wichita Falls Daily Times*, March 21, 1949; Louise Kelly, *Wichita County Beginnings* (Burnet, Tx.: Eakin Press, 1982), 43–45; Johnnie R. Morgan, *The History of Wichita Falls* (Wichita Falls: Nortex Press, 1971), 87–90; W. J. L. Sullivan, *Twelve Years in the Saddle for Law and Order on the Frontiers of Texas* (originally published by W. J. L. Sullivan, 1909. Reprint, Lincoln: University of Nebraska Press, 2001), 227–229; Albert Bigelow Paine, *Captain Bill McDonald, Texas Ranger* (Austin: State House Press, 1986), 199–213; Glenn Shirley, *West of Hell's Fringe* (Norman: University of Oklahoma Press, 1978), 347–348.

8. Sullivan, *Twelve Years in the Saddle for Law and Order*, 182–183.

9. *Wichita Daily Times*, April 9, 1908; *Wichita Daily Times*, March 21, 1920; Morgan, *The History of Wichita Falls*, 87–90.

10. *Dallas Morning News*, February 27, 1896.

11. *Wichita Daily Times*, March 21, 1920.

12. *Wichita Daily Times*, April 9, 1908.

13. *Wichita Daily Times*, July 1, 1951.

14. *Wichita Daily Times*, April 9, 1908.

15. *Wichita Daily Times*, March 21, 1920.

16. *Dallas Morning News*, February 27, 1896.

17. *Wichita Daily Times*, April 9, 1908.

18. Paine, *Captain Bill McDonald*, 207–213.

19. *Wichita Daily Times*, June 10, 1951.

20. Paine, *Captain Bill McDonald*, 212.

21. *Wichita Daily Times*, June 17, 1951.

22. *Dallas Morning News*, February 28, 1896.

23. *Fort Worth Gazette*, February 28, 1896.

24. *Dallas Semi-Weekly News*, February 28, 1896.

25. *Wichita Daily Times*, July 1, 1951.

26. *Dallas Morning News*, February 27, 1896.

27. *Dallas Morning News*, February 27 and 28, 1896; *Wichita Daily Times*, July 7, 1951.

28. *Dallas Semi-Weekly News*, February 28, 1896.

29. *Wichita Daily Times*, April 9, 1908.

30. *Wichita Daily Times*, February 27 and 28, 1896; *Fort Worth Gazette*, February 26, 27, and 28, 1896; *Dallas Semi-Weekly News*, February 28, 1896.

31. *Dallas Morning News*, February 27, 1896; *Dallas Semi-Weekly News*, February 28, 1896.

32. *Wichita Daily Times*, June 24, 1951.

33. *Wichita Daily Times*, March 21, 1920.

34. *Fort Worth Gazette*, February 27, 1896.

35. In a fascinating study of how newspapers in America covered sensational crimes and criminal trials during the last half of the nineteenth century and the first years of the twentieth century, professor Richard F. Hamm has traced the stages of journalistic development. Richard F. Hamm, *Murder, Honor, and Law: Four Virginia Homicides from Reconstruction to the Great Depression* (Charlottesville: University of Virginia Press, 2003). In his introduction (pp. 1–11), he finds there were three distinct periods of press development:

> In the first period, during the middle decades of the nineteenth century, the partisan tradition dominated the press. Newspapers blended news and editorial commentary together and slanted it in favor of their party. In the second period, from 1890 through 1920, sensational and independent journalism eclipsed partisan journalism. Independent journalism promoted "objective" news and separated out its political and editorial opinions from "news." Sensational newspapers engaged in spectacular stunts and used simple language and prolific illustrations to attract readers. The final period, beginning in the 1920s . . . saw convergence in coverage. The idea of objective reporting was now used to tone down the sensational press, while at the same time daily newspapers assimilated the former hallmarks of the sensational press.

36. *Dallas Semi-Weekly News,* March 6 and 7, 1896.

37. The voices of the citizens' committee (and other like-minded groups) were heard in the halls of Congress, and their demands eventually carried the day, although it would be more than a decade before it all came to full fruition. To greatly oversimplify the matter, the impetus—and the driving force—for this final conquest was a firm belief by most Americans in what we now refer to as the "Manifest Destiny" doctrine. Originally all of the modern State of Oklahoma was "Indian Territory" governed primarily by the tribes themselves. In 1890, Congress created the Oklahoma Territory out of the western part of what is now the state of Oklahoma. This decision was the product of years of agitation by land-hungry whites, and the efforts of the nation's lawmakers to diminish or eliminate tribal authority. In 1898, Congress passed the Curtis Act, which abolished the tribal courts and declared that Indian law was unenforceable in federal courts. Finally, in 1907 Congress admitted the State of Oklahoma into the union by combining the Indian Territory and the Oklahoma Territory. The "Indian Territory" was no more. For an in depth discussion of the twisted history of how it all finally came about—and why—see Jeffrey Burton, *Indian Territory and the United States, 1866–1906: Courts, Government, and the Movement for Oklahoma Statehood* (Norman: University of Oklahoma Press, 1995).

38. All of the above exchanges between the Dallas, Fort Worth, and Wichita Falls newspapers are quoted in *Fort Worth Gazette,* April 2, 1896.

39. *Dallas Morning News,* February 28, 1896.

40. *Wichita Daily Times,* April 9, 1908

41. *Wichita Daily Times,* July 1, 1951 (quoting Arch D. Anderson's letter to *Dallas Morning News.*)

42. *Wichita Daily Times,* April 9, 1908.

43. *Fort Worth Gazette,* April 2, 1896 (the Wichita Falls citizens' committee's heated responses to Judge Kilgore's blast was printed in the *Fort Worth Gazette,* April 7, 1896.)

44. Paine, *Captain Bill McDonald,* 213.

45. Letter dated April 4, 1896, from Captain W. J. McDonald to Texas adjutant general W. H. Mabry; Adjutant General's Correspondence Files, Texas State Archives, Austin, Texas. See also, Walter Prescott Webb, *The Texas Rangers* (Austin: University of Texas Press, 1935), 446–447.

46. Coombes, *The Prairie Dog Lawyer,* 274. Judge Miller was born in Mississippi in 1861. His father was killed in the Civil War, and shortly thereafter, in 1870, his mother died, leaving him an orphan at age nine. Nevertheless, in 1884 he managed to obtain his law degree from Cumberland University. He migrated westward to Graham, Texas, where he began his practice and was soon named county attorney for Young County. Moving then to Wichita Falls, he was elected district attorney there in 1888, and district judge in 1890, and re-elected in 1894 to another

four-year term. Charles E. Coombes called Miller one of the three "great" lawyers of his day. (The other two were Wichita Falls lawyers A. H. Carrigan and J. B. Barwise.) Coombes said of the three: "These three great lawyers . . . had a great influence on the making of Texas jurisprudence and in establishing the high ethics of the legal profession in the state."

47. *Fort Worth Gazette,* April 29, 1896; *Wichita Daily Times,* July 1, 1951.

48. Five murder indictments for the lynching of Lewis and Crawford were returned on May 6, 1896, by the grand jury in the 30th Judicial District Court of Wichita County. They were returned against Marion Potter, Cause No. 604; Frank Smith, Cause No. 605; W. E. Cobb, Cause No. 606; Dick Quinn, Cause No. 607; and F. M Davis, Cause No. 608.

49. Louise Kelly, *Wichita County Beginnings* (Burnet, Tex.: Eakin Press, 1982), 45. See also, *Wichita Daily Times,* July 1, 1951.

50. *Dallas Morning News,* May 9, 1896. The four indictments transferred to Vernon were filed in the 46th Judicial District Court of Wilbarger County as follows: F. M. Davis, Cause No. 940; Dick Quinn, Cause No. 941; W. E. Cobb, Cause No. 942; and Frank Smith, Cause No. 943.

51. Marion Potter, Cause No. 3441, Cooke County District Court.

52. *Dallas Morning News,* May 9, 1896.

53. Although the district attorney and the district judge, as well as witnesses, may appear before the grand jury while it is *investigating* the case, when that phase of the proceeding is concluded and the grand jury begins its *deliberations* on the issue of whether or not to return an indictment, then no one is allowed to be present except the grand jury members themselves. The Wilbarger County court records do not reflect whether Judge Brown, before dismissing the indictments, held an evidentiary hearing to test the defendants' allegations that Judge Miller and District Attorney Carter were, in fact, present during deliberations.

54. *Wichita Falls Record News,* March 21, 1944.

55. *Wichita Daily Times,* July 1, 1951.

56. Coombes, *The Prairie Dog Lawyer,* 274.

57. *Fort Worth Gazette,* April 5, 1896. The Texas Court of Criminal Appeals wasn't the ony court being roundly criticized for reversing murder convictions on technicalities. The U.S. Supreme Court received harsh criticism for doing the same thing from federal judge Isaac C. Parker, the famous "hanging judge" who presided over the federal district court for the Western District of Arkansas from 1875 to 1896. At that time federal courts (including Judge Parker's court) had jurisdiction over murders committed in the Indian Territory where a non-Indian was involved. After a number of murder convictions out of his court had been reversed by the U.S. Supreme Court, Judge Parker had had enough. He railed: "The appellate court exists mainly to stab the trial judge in the back and enable the criminal to go free." On his deathbed, in 1896, Judge Parker was still fuming at the high court

for reversing murder convictions "upon the flimsiest technicalities." He said, "I would that the law would provide against the reversal of cases unless innocence was manifest. . . . I would have brushed aside all technicalities that do not affect the guilt or innocence of the accused." Fred Harvey Harrington, *Hanging Judge* (Norman: University of Oklahoma Press, 1951), 179–187. See also, Robert H. Tuller, *"Let No Guilty Man Escape": A Judicial Biography of "Hanging Judge" Isaac C. Parker* (Norman: University of Oklahoma Press, 2001); Michael J. Brodhead, *Isaac C. Parker: Federal Justice on the Frontier* (Norman: University of Oklahoma Press, 2003).

58. Article 723, *The Texas Code of Criminal Procedure*; Gammel, comp., *Laws of Texas*, vol. 10, 25th Legislature (1897), p. 17.

59. H.B. No. 30; Gammel, comp., *Laws of Texas*, vol. 10, 25th Legislature (1897, special session), p. 1480.

60. Keith Carter, "The Texas Court of Criminal Appeals," 11 *Tex. L. Rev.* 185 (1933): 196.

61. Until recent times, defendants were entitled to appeal any conviction directly to the Texas Court of Criminal Appeals in Austin—the supreme court of criminal appeals in the state. Nowadays, the convicted defendant is entitled to appeal his conviction to an intermediate regional court of appeals. If unsuccessful there, he may petition the Texas Court of Criminal Appeals to consider the merits of his appeal. However, the Texas Court of Criminal Appeals has discretionary authority to decide whether or not to consider that appeal. In a great majority of cases, it refuses to hear such appeals.

62. Michael Hall, "And Justice for Some," *Texas Monthly* (November 2004): 153–157, 259–263.

63. Edward L. Ayers, *Vengeance and Justice*, 33.

The 1890s Wells Fargo Murder Trials

1. Testimony of witnesses W. J. Conaster, J. N. Webb, Doc Walton, and Mrs. John Miller taken from the transcript of the trial of Joe Blake in Cause No. 939, Wilbarger County, Texas, District Court and from the transcript of the trial of Jim Harbolt in Cause No. 647, Donley County, Texas, District Court.

2. Testimony of John Kirkham taken from the transcripts of the trials of Joe Blake and Jim Harbolt cited in the preceding note.

3. Walter Prescott Webb, "George W. Arrington: The Iron-Handed Man of the Panhandle," *Panhandle-Plains Historical Review* 8 (1935): 7–20. See also, Allen G. Hatley, "Cap Arrington: Adventurer, Ranger and Sheriff" *Wild West* (June 2001). During the Civil War, Arrington fought for the Confederacy at both battles of Manassas, at Harpers Ferry, and at Antietam, where he was wounded. He soldiered

with Robert E. Lee at the Battle of Gettysburg, during which retreat he was captured by Union forces. He was imprisoned, but not for long. Arrington escaped and made his way back to Confederate lines. During the last year of the war he was attached to a famous guerilla band—Colonel John Singleton Mosby's Rangers. Actually, Arrington was born December 23, 1844, bearing the name, John C. Orrick Jr. However, in 1867, he killed a black man named Alex Webb in Alabama for reasons not recorded. He then changed his name to Arrington and fled first to Mexico and then Texas, thus outrunning a murder indictment.

4. For years glowing accounts of the brave exploits of the "Three Guardsmen" and their boss, U.S. marshal E. D. Nix have been told and retold by western historians. Turns out that many of these tales of heroic bravery were based on the uncorroborated accounts of the subjects themselves. Recent research, however, has revealed that they did more "shooting from the lip" than from the hip. Chris Madsen, particularly, was a master at self-aggrandizement and the unabashed spinner of tall tales. For instance, he claimed that before immigrating to the United States from his native Denmark, he had at age fourteen joined the Danish army, that he later saw combat as a French Foreign Legionnaire in Algiers and that, still later, as a French partisan he fought against the Germans. All such background information was accepted as holy writ by American journalists and historians. But a recent historian, after exhaustive research, could find no records of Madsen every having served in any of these armies. Instead, the Danish records revealed that he was an intelligent and calculating scoundrel who had served several prison sentences in Denmark for fraud and forgery before immigrating to the United States. (He may have been deported as a habitual criminal.) After arrival in the United States in 1876 he did enlist in the U.S. Army and saw service in the Indian wars with the Fifth Cavalry for fifteen years, although his accounts greatly exaggerate his importance in several encounters. Later he did volunteer for Teddy Roosevelt's Rough Riders during the Spanish-American War, but again his role was less than heroic. He was a quartermaster sergeant, and Tampa, Florida, was the closest he ever got to Cuba. Madsen was first named as a deputy U.S. marshal of the Oklahoma Territory in 1891, and he served as a deputy U.S. marshal for a number of years until his retirement in 1916. While his record of service as a federal officer during the bloody outlaw era of the Oklahoma and Indian territories was commendable, he was never shy when it came to claiming credit for kills or captures or inflating his role therein. Nancy B. Samuelson, *Shoot from the Lip: The Lives, Legends and Lies of the Three Guardsmen of Oklahoma and U.S. Marshal Nix* (Eastford, Conn., Shooting Star Press, 1998), 10–20, 83–94, and 128–134. Compare Samuelson's research and findings on the "Three Guardsmen" and Marshal Nix with the previously accepted versions such as that written by Bill Tilghman's widow, Zoe A. Tilghman, *Outlaw Days: A True History of Early-Day Oklahoma Characters* (Oklahoma City: Harlow Publishing Co., 1926),

and Zoe A. Tilghman, *Marshal of the Last Frontier: Life and Services of William Matthew (Bill) Tilghman* (Glendale: Arthur H. Clark Co., 1964); and the account given by Chris Madsen to Homer Croy, *Trigger Marshal: The Story of Chris Madsen* (New York: Duell, Sloan and Pearch, 1958).

5. Colonel Bailey C. Hanes, *Bill Doolin-Outlaw O. T.* (Norman: University of Oklahoma Press, 1968), 3–23. Glenn Shirley, *Six-Gun and Silver Star* (Albuquerque: University of New Mexico Press, 1955), 142–143.

6. Texas Prison Convict Record ledger for George Isaacs, No. 15, 531, Texas State Archives, Austin, Texas.

7. *Cheyenne Sunbeam* (Robert Mills County, Oklahoma Territory), December 1, 1894.

8. Minnie Timms Harper and George Dewey Harper, *Old Ranches* (Dallas: Dealy and Lowe, 1936), 54–56. During the famous 1883 "cowboy strike" in the Texas Panhandle, six T Anchor hands quit the ranch, leaving only twenty-five-year-old George Isaacs, one other cowboy, and a cook to man the ramparts. The owners thereupon promoted George to foreman.

9. The testimony of George Isaacs and other witnesses taken at the trial of George Isaacs held in the Hardeman County District Court (Cause No. 334) on October 31, 1895, is summarized in the appellate opinion of the Texas Court of Criminal Appeals in *Isaacs v. State*, 38 S.W. 40 (Tex.Ct.Crim.App. 1896).

10. Zoe A. Tilghman, *Outlaw Days: A True History of Early-Day Oklahoma Characters* (Oklahoma City: Harlow Publishing Co., 1926), 76–78. See also, Richard S. Graves, *Oklahoma Outlaws* (Ft. Davis, Tx.: Frontier Book Co., 1968), 82–83.

11. Sallie B. Harris, *Cowmen and Ladies: A History of Hemphill County* (Canyon, Tex.: Staked Plains Press, Inc., 1977), 7–8.

12. *Cheyenne Sunbeam* (Roger Mills County, Oklahoma Territory), December 1, 1894.

13. Testimony of A. B. Harding taken from transcript of trial of Joe Blake in Cause No. 939, District Court of Wilbarger County, Texas, and from the transcript of the trial of Jim Harbolt in Cause No. 647, District Court of Donley County, Texas.

14. Testimony of Dr. A. M. Newman in Joe Blake trial and the Jim Harbolt trial.

15. Testimony of Captain G. W. Arrington in Joe Blake trial and the Jim Harbolt trial.

16. Testimony of A. B. Harding in Joe Blake trial and the Jim Harbolt trial.

17. Testimony of J. A. Chambers in Joe Blake trial and the Jim Harbolt trial.

18. On May 21, 1895, the grand jury of the 31st Judicial District Court of Hemphill County returned four indictments: Cause No. 108, against Joe Blake for the murder of Sheriff Tom T. McGee; Cause No. 109 against Jim Harbolt for the murder of sheriff McGee; Cause No. 110, against George Isaacs and Jim Harbolt

for the McGee murder; and Cause No. 111, against Joe Blake, Jim Harbolt, George Isaacs, Will Blake (aka "Tulsa Jack" Blake), Sam Blake, George "Bitter Creek" Newcomb, and Dan McKenzie for conspiracy to rob the Wells Fargo Express.

19. Cause No. 334, Hardeman County District Court.

20. Cause No. 939, Wilbarger County District Court.

21. Cause No. 647, Donley County District Court.

22. Cause No. 335, Hardeman County District Court.

23. *Quanah Tribune-Chief,* February 17, 1931.

24. Thomas F. Turner, "Prairie Dog Lawyers," *Panhandle-Plains Historical Review* 2 (1929): 116; H. C. Randolph, *Panhandle Lawyers* (Amarillo, Tex.: Russell Stationery, 1931), 22–23.

25. Turner, "Prairie Dog Lawyers," 117.

26. *Quanah Chief,* October 24, 1895.

27. *Quanah Tribune-Chief,* February 17, 1931.

28. *Quanah Tribune-Chief,* April, 16, 1916.

29. *State v. Grant Pettyjohn* for suborning perjury: Cause Nos. 399, 406, 407, and 436.

30. *State v. Bert Sexton* for perjury: Cause Nos. 405 and 437. *State v. John Shumate* for perjury: Cause No. 404.

31. *Daily Oklahoman,* Novovember 21, 1895; *Taloga Times,* September 13, 1906.

32. Testimony of Dan McKenzie quoted in appellate opinion: *Isaacs v. State,* 38 S. W. 40 (Tex.Ct.Crim.App. 1896).

33. Tilghman, *Outlaw Days,* 76–78; Graves, *Oklahoma Outlaws,* 82–83.

34. Email dated May 30, 2002, addressed to author from Dr. Robert J. Chandler, Senior Research Historian, Historical Services, Wells Fargo Bank, 420 Montgomery St., San Francisco, Calif. 94163. Dr. Chandler cites the 1888 Wells Fargo Instructions (then in effect). Paragraph 221 states, in part: "In delivering money sealed with the "Public" seal . . . In no case shall [the packet] be opened and contents counted . . . nor will the Company be responsible for any discrepancy in the amount or character of the money."

35. *Isaacs v. State,* 38 S. W. 40 (Tex.Ct.Crim.App. 1896).

36. Testimony of Dan McKenzie in the transcript of the trial of Joe Blake in Cause No. 939, Wilbarger County District Court.

37. *Harbolt v. State,* 40 S.W. 983 (Tex.Ct.Crim.App. 1897); *Blake v. State,* 43 S. W. 107 (Tex.Ct.Crim.App. 1897).

38. Charles K. Cary, *Kaffir Woolies* (Laverne, Okla.: Dewey County Jailhouse Museum, 1999), 26.

39. *Territory of Oklahoma v. Lew Herring and William Kopp,* Vol. 1, Pg. 13, "D" County, O.T. Criminal Docket Book.

40. Samuelson, *Shoot from the Lip*, 69–70.

41. Testimony of W. C. (Bill) Isaacs taken from transcript of trial of Joe Blake, Cause No. 939, Wilbarger County District Court.

42. Testimony of A. B. Harding taken from transcript of trial of Joe Blake, Cause No. 939, Wilbarger County District Court.

43. *Harbolt et al.* [Sam Isaacs and W. C. Isaacs] *v. State*, 44 S.W. 1110 (Tex.Ct.Crim.App. 1898).

44. Dewey County was named for the famous American naval hero Commander George Dewey (1837–1917), famed for completely destroying the Spanish fleet during the Spanish-American War at the Battle of Manila Bay. (Think: "Fire when ready, Gridley.") It is indeed ironic that landlocked Dewey County, hundreds of miles from any sea, was named for a naval hero, as also is the fact that its county seat, Taloga, sits on the bank of the Canadian River, a watercourse that is hundreds of miles from Canada.

45. Dewey County Historical Society (DCHS), *Spanning the River: Dewey County Family Histories*, Vol. 1 (San Angelo, Tex.: Newsfoto Yearbook Co., 1976), 499–500. Homer Croy, "Where the Outlaws Hid," *True West Magazine* (October 1962).

46. Croy, "Where the Outlaws Hid."

47. Robert E. King, "Till the Drums Beat Again: The Fred Hoffman Story," (Unpublished treatise, 2002, available for review at the Oklahoma State Archives, Oklahoma City, Oklahoma), 1–4.

48. See the "D" County map captioned "Murder in a Nest of Outlaws," accompanying this story in which the locations of known outlaws and outlaw sympathizers are noted. The map is adapted from the map printed in DCHS, *Spanning the River*, inside cover; and a Taloga area map in King, "Till the Drums Beat Again," 43. Information about, as well as the locations of, known outlaws and outlaw sympathizers was obtained from DCHS, *Spanning the River*, 499–502; King, "Till the Drums Beat Again," 5–25, 30–49; personal interviews by the author with Robert E. King and Ms. Patsy Smart, local Dewey County historians, on March 21, 2003, in Seiling, Oklahoma; and a six-part series of "Dewey County Memories" written by former Dewey county attorney George E. Black, appearing in six weekly installments of the *Taloga-Times Advocate*, April 17, April 24, May 1, May 8, May 15, and May 22, 1941.

49. DCHS, *Spanning the River*, 500; Cary, *Kaffir Woolies*, 26, 44.

50. *Taloga Tomahawk*, March 8, 1894; *Taloga Tomahawk*, April 7, 1894; King, "Till the Drums Beat Again," 14, 46. Editor Pettyjohn, however, seems to have overlooked another news story of considerable interest during this time period. Vol. 1, pg. 11 of the "D" County Criminal Docket book reflects that Grant Pettyjohn was charged with breaking into the Office of Registry of Deeds and stealing a deed from J. R. Dean to Thomas O'Toole.

51. *Oklahoma Daily Press-Gazette*, March 14, 1894; *Oklahoma State Capital*, March 13 and 14, 1894; *Guthrie Daily Leader*, March 14 and 15, 1894.

52. King, "Till the Drums Beat Again," 44. For years, Lee Moore was thought to be the half brother of Alfred Son. However, when he married Amos Chapman's daughter, Minnie Chapman, at Watonga, Blaine County, Oklahoma Territory, on February 25, 1896, he listed his name as "J. Lee Moore alias Son" on the Affidavit on Application for Marriage License, giving his father's name as J. W. Son and his mother's maiden name as Sarah Logan. The Son family had originally settled in Brown County, Texas, and the federal census for 1880 lists five-year-old Alfred Son as being the child of John W. and Sarah Son.

53. Robert E. King, interview by author, Seiling, Oklahoma, March 21, 2003; King, "Till the Drums Beat Again," 40, 44.

54. Glenn Shirley, *Temple Houston: Lawyer with a Gun* (Norman: University of Oklahoma Press, 1980), 256. Colonel Bailey C. Hanes, *Bill Doolin-Outlaw O.T.* (Norman: University of Oklahoma Press, 1968), 60, 65. Shirley states that "*Alfred Son* was *not* an outlaw," although he states that he was a friend of McKenzie, Harbold [*sic*], and Red Buck Weightman. Hanes states that "*Alf Sohn* [*sic*] was a lesser member of Doolin's gang: "Of Alf Sohn [*sic*], little is known except that he was another cowboy of unknown origin who rode with Doolin on a few occasions but was not a regular in the real sense."

55. *The Territory of Oklahoma v. Dick Yeager (alias Zip Wyatt), Bailey Son, Alford* [sic] *Son, Dan McKinzie* [sic] *and Grant Pettyjohn*, Cause No. 15, Second Judicial District Court of "D" County.

56. At that time (the 1890s) the lands that would later (in 1907) become the State of Oklahoma were divided into two parts: the Oklahoma Territory (western part of what is now Oklahoma) and the Indian Territory (eastern part.) As we have seen, both parts were wild and violent. However, the judicial systems in the Oklahoma Territory and the Indian Territory were as different as daylight and dark. In the Oklahoma Territory murder cases were tried in district "territorial" courts very similar to the state district courts in Texas, and the criminal laws and the court practices and procedures were also similar. Appeals from convictions were directed to the Oklahoma Territory Supreme Court, similar to the Texas Court of Criminal Appeals. In the Indian Territory, meanwhile, no state or territorial courts existed. The five "Civilized Tribes" (Chocktaw, Creek, Chickasaw, Seminole, and Cherokee) each had its own district within the Indian Territory, and each had its own tribal court governed by its own tribal laws in murder prosecutions—unless a non-Indian was a party involved in the homicide. In that event, the murder case was prosecuted in a federal court, pursuant to federal criminal statutes and under federal rules of procedure. Either way—tribal court or federal court—the criminal justice system bore scant resemblance to the Texas and Oklahoma Territorial judiciaries. Plus, there was no provision for appealing federal murder convictions until after 1889.

Thereafter, appeals from murder convictions were made directly to the U.S. Supreme Court. Most Indian Territory murder cases tried in federal court prior to 1896 were tried in the federal district court for the Western District of Arkansas at Fort Smith, a court presided over by the fearsome "hanging judge," Isaac C. Parker. See Fred Harvey Harrington, *Hanging Judge* (Norman: University of Oklahoma Press, 1951); Jeffrey Burton, *Indian Territory and the United States, 1866–1906: Courts, Government, and the Movement for Oklahoma Statehood* (Norman: University of Oklahoma Press, 1995); Roger H. Tuller, *"Let No Guilty Man Escape": A Judicial Biography of "Hanging Judge" Isaac C. Parker* (Norman: University of Oklahoma Press, 2001); and Michael J. Brodhead, *Isaac C. Parker: Federal Justice on the Frontier* (Norman: University of Oklahoma Press, 2003).

57. *Alfred Son v. Territory of Oklahoma,* 5 Okla. Rep. 526, 49 P. 923 (Okla. Sup.Ct. 1897); Shirley, *Temple Houston,* 259.

58. Shirley, *Temple Houston,* 161.

59. Background and early career adventures of Temple Houston obtained from Shirley, *Temple Houston,* and Hank Bass, "Temple Lea Houston—Gun-Toting, Bible-Quoting Lawyer of the Old West" *Texas Bar Journal* 64, no. 1 (January 2001): 69.

60. Harris, *Cowmen and Ladies,* 41. See also H. C. Randolph, *Panhandle Lawyers* (Amarillo, Tex: Russell Stationery, 1931), 17–21.

61. Shirley, *Temple Houston,* 257.

62. *Taloga Times-Advocate,* April 17, 1941, et seq. (recollections of early "D" County by former "D" County attorney George E. Black).

63. Shirley, *Temple Houston,* 257.

64. *Taloga Times-Advocate,* April 17, 1941, et seq. (Recollections of former "D" county attorney George E. Black). See also Evett Dumas Nix, *Oklahombres* (St. Louis: Eden Publishing House, 1929), 143–144; Ramon Adams, *Burrs Under the Saddle* (Norman: University of Oklahoma Press, 1964), 20; and Hanes, *Bill Doolin—Outlaw O.T.,* 61–62. The three latter sources relate that Bill Doolin expelled Red Buck from the gang for the wanton and unnecessary slaying of an old and unarmed preacher named Godfred, whose only transgression consisted of exhibiting the temerity to protest the theft of his horse by the outlaws in order to replace a mount that had just been shot out from under them by a pursuing posse. But see Shirley, *West of Hell's Fringe* (Norman: University of Oklahoma Press, 1978), 276, 456.

65. Leslie McRill, "Old Ingalls: The Story of a Town That Will Not Die," *Chronicles of Oklahoma* 36, no. 4 (Winter 1958–1959): 441.

66. Shirley, *Temple Houston,* 257–258.

67. DCHS, *Spanning the River,* 502; Glenn Shirley, *West of Hell's Fringe* (Norman: University of Oklahoma Press, 1978), 348–351.

68. *Alfred Son v. Territory of Oklahoma,* 5 Okla.Rep. 526, 49 P. 923 (Okla. Sup.Ct. 1897).

69. Shirley, *Temple Houston,* 260–261.

70. It is both interesting and instructive to compare the Texas and Oklahoma Territory murder trials. Compare, for instance, the Texas murder trials of Bill Longley (Giddings, Texas, 1877) and John Wesley Hardin (Comanche, Texas, 1877) with the 1925 Oklahoma murder trial of Wiley Lynn for the killing of frontier lawman Bill Tilghman, as described in Johnny D. Boggs, *Great Murder Trials of the Old West* (Plano: Republic of Texas Press, 2003). A significant contribution to understanding the struggle to control violence on the western frontier and to establish an effective rule of law is told by John W. Davis, *A Vast Amount of Trouble* (Niwot: University Press of Colorado, 1993). Davis, himself a Wyoming lawyer and historian, accurately captures 1909 Wyoming and tells of the time and the place and the way the people thought, felt, acted, and interacted with one another. The "Spring Creek Massacre" of 1909 is the crime. One night seven masked raiders, all cattlemen enraged at sheepherders who had encroached upon "their" free range, swooped down on a sheep camp and killed three unarmed men. Davis then gives an in-depth analysis of the prosecution. Much to the amazement of nearly everyone, a Wyoming jury found the first defendant guilty and sentenced him to be hanged. Startled by this unexpected turn of events, four of the other defendants quickly cut deals to plead guilty for lesser sentences. It was a watershed event in the history of Wyoming, and Davis not only analyzes the crime and the trial; but he also examines the aftermath and puts it into perspective.

71. *Taloga Times-Advocate,* April 17, 1941, et seq.

72. DCHS, *Spanning the River,* 501.

73. King, "Till the Drums Beat Again," 5, 7, 17.

74. *Territory v. Amos Chapman,* Vol. 1, Pg, 70 "D" County Criminal Docket Book; *Territory v. Lee Moore,* Vol. 1, Pg. 72, "D" County Criminal Docket Book.

75. Robert E. King, interview by Bill Neal, Seiling, Oklahoma, March 21, 2003.

76. Testimony of witnesses in the Joe Blake and Jim Harbolt murder trials: Dan McKenzie, Mrs. Dan McKenzie, daughter Stella McKenzie; and those who saw the four horseman riding toward Canadian the day Sheriff McGee was murdered, J. W. Conaster, Doc Walton, and J. N. Webb; plus a cryptic reference in Joe Blake's intercepted jailhouse letter to Dan McKenzie dated August 11, 1895, wherein he described the outlaw as the "big fellow with sideburns."

77. Robert E. King, interviewed by Bill Neal, Seiling, Oklahoma, March 21, 2003. Of all the known outlaws and outlaw associates active at that time and place, Mr. King notes only four were "tall men": Bill Doolin, Zip Wyatt, Charlie Pierce, and outlaw associate Jim Riley. Of these, Mr. King considers Charlie Pierce, a known member of the Bill Doolin gang, the most likely "Jim Stanley" poser. He

was tall with a light complexion. He was a half brother of Will "Tulsa Jack" Blake and Joe Blake and his best friend and colleague in crime was Bitter Creek Newcomb.

78. Robert E. King, interviewed by Bill Neal, Seiling, Oklahoma, March 17, 2003.

79. *Lawton News-Reporter,* December 10, 1903; *Taloga Advocate,* December 17, 1903.

80. *McCracken [Kansas] Enterprise,* August 31, 1906; *Taloga Times,* September 13, 1906.

81. Shirley, *Temple Houston,* 260–261. Although Glenn Shirley is the dean of Oklahoma/Indian Territory lawmen/outlaw history experts, his brief account of the 1894 Wells Fargo attempted robbery at Canadian, Texas, and the resultant murder of Hemphill County sheriff Tom McGee and later, U.S. Commissioner Fred Hoffman in the Oklahoma Territory, has several errors:

a. *George Isaacs was, "a wealthy cattleman of Canadian, Texas."* It is true that George's three brothers (Bill, Sam, and John) were wealthy cattlemen of Canadian, Texas, but George was the black sheep of the family, a self-described "laborer" and a "poor man" who hung out with Oklahoma Territory outlaws, including Bill Doolin, around Chickasha.

b. Other minor errors in Shirley's account of the Wells Fargo shootout at the Canadian, Texas, depot: 1. *Sheriff McGee was "riddled with lead."* He was hit only once, although mortally; 2. *Several persons were wounded in the shootout.* Only Sheriff McGee was shot; 3. *The Wells Fargo Express packages which supposedly contained $25,000 contained $200.* They contained $500; 4. *George's co-conspirators included Jim Harbold* (correct name, Jim Harbol*t*), *and* Jake *McKenzie* (correct name, *Dan* McKenzie).

Pardon Me, Please!

1. For a perceptive discussion of the history of pardons, including the many justifications advanced therefore, both practical and theoretical applications, and abuse of the power to pardon, see Kathleen Dean Moore, *Pardons: Justice, Mercy and the Public Interest* (New York: Oxford University Press, 1989).

2. *Brown v. State,* 38 S.W. 1008 (Tex.Crim.App. 1897).

3. *Brown v. State,* 43 S.W. 986 (Tex.Crim.App. 1898).

4. When Dent was received by the Texas prison system on March 17, 1898, he didn't see fit to favor prison officials with either his true name or the fact that he had two prior, out-of-state felony convictions—one in Missouri and one in Colorado. The prison's intake records show his name as "J. W. Brown," and there is no

entry for prior convictions. Convict Record Ledger, Texas State Penitentiary Records, Inmate J.W. Brown, No. 16,314, Texas State Archives, Austin, Texas. However, when he was received by prison officials on June 28, 1901, on his next visit to the penitentiary (discussed later in the story), his true identity (William J. Dent) had been discovered, and the two prior, out-of-state felony convictions are listed on his Convict Record Ledger (inmate No. 20,538).

5. Letter dated July 13, 1899, from "J. W. Brown" to Governor Joseph D. Sayers, pleading for a pardon. Governor's Executive Record Books, Pardon No. 19573, Texas State Archives, Austin, Texas. (All other letters and documents relating to the pardon of J. W. Brown/W. J. Dent are taken from this source.)

6. Letter dated July 8, 1899, (purporting to be) from W. M. C. Hill, Financial Agent Texas State Penitentiaries, to Governor Joseph D. Sayers.

7. Actually U.S. district judge John J. Jackson sent *two* letters to Governor Sayers upon behalf of his nephew, W. J. Dent. One dated June 1, 1899, and the next dated July 26, 1899. In addition to the contents quoted in the text, Judge Jackson took it upon himself to straighten out the name discrepancy, stating that *he* had first referred to his nephew, the convict, as "J. W. Brown" when his real name was "W. J. Dent," and that he now wished to correct *his* mistake.

8. West Virginia governor George W. Atkinson also wrote *two* letters to Governor Sayers pleading for a pardon, the first dated June 2, 1899, and the second dated August 25, 1899.

9. Pardon No. 19573 (W. J. Dent, 16,314), dated August 28, 1899, Governor's Executive Record Books. The recitations for granting Dent a full pardon included pleas for pardon by Dent's esteemed uncle, U.S. District Court Judge Jackson, West Virginia Governor Atkinson, and prison officials who cited Dent's good conduct in prison. The last reason given was "his past good record as a citizen." (Although Judge Jackson and Governor Atkinson had admitted to Governor Sayers that in the past, W. J. had indeed engaged in "wild methods of living" from time to time, yet nobody had gotten around to informing Governor Sayers of Dent's two out-of-state felony convictions.)

10. Convict Record Ledger for George Isaacs, No. 15, 531, under "Remarks" entry it states: "Escaped August 30, 1899, by means of a forged pardon."

11. *Quanah Tribune-Chief,* February 17, 1931.

12. *Dent v. State,* 65 S.W. 627 (Tex.Ct.Crim.App. 1901). The Court of Criminal Appeals held that when the jury found beyond a reasonable doubt that W. J. Dent had, in fact, forged George Isaacs's pardon, and thus provided the means of Isaacs's escape from prison, he came within Texas's accessory after the fact statute. That is, Dent gave the principal, George Isaacs, "aid in order that he (Isaacs) [might] evade the execution of his sentence." Dent thus became an accessory after the fact in the

murder of Sheriff McGee. The dissenting judge thought that stretched the accessory statute beyond its intent and meaning:

> the sentence of a felon is executed when he is lodged within the penitentiary and is undergoing his punishment. . . . In absence of a prison breach statute, the law is done with him.

13. W. J. Dent must have been the source of only one of many disgruntlements during the good governor's reign. Governor Sayers seems to have suffered chronic dyspepsia as a result of matters of government on his plate. He later opined: "A Texas governor has only two happy days—the day he is inaugurated and the day he retires." *Dallas Morning News*, December 19, 2003.

14. Pardon No. 10654 (W. J. Dent, No. 20,538), dated May 16, 1911. Governor's Executive Record Books.

15. Kent Biffle, *Dallas Morning News*, August 18, 2002

16. James L. Haley, *Texas: From Spindletop through World War II* (New York: St. Martin's Press, 1993); 144–147.

17. Recent research indicates that the Fergusons did, in fact, pocket payoffs for pardons, although many were also granted to indigent inmates. May Nelson Paulissen and Carl McQueary, *Miriam: The Southern Belle Who Became the First Woman Governor of Texas* (Austin: Eakin Press, 1995), 155–166. Also see Norman D. Brown, *Hood, Bonnet, and Little Brown Jug: Texas Politics, 1921–1928* (College Station: Texas A&M University Press, 1984), 270–274; and Moore, *Pardons: Justice Mercy and the Public Interest*, 63.

18. Haley, *Texas: From Spindletop through World War II*, 145; Paulissen, *Miriam*, 155.

19. Ibid.

20. Brown, *Hood, Bonnet, and Little Brown Jug*, 272.

21. Charlie E. Coombes, *The Prairie Dog Lawyer* (Dallas: The University Press, 1945), 51–53.

22. The story of the killing of H. E. Nichols by Miss Ruby Britain and her murder trial have been compiled from these sources: *Wichita Daily Times*, August 16, 1934; *Baylor County Banner*, August 16, 1934; and the appellate opinion set out in *Britain v. State*, 86 S.W. 2d 457 (Tex.Ct.Crim.App. 1935).

23. Jack Jones, Baylor County resident historian, interviewed by Bill Neal, Seymour, Texas, April 18, 2001.

24. Ibid.

25. Ibid. The same story was recounted (without any prompting) by retired district judge Clyde Whiteside (himself a former district attorney of the 50th Judicial District) to Bill Neal on April 4, 2002, Benjamin, Texas.

26. Proclamation of Pardon No. 28037 signed September 12, 1935, by acting

governor of Texas John S. Redditt, Governor's Executive Record Books, Texas State Archives, Austin, Texas.

27. Interview of Jack Jones.

More Scandalous Adventures of the Isaacs Family

1. Carol Morse, interviewed by Bill Neal, August 10, 2004, Ardmore Oklahoma. The background of the William Rufus and Mary Horton Ellis family as well as the history of Lizzie Ellis Byrne Isaacs up to and through the 1910 federal census have been obtained from Ms. Morse.

2. *The Daily Oklahoman,* February 11, 1898. The article also mentions that Lizzie's husband, George Isaacs, was then serving a life sentence in the Texas penitentiary for the murder of the sheriff at Canadian, Texas, during the aborted Wells Fargo robbery. It also briefly recounts the facts set out in the text relating to the murder of Sterling Elder by Lizzie and her brother John Ellis, and it reported that John Ellis was out on bond awaiting trial. The outcome of that trial has also been lost to time (documentation has not been located to date), although it is known that Ellis was not hanged because death records indicate he died on November 5, 1934, in Carter County, Oklahoma. A brief report of Lizzie's murder conviction was also printed in the February 10, 1898, edition of the *Dallas Morning News.*

3. Carol Morse interview.

4. Foard County, Texas, Death Certificate of Mrs. Helen Gertrude Sparks, No. 145, Foard County Courthouse, Crowell, Texas, and Crowell Cemetery records, Crowell, Texas.

5. *Foard County News,* January 7, 1916.

6. *Quanah Tribune-Chief,* January 6, 1916. See also Foard County, Texas, Death Certificate of Mrs. Jessie Sparks, No. 172, Foard County Courthouse, Crowell, Texas, and Crowell Cemetary records, Crowell, Texas.

7. *The Quannah Tribune-Chief,* April 6, 1916. See also Foard County, Texas, Death Certificate of Thomas Niri Sparks, No. 185, Foard County Courthouse, Crowell, Texas, and Crowell Cemetery records, Crowell, Texas.

8. *Quanah Tribune-Chief,* November 16, 1916.

Murder and Mayhem in the Knox County Courthouse

1. Josephine Hooper Campbell, *Knox County History* (Haskell, Tex.: Haskell Free Press, 1966), 59; Jack Jones, "Museum News," *Baylor County Banner,* July 22, 1999.

2. John Bunyon Rhea, "Revenge," *Wichita* [Falls, Texas] *Heritage Magazine* (Spring 1990): 30.

3. *Mary E. Jones v. Dr. L. P. Jones,* filed April 29, 1904, Cause No. 532 in the 50th Judicial District Court of Knox County, Texas.

4. The text account of the killing of Mary Jones by her husband, Dr. L. P. Jones, is compiled from the following news accounts: *Baylor County Banner,* August 26, 1904; *Haskell Free Press,* August 27, 1904; and Jack Jones, "Museum News," *Baylor County Banner,* July 15, 1999.

5. Jack Jones, "Museum News," *Baylor County Banner,* July 22, 1999, and July 29, 1999.

6. Jack Jones (resident Baylor County historian) interviewed by Bill Neal, Seymour, Texas, October 23, 1999. Another yarn that Brookerson told on himself to Jack Jones went like this: As is the case with many newly elected prosecutors, over-zealousness often leads to surprising, unanticipated, and, at least from the prosecutor's perspective, undesirable results. At any rate, shortly after his election, Brookerson decided to bring every criminal—large or small—to book for their transgressions, and make a name for himself in the process. In those days Knox County was completely "dry." Brookerson was aware, however, that there were a substantial number of Knox citizens who were not taking this law very seriously— particularly those of German ancestry who were congregated in small rural enclaves like the Rhineland community. Brookerson took it upon himself to organize an informal task force consisting of himself and a couple of deputies. Together they worked hard, stayed up late, and diligently put together several well-documented bootlegging cases. Brookerson was "chomping at the bit" to get to trial and put a stop to this flagrant flouting of the liquor laws. His first defendant was, fittingly, a rotund, jolly old German farmer from the Rhineland community. Brookerson put his airtight case to a jury and sat back to await the expected conviction. To his surprise—and dismay—it took the six-man jury only about five minutes to return with a verdict: not guilty. He was even more flabbergasted when the old defendant immediately jumped up, ran across the courtroom, and shook his hand. In a thick German brogue, and while still shaking his hand, he thanked Brookerson profusely for putting "three of my best customers" on the jury. Brookerson became a much wiser—and better—prosecutor, and the rest of his Teutonic bootleg beer cases were quietly scuttled.

7. *Wichita Falls Times,* November 20, 1895.

8. Rhea, "Revenge," 27–28.

9. Rhea, "Revenge," 28.

10. Vol. 12, Pg. 245, Deed Records of Knox County, Texas.

11. Rhea, "Revenge," 28.

12. Ibid.

13. Rhea, "Revenge," 28–29.

14. *Ellen Mitchell v. J. J. (Red) Mitchell,* filed January 12, 1916, Cause No. 146 in the 50th Judicial District Court of King County, Texas.

15. *J. J. Mitchell v. Ellen Mitchell,* filed June 24, 1916, Cause No. 1034 in the 50th Judicial District Court of Knox County, Texas.

16. Answers by Mrs. Cordie Jones to written interrogatories propounded to her by J. J. Mitchell's attorney, D. J. Brookerson, in Ellen Mitchell's King County divorce case.

17. Rhea, "Revenge," 29.

18. Rhea, "Revenge," 30.

19. Motion for Continuance dated March 20, 1917, and filed by George Douglas, *State v. George Douglas,* Cause No. 1038, Knox County, Texas District Court.

20. Holographic will of J. J. Mitchell dated September 1, 1916, Vol. 13, Pg. 32, King County, Texas Deed Records; also appears in Cause No. 185 on the Probate Docket of Knox County, Texas.

21. *J. J. Mitchell v. Ellen Mitchell,* Cause No. 1034, Knox County, Texas District Court.

22. Rhea, "Revenge," 29.

23. All murder indictments returned in the Knox County District Court: *State v. George Douglas,* No. 1027 (murder of Joel Reed); *State v. George Douglas,* No. 1028 (murder of J.J. Mitchell); *State v. William M. Winter,* No. 1073 (murder of J. J. Mitchell); and *State v. William M. Winter,* No. 1074 (murder of Joel Reed).

24. Rhea, "Revenge," 29.

25. *Abilene Daily Reporter,* March 21, 1917.

26. Rhea, "Revenge," 29.

27. Rhea, "Revenge," 31.

28. *Abilene Daily Reporter,* March 20, 21, and 22, 1917; *Fort Worth Star-Telegram,* March 21, 1917; *Foard County News* and *Crowell Index,* March 23, 1917.

29. *Abilene Daily Reporter,* March 20, 1917.

30. Rhea, "Revenge," 32.

31. Rhea was probably right. He survived World War I and was honorably discharged as a first lieutenant. He lived until 1985, when he died at the ripe old age of ninety-five. After World War I, he practiced law in Wichita Falls for many years and served as the first full-time city attorney for that town. *Wichita Falls Times,* November 20, 1985.

32. Indictments returned by Knox County District Court against Will Mitchell: No. 1070 (murder of George Douglas); No. 1071 (assault with intent to murder J. F. Cunningham); and No. 1072 (assault with intent to murder Henry Delk).

33. Cause No. 1334, Baylor County District Court.

34. Rhea, "Revenge," 32.

35. *State v. W. M. Winters,* Cause Nos. 1073 and 1074, respectively, on the docket of the Knox County District Court.

36. Rhea, "Revenge," 32.

37. For a historical perspective on the insanity defense see John Phillip Reid,

Chief Justice: The Judicial World of Charles Doe (Cambridge: Harvard University Press, 1967), 109–221. Reid discusses the famous "M'Naghten" test for insanity adopted by most American jurisdictions. The M'Naghten rule was imported from England. It provided that "to establish a defense on the ground of insanity, it must be clearly proved that, at the time of the committing of the act, the party accused was laboring under such a defect of reason, from disease of the mind, as not to know the nature and quality of the act he was doing; or, if he did know it, that he did not know what he was doing was wrong. *M'Naghten's Case,* 10 Cl. & F. 200, 210; 8 Eng. Rep. 718, 722 (1843). Some American jurisdictions tacked on the "irresistible impulse" to the traditional M'Naghten test. Under the latter doctrine, the defendant could be found to be legally insane at the time of the act, even though he knew what he was doing and knew it was wrong, if, by reason of some mental disease, he was rendered incapable of resisting an impulse that led to the commission of the act. *Commonwealth v. McCann,* 325 Mass. 510, 515; 91 N.E.2d 214, 217 (1950).

38. Deposition of county judge J. D. Goff, County Court of White County, Tennessee, Cause No. 1070 in the Knox County, Texas, District Court and, upon change of venue, Cause No. 1334 in the Baylor County, Texas, District Court, and upon change of venue, Cause No. 2312 in the Wilbarger County, Texas, District Court.

39. Deposition of Dr. E. W. Mitchell, superintendent of the Eastern Hospital for the Insane at Bearden, Tennessee, in the above prosecution.

40. Deposition of Mrs. George Steakley of Paducah, Texas, in the above prosecution.

41. Deposition of Dr. E. W. Mitchell. Will Mitchell's background of mental aberrations, "lunacy episodes," and commitments are compiled from written deposition testimony introduced during Will Mitchell's trials: *State v. Will Mitchell,* Cause No. 1070, Knox County District Court; Cause No. 1334, Baylor County District Court; and Cause No. 2312, Wilbarger County District Court. Depositions included that of Mrs George Steakley of Paducah, Texas (Will Mitchell's niece who grew up in the Sparta, Tennessee, community where Will was raised); E. W. Mitchell, MD (no relation to Will) who was superintendent of the Eastern Hospital for the Insane, Bearden, Tennessee; and White County, Tennessee, county judge J. D. Goff, who was present during Will's first lunacy trial and who personally delivered Will and his possum to the mental institution.

42. Deposition in the above cause of W. J. Howard, Wichita County justice of the peace and formerly a sheriff of that county.

43. "Incompetency to stand trial" is a very different animal from "insanity at the time of the crime." The former relates to the defendant's present mental state and merely prevents a criminal trial to determine guilt or innocence from proceeding forward until such time as the defendant becomes competent—if ever. The latter relates to the defendant's mental state at the time of the crime, and such a find-

ing is made at the guilt-or-innocence trial itself (after the defendant has been found to be competent to stand trial) and results in an acquittal ("not guilty by reason of insanity"), which of course prevents any further prosecution under the double jeopardy doctrine. Under present Texas law, a defendant is incompetent to stand trial for an offense if he does not have: (a) sufficient present ability to consult with his lawyer with a reasonable degree of rational understanding, or (b) a rational as well as a factual understanding of the proceeding against him. If the incompetency issue is raised, then the defendant has the burden of proving by a "preponderance of the evidence" that he is incompetent. *Article 46.02, Texas Code of Criminal Procedure.* Texas has streamlined the definition of insanity since the old M'Naghten days. A defendant is to be found insane under today's test if, at the time of the criminal conduct charged against him, he, as a result of severe mental disease or defect, did not know that his conduct was wrong. The Texas statute then qualifies that simple test somewhat by providing that the term "mental disease or defect" does not include an abnormality manifested only by repeated criminal or otherwise antisocial conduct. Insanity at the time of the crime is an affirmative defense to prosecution, but again, the defendant bears the burden of proving to a jury "by a preponderance of the evidence" that he was, in fact, insane. *Section 8.01, Texas Penal Code; Article 46.03, Texas Code of Criminal Procedure.*

44. Vol. 10, Pg. 131, Minutes of the District Court of Wilbarger County: Dismissal of *State v. Will Mitchell,* Cause No. 2362, Wilbarger County District Court. (There is a confusion in the Wilbarger County District Court records of this case—sometimes the Cause No. is referred to as No. 2312, sometimes 2362, and sometimes 2394.)

45. *Estate of J. J. Mitchell,* deceased, Cause No. 185 on the Probate Docket of Knox County.

46. Recitations appearing in Vol. 2, pg. 11 of the Probate Docket of King County in Cause No. 2, Guardianship of minor children of Ellen Mitchell and J. J. Mitchell, deceased, to wit: Anna May Mitchell, Sallie Lee Mitchell, and J. P. Mitchell—Ellen Mitchell Barkley, guardian.

47. The tactic of delaying a criminal trial by any means possible and for as long as possible was one of the most common and successful weapons employed by every criminal defense lawyer on the western frontier. Gordon Morris Bakken, *Practicing Law in Frontier California* (Lincoln: University of Nebraska Press, 1991), 111–112; Edward L. Ayers, *Vengeance and Justice: Crime and Punishment in the 19th Century American South* (New York: Oxford University Press, Inc., 1984), 268–269.

Strychnine in the Bride's Flour

1. Vol. 1, Pg. 385, Foard County Marriage Records, (Fred Bell and Suetta Gafford, Dec. 9, 1918).

NOTES

2. Foard County Death Certificate Records (Suetta Gafford Bell, February 10, 1919).

3. *Quanah Tribune-Chief,* July 3, 1919; *Foard County News,* July 4, 1919.

4. *Foard County News,* June 27, 1919; Betty Ingle Gibson, http://boards .ancestry.com/mbexec?htx'message&r'an&p'localities,northam.usa.states.texas-counties.foard "Steve Bell." April 30, 2001 MyFamily.com, Inc. and its subsidiaries, (Ancestry.com) July 22, 2001.

5. *Foard County News,* March 30, 1917.

6. *Foard County News,* March 23, 1917; *Foard County News,* July 4, 1919.

7. *Foard County News,* June 27, 1919.

8. *Foard County News,* August 31, 1917.

9. *Dallas Morning News,* June 23, 1919.

10. Clark Hitt, interview by Bill Neal, Crowell, Texas, February 24, 2002. Hitt also produced a supporting letter from longtime Crowell resident James Welch addressed to Faye Statser, dated May 25, 1998, supporting this observation, a copy of which is in this author's files.

11. *Foard County News,* August 31, 1917.

12. Jim Lois Gafford Johnson, interview by Judy Payne, Amarillo, Texas, August 8, 2001.

13. Jim Lois Gafford Johnson interview, August 8, 2001.

14. 1918 Foard County Death Certificate Records (Suetta Gafford Bell, February 9, 1919).

15. Newspaper accounts of the shootout are compiled from *Dallas Morning News,* June 23, 1919; *Fort Worth Star-Telegram,* June 23, June 24, and June 25, 1919; *Foard County News,* June 27, 1919.

16. *Fort Worth Star-Telegram,* June 24, 1919

17. Grand jury indictments returned on June 21, 1919, against Myrtle Gafford in the District Court of Foard County include No. 318 (murder of Senator Steve Bell by shooting him with a pistol); No. 319 (assault with intent to kill Fred Bell); and No. 320 (assault with intent to kill Everett Bell). When transferred to the Hardeman County District Court in Quanah, these indictments had been renumbered Cause Nos. 1009, 1010, and 1011, respectively.

18. The story of the murder trial of Myrtle Gafford has been compiled from the following sources: Court records in Cause No. 1009, Hardeman County District Court, and newspaper accounts of the trial in *Wichita Daily Times,* March 16, 17, 18, 19, and 20, 1920; *Fort Worth Star-Telegram,* March 17, 18, 19, and 20. 1920; *Foard County News,* March 19 and 26, 1920; and *Quanah Tribune-Chief,* March 18 and 25, 1920.

19. *Fort Worth Star-Telegram,* March 16, 1920.

20. *Wichita Daily Times,* March 18, 1920.

21. *Wichita Daily Times,* March 19, 1920.

22. *Foard County News,* March 19, 1920.

23. Ibid.

24. *Quanah Tribune-Chief,* March 18, 1920.

25. Ibid.

26. *Wichita Daily Times,* March 18, 1920.

27. Ibid.

28. Billy Mitchell, "Judge A. J. Fires, Childress Pioneer," *Panhandle-Plains Historical Review* 19 (1946): 27.

29. Retired Texas district court Judge T. Forbis, interview by Bill Neal, Childress, Texas, November 15, 2001.

30. Two authors in recent books have demonstrated how the honor defense worked for female as well as male defendants. Richard Wightman Fox, *Trials of Intimacy: Love and Loss in the Beecher-Tilton Scandal* (Chicago: University of Chicago, 1999); Michael Grossberg, *A Judgment for Solomon: The D'Hauteville Case and Legal Experiences in Antebellum America* (New York: Cambridge University Press, 1996).

31. The "honor code," the basis of "the unwritten law," is commonly associated with the Old South. But it was by no means limited to the southern states. Until well after the turn of the century lawyers in Texas and the western states continued to invoke lex non scripta. The heavy migration of southerners to Texas and the western states both before and after the Civil War doubtless accounted for this cultural export. Clare V. McKanna Jr., *Homicide, Race and Justice in the American West, 1880–1920* (Tucson: University of Arizona Press, 1997), 66–67. Also see the California cases collected in Gordon Morris Bakken, "The Limits of Patriarchy: The 'Unwritten Law' in California," in Gordon Morris Bakken, ed., *California History: A Topical Approach* (Wheeling, Ill.: Harlan Davidsor, Inc., 2003), 84–107. In the two murder cases analyzed in that work, women successfully relied upon "the unwritten law" defense—just as did Myrtle Gafford.

32. *Wichita Daily Times,* March 18, 1920.

33. *Quanah Tribune-Chief,* March 18, 1920.

34. *Fort Worth Star-Telegram,* March 18, 1920; *Foard County News,* March 19, 1920.

35. *Wichita Daily Times,* March 17, 1920.

36. Anonymous source who required anonymity, interview by Bill Neal, Crowell, Texas, February 24, 2002. The author has known this source personally for many years and believes the source to be not only credible but also knowledgeable as to the information provided. The source believes that the three Crowell doctors who performed the autopsy upon Suetta Gafford's body concluded that the cause of her death was blood poisoning resulting from a botched abortion attempt, the instrument used in the attempt having most likely been a ladies' long-needle hat pin.

37. *Wichita Daily Times,* March 18, 1920.

38. *Quanah Tribune-Chief,* March 18, 1920. *Fort Worth Star-Telegram,* March 19, 1920.

39. *Quanah Tribune-Chief,* March 18, 1920.

40. *Wichita Daily Times,* March 19, 1920.

41. *Quanah Tribune-Chief,* March 25, 1920.

42. Anonymous source interview, February 24, 2002.

43. Jim Lois Gafford Johnson interview, August 8, 2001.

44. Ibid.

45. Judge Charlie Bell, interview by Bill Neal, Crowell, Texas, May 3, 2001.

46. Anonymous source interview, February 24, 2002.

47. Judge Charlie Bell interview, May 3, 2001.

48. Except as specifically noted otherwise, the following story of the establishment of Texas Tech University and the decision of where to locate it has been compiled from the following sources: Matthew Henry, http://www.redraiders.com/ techs 75th/ "Beginnings: Tech's Roots Based in Effort to Start West Texas College," *Lubbock Avalanche-Journal* 1998 (Accessed November 2, 2001); Jane Gilmore Rushing and Kline N. Nall, *Evolution of a University: Texas Tech's First Fifty Years* (Austin: Madrona Press, Inc., 1975); Clifford L. Gibbs, "The Establishment of Texas Technological College," M.A. thesis, Texas Technological College, 1939; *Lubbock Morning Avalanche,* August 1, 1923, August 28, 1923, and January 20, 1946.

49. *Foard County News,* July 4, 1919.

50. The Texas legislature, in the bill creating Texas Tech, specified that it had to be located somewhere north of the twenty-ninth parallel and west of the ninety-eighth meridian, which meant that it could be no further south than an east-west line running roughly halfway between Houston and Austin, no further north than the Red River and the Oklahoma boundary (which thus included all the Texas Panhandle), no further east that a north-south line running about forty-five miles west of Fort Worth, and no further west than the New Mexico border. The geographical center of the area would, therefore, be roughly in the vicinity of Abilene and Sweetwater. *Lubbock Morning Avalanche,* July 25, 1923.

51. Matthew Henry, "Beginnings: Tech's Roots Based in Effort to Start West Texas College." See also, *Lubbock Morning Avalanche,* August 1, 1923, August 28, 1923, and January 20, 1946, and *University Daily,* December 8, 1969.

. . . And the Perpetrator Walked

1. Glenn Shirley, *Temple Houston: Lawyer with A Gun* (Norman: University of Oklahoma Press, 1980), 3–7. Temple Houston didn't carry "Old Betsy" solely as a dramatic prop, and he ordinarily didn't shoot blanks either. In 1895, while practicing law in Woodward, Oklahoma Territory, he locked horns with the Woodward

County probate judge J. D. F. Jennings. Jennings's four sons, Al, Frank, John, and Ed, were all lawyers and practiced in their father's court. Every time Temple came up against one of the Jennings boys in their father's court, Temple's client lost— even when the law seemed clearly on his side. "Don't pass me any more deals from a cold deck," Houston warned. After another such courtroom defeat, Houston encountered sons Ed and John in Jack Garvey's saloon in Woodward. Tempers flared, words were exchanged, and guns were drawn. Temple shot Ed in the head, killing him on the spot, and then either he or his companion, Jack Love, shot John's left arm off as he was trying to get out the front door. The remaining Jenningses saw fit to leave town post haste, and Temple Houston had no further trouble with them. Houston was tried and acquitted. Later, brothers Al and Frank Jennings fell in with other Oklahoma Territory outlaws. They were not very successful on that side of the law either, and soon both ended up in the federal penitentiary. See Jim Gober, *Cowboy Justice: Tale of a Texas Lawman* (Lubbock: Texas Tech University Press, 1997), 186–187; Shirley, *Temple Houston*, 212–223.

2. Mrs. Betty B. McAdams (granddaughter of J. J. McAdams) interview by Bill Neal, Foard County, Texas, December 31, 1999; Carmen Taylor Bennett, *Our Roots Grow Deep: A History of Cottle County* (Floydada, Tex.: Blanco Offset Printing, Inc., 1970), 15–22.

3. *State of Texas v. J. J. McAdams*, Cause No. 2482 in the District Court of Cooke County, Texas.

4. Hank Bass, "Temple Lea Houston: Gun Toting, Bible-Quoting Lawyer of the Old West," *Texas Bar Journal* 64, no. 1 (January, 2001): 69; Sallie B. Harris, *Cowman and Ladies: A History of Hemphill County* (Canyon, Tex.: Staked Plains Press, Inc., 1977), 41; H. C. Randolph, *Panhandle Lawyers* (Amarillo: Russell Stationery, 1931), 17–21; Glenn Shirley, *Temple Houston*, ix–x.

5. Billy Mitchell, "Judge A. J. Fires, Childress Pioneer," *Panhandle-Plains Historical Review* 19 (1946): 24–28. See also Leroy Reeves, "The History of Childress County," M.A. thesis, West Texas State College, 1951; Michael Graham Ehrle, *The Childress County Story* (Childress, Tex.: Ox Bow Printing Co., 1971).

6. *State v. J .J. McAdams*, Cause No. 24 on the docket of the Childress County District Court.

7. *State v. J. J. McAdams*, Cause No. 473 on the docket of the Wilbarger County District Court.

8. Recitations in defendant's attachment for the witness A. G. Carruth on file in *State of Texas v. J. J. McAdams*, Cause No. 1 on the docket of the Cottle County District Court.

9. Everett Dick, *The Dixie Frontier: A Social History* (Norman: University of Oklahoma Press, 1993), 232.

10. Luke Gournay, *Texas Boundaries: Evolution of the State's Counties* (College Station: Texas A&M University Press, 1995), 33.

11. Apparently other sparsely populated West Texas counties faced the same problem in attempting to officially organize themselves. Noted Panhandle historian J. Evetts Haley in commenting on the organization of Donley County wrote: "As in the case of counties already organized, they had to go beyond their political bounds to muster the required [150] signatures. The procedure was slightly irregular, but what was a county line between Western friends." J. Evetts Haley, *Charles Goodnight: Cowman and Plainsman* (Norman: University of Oklahoma Press, 1936), 370–371.

12. Bennett, *Our Roots Grow Deep,* 22. Meanwhile, a few miles to the south, proponents of county organization in Fisher County (the county seat of which is Roby) overcame their lack of people problem in 1886 by scribbling in the names of their pet dogs on the petition. Opponents mounted a hotly contested challenge, but eventually the dog lovers prevailed, and Fisher County was organized. George S. Anderson, "West Texas and Its Press as I Have Known Them," *West Texas Historical Association Year Book* 18 (1942): 5. And out west of there a few years later (1893) similar shenanigans were apparently employed to bring about the organization of sparsely populated Glasscock County (Garden City). Ellis Douthit, "Some Experiences of a West Texas Lawyer," *West Texas Historical Association Year Book* 18 (1942): 41–42.

13. *Childress Index,* July 14, 1938; Shirley, *Temple Houston,* 266–271.

14. J. W. Williams, *The Big Ranch Country* (Wichita Falls: Nortex Offset Publications, Inc., 1971), 38–39.

15. Shirley, *Temple Houston,* 271.

16. *Childress Index,* July 14, 1938; Shirley, *Temple Houston,* 266–271.

17. Shirley, *Temple Houston,* 271.

18. Shirley, *Temple Houston,* 308.

19. Thomas F. Turner, "Prairie Dog Lawyers," *Panhandle-Plains Historical Review* 2 (1929): 116.

20. W. J. L. Sullivan, *Twelve Years in the Saddle for Law and Order on the Frontier of Texas* (originally published by W. J. L. Sullivan, 1909. Reprint, Lincoln: The University of Nebraska Press, 2001), 170–171.

21. King County Historical Society, *King County: Windmills and Barbed Wire* (Quanah: Nortex Press, 1976), 16. Also see Baylor County Historical Society, *Salt Pork to Sirloin: The History of Baylor County from 1870 to 1930* (Quanah: Nortex Press, 1972), 8–9, and Sarah Ann Britton, *The Early History of Baylor County* (Dallas: The Story Book Press, 1955), 165.

22. Ralph Powell, interview by Bill Neal, on June 14, 2005, Matador, Texas. Ralph Powell is the son of Jessie Celia Blanks Powell who, as of that date was ninety-seven years old. Ralph Powell has heard his mother tell about the 1916 racial incident in Seymour, and in addition, on December 25, 2001, she wrote an informal family history (unpublished) in which she recounted the event as set forth

in the text herein. A copy of that account is in the author's files courtesy Ralph Powell.

23. Article 1220, *Texas Penal Code*: "a homicide is justifiable when committed by the husband upon a person of any one taken in adultery with the wife; provided the killing takes place before the parties to the act of adultery have separated."

24. For a colorful examination of this quaint old "license-to-kill-the-cuckold-maker" statute, and how the Texas appellate court struggled to interpret it and to apply it to specific (and always lascivious) factual situations, all the while attempting to maintain some degree of judicial decorum in that Victorian era, see Paul Kens, "Don't Mess Around in Texas: Adultery and Justifiable Homicide in the Lone Star State," in Gordon Morris Bakken, ed., *Law in the Western United States* (Norman: University of Oklahoma Press, 2000), 114–17.

25. *Fort Worth Star-Telegram*, November 18 and 19, 1941; *Fort Worth Star-Telegram*, February 24, 1913.

26. This story is taken entirely from a forty-five-page pamphlet written by Colonel Hallum, the title of which is almost as lengthy as his jury oration: John Hallum, *Address to the Jury by Col. John Hallum in Self Defense in the Case of the State of Texas Against Him: An Indictment for the Shooting a Minister of the Gospel, Together with the Extraordinary Facts and Remarkable Incidents Connected with the Trial and Prosecution* (Muskogee, Okla.: The Phoenix Press, 1911). The only known copy of this rare 1911 edition may be found in the Jamail Center for Legal Research, Tarlton Law Library, University of Texas Law School in Austin, Texas. Prosecution was had in the case of *The State of Texas v. John Hallum*, Cause No. 1113 in the district court of Bowie County, Texas.

27. The text story of the Boyce-Sneed feud, the killings and the four ensuing murder trials are taken primarily from Clara Sneed's story: Clara Sneed, "Because This Is Texas: An Account of the Sneed-Boyce Feud," *Panhandle-Plains Historical Review* 72 (1999): 1–99, supplemented by accounts of the four murder trials (held in 1912 and 1913) as reported in the *Fort Worth Star-Telegram*. Jury arguments cited in the text were taken from trial accounts appearing in the *Fort Worth Star-Telegram*, February 22, 23, and 24, 1912, and February 24, 1913.

28. The three following anecdotes of jury shenanigans are taken from Thomas F. Turner, "Prairie Dog Lawyers," *Panhandle-Plains Historical Review* 2 (1929): 120–122. A slightly different version of the Jack Ryan anecdote is told by Glenn Shirley in his book *Temple Houston*, 74–76.

29. *Northern v. State*, 203 S.W.2d 206 (Tex.Ct.Crim.App. 1947). Fortunately for the cause of justice, the court did allow the state to re-indict and correct the egregious error in its indictment. Buster Northern was again tried, convicted, and sentenced to death. This time the court affirmed, and Buster finally got his after all. *Northern v. State*, 216 S.W.2d 192 (Tex.Ct.Crim.App. 1948).

30. *Gragg v. State*, 186 S.W.2d 243 (Tex.Ct.Crim.App. 1945).

31. *Jackson v. State*, 34 Tex.Cr.Rep. 38, 28 S.W. 815 (Tex.Ct.Crim.App. 1894).

32. *Vaughan v State*, 607 S.W.2d 914 (Tex.Ct.Crim.App., 1980).

33. J. F. H. Claiborne, *Mississippi as a Province, Territory, and State* (Jackson: Power and Barksdale, 1880), 482; Reuben Davis, *Recollections of Mississippi and Mississippians* (Boston: Houghton Mifflin, 1889), 104; Edward L. Ayers, *Vengeance and Justice: Crime and Punishment in the 19th-Century American South* (New York: Oxford University Press, Inc., 1984), 32.

34. Hon. John T. Forbis (retired judge of the 100th Judicial District Court of Texas) interview by Bill Neal, Childress, Texas, November 25, 2001.

Afterword

1. Gordon Morris Bakken, *Practicing Law in Frontier California* (Lincoln: University of Nebraska Press, 1991), xi–xiii; Richard F. Hamm, *Murder, Honor, and Law: Four Virginia Homicides from Reconstruction to the Great Depression* (Charlottesville: University of Virginia Press, 2003), 213.

2. Daniel Joseph Singal, *The War Within: From Victorian to Modernist Thought in the South, 1919–1945* (Chapel Hill: University of North Carolina Press, 1982), 346.

3. Warren quoted in Edward L. Ayers, *Vengeance and Justice: Crime and Punishment in the 19th-Century American South* (New York: Oxford University Press, 1984), 270.

4. W. Eugene Hollon, *Frontier Violence: Another Look* (New York: Oxford University Press, 1974), 43. Hollon makes this observation:

> One reason the heritage of the Texas frontier has survived so late into the twentieth century is that the physical frontier survived there perhaps longer than in any other region. Texas spent more than half a century trying to solve its Indian problem, while most frontier states took only a decade or two to do so. . . . During the Civil War [the Indians] pushed the frontier line of settlements back a hundred miles or more in parts of western Texas. The settlers retaliated, and more often than not the victims on both sides were the innocent, rather than the perpetrators of the crime.

5. Richard B. McCaslin, *Tainted Breeze: The Great Hanging at Gainesville, Texas, 1862* (Baton Rouge: Louisiana State University Press, 1994).

6. Hollon, *Frontier Justice*, 52–53.

7. Benjamin Heber Johnson, *Revolution in Texas: How a Forgotten Rebellion and Its Bloody Suppression Turned Mexicans into Americans* (New Haven: Yale University Press, 2003), 1–6.

8. J. T. Gibbs, *Race and Justice: Rodney King and O. J. Simpson in a House Divided* (San Francisco: Jossey-Bass, 1996); Wayne K. Hobson, "Narratives in Black

and White: The O. J. Simpson Trials as Social Drama" in John W. Johnson, ed., *Historical U.S. Court Cases: An Encyclopedia,* 2nd ed., vol. 1 (New York: Routledge, 2001), 139–145; Vincent Bugliosi, *Outrage: The Five Reasons Why O. J. Simpson Got Away with Murder* (New York: Bantam Doubleday Dell Publishing Group, Inc., 1996).

9. *United States v. United Mine Workers,* 330 U.S. 258, 312 (1947).

BIBLIOGRAPHY

Books

Adams, Ramon. *Burrs under the Saddle.* Norman: University of Oklahoma Press, 1964.

Ayers, Edward L. *Vengeance and Justice: Crime and Punishment in the American South.* New York: Oxford University Press, 1984.

Bakken, Gordon Morris. "The Limits of Patriarchy: The Unwritten Law in California." In *California History: A Topical Approach,* edited by Gordon Morris Bakken. Wheeling, W. Va.: Harlan Davidsor, Inc., 2003.

Bakken, Gordon Morris. *Practicing Law in Frontier California.* Lincoln: University of Nebraska Press, 1991.

Baylor County Historical Society. *Salt Pork to Sirloin: The History of Baylor County from 1870 to 1930.* Quanah, Tex.: Nortex Press, 1972.

Bennett, Carmen Taylor. *Our Roots Grow Deep: A History of Cottle County.* Floydada, Tex.: Blanco Offset Printing, 1970.

Boggs, Johnny D. *Great Murder Trials of the Old West.* Plano: Republic of Texas Press, 2003.

Britton, Sarah Ann. *The Early History of Baylor County.* Dallas: The Story Book Press, 1955.

Brodhead, Michael J. *Isaac C. Parker: Federal Justice on the Frontier.* Norman: University of Oklahoma Press, 2003.

Brown, Norman D. *Hood, Bonnet, and Little Brown Jug: Texas Politics, 1921–1928.* College Station: Texas A&M University Press, 1984.

Brown, Richard Maxwell. *No Duty to Retreat: Violence and Values in American History and Society.* New York: Oxford University Press, 1991.

Bugliosi, Vincent. *Outrage: The Five Reasons Why O. J. Simpson Got Away with Murder.* New York: Bantam Doubleday Dell Publishing Group, Inc., 1996.

Burton, Jeffrey. *Indian Territory and the United States, 1866–1906: Courts, Government, and the Movement for Oklahoma Statehood.* Norman: University of Oklahoma Press, 1995.

Calhoun, Daniel H. *Professional Lives in America.* Cambridge: Harvard University Press, 1965.

Campbell, Harry H. *The Early History of Motley County,* 2nd ed., Wichita Falls, Tex.: Nortex Offset Publications, Inc., 1971.

Campbell, Josephine Hooper. *Knox County History.* Haskell, Tex.: The Haskell Free Press, 1966.

Cary, Charles K. *Kaffir Woolies.* Laverne, Okla.: Dewey County Jailhouse Museum, 1999.

Cashion, Ty. *A Texas Frontier: The Clear Fork Country and Fort Griffin, 1849–1887.* Norman: University of Oklahoma Press, 1996.

Claiborne, J. F. H. *Mississippi as a Province, Territory, and State.* Jackson, Miss.: Power and Barksdale, 1880.

Cobb, Berry B. *A History of Dallas Lawyers, 1840 to 1890.* Dallas: The Bar Association of Dallas, 1934.

Coombes, Charles E. *The Prairie Dog Lawyer.* Dallas: University Press in Dallas, 1945.

Croy, Homer. *Trigger Marshal: The Story of Chris Madsen.* New York: Duell, Sloan, and Pearce, 1958.

Davis, John W. *Goodbye Judge Lynch: The End of a Lawless Era in Wyoming's Big Horn Basin.* Norman: University of Oklahoma Press, 2005.

Davis, John W. *A Vast Amount of Trouble: A History of the Spring Creek Raid.* Niwot: University Press of Colorado, 1993.

Davis, Reuben. *Recollections of Mississippi and Mississippians.* Boston: Houghton Mifflin, 1889.

DeArment, Robert K. *Bravo of the Brazos: John Larn of Fort Griffin, Texas.* Norman: University of Oklahoma Press, 2000.

Dewey County Historical Society. *Spanning the River: Dewey County Family Histories,* vol. 1. San Angelo, Tex.: Newsfoto Yearbook Co., 1976.

Dick, Everett. *The Dixie Frontier: A Social History.* Norman: University of Oklahoma Press, 1993.

Ehrle, Michael Graham. *The Childress County Story.* Childress, Tex.: Ox Bow Printing Co., 1971.

Fox, Richard Wightman. *Trials of Intimacy: Love and Loss in the Beecher-Tilton Scandal.* Chicago: University of Chicago Press, 1999.

Frantz, Joe B. *The History of Violence in America: Historical and Comparative Per-*

spectives. Edited by Hugh Davis Graham and Ted Robert Gurr. New York: Frederick A. Praeger, Publishers, 1969.

Gard, Wayne. *Frontier Justice.* Norman: University of Oklahoma Press, 1949.

Gibbs, J. T. *Race and Justice: Rodney King and O. J. Simpson in a House Divided.* San Francisco: Josey-Bass, 1996.

Gober, Jim. *Cowboy Justice: Tale of a Texas Lawman.* Lubbock: Texas Tech University Press, 1997.

Gournay, Luke. *Texas Boundaries: Evolution of the State's Counties.* College Station: Texas A&M University Press, 1995.

Graves, Robert S. *Oklahoma Outlaws.* Ft. Davis, Tex.: Frontier Book Co., 1968.

Grossberg, Michael. *A Judgment for Solomon: The D'Hauteville Case and Legal Experiences in Antebellum America.* New York: Cambridge University Press, 1996.

Haley, James L. *Texas: From Spindletop through World War II.* New York: St Martin's Press, 1993.

Haley, J. Evetts. *Charles Goodnight-Cowman and Plainsman.* Norman: University of Oklahoma Press,1936.

Hallum, Col. John. *Address to the Jury by Col. John Hallum in Self Defense in the Case of the State of Texas Against Him: An Indictment for Shooting a Minister of the Gospel, Together with the Extraordinary Facts and Remarkable Incidents Connected with the Trial and Prosecution.* Muskogee, Okla.: The Phoenix Press, 1911.

Hamm, Richard F. *Murder, Honor, and Law: Four Virginia Homicides from Reconstruction to the Great Depression.* Charlottesville: University of Virginia Press, 2003.

Hanes, Col. Bailey C. *Bill Doolin—Outlaw O.T.* Norman: University of Oklahoma Press, 1968.

Harper, Minnie Timms and George Dewey Harper. *Old Ranches.* Dallas: Dealy and Lowe, 1936.

Harrington, Fred Harvey. *Hanging Judge.* Norman: University of Oklahoma Press, 1951.

Harris, Sallie B. *Cowmen and Ladies: A History of Hemphill County.* Canyon, Tex.: Staked Plains Press, Inc., 1977.

Hatley, Allen G. *Bringing the Law to Texas: Crime and Violence in Nineteenth Century Texas.* LaGrange, Tex.: Centex Press, 2002.

Hobson, Wayne K. "Narratives in Black and White: The O. J. Simpson Trials as Social Drama." In *Historical U.S. Court Cases: An Encyclopedia,* edited by John W. Johnson, 2nd ed., vol. 1. New York: Routledge, 2001.

Hollon, W. Eugene. *Frontier Violence: Another Look.* New York: Oxford University Press, 1974.

Howe, Mark DeWolfe, ed. *Holmes-Laski Letters: The Correspondence of Mr. Justice Holmes and Harold J. Laski, 1916–1935.* Cambridge: Harvard University Press, 1953.

Johnson, Benjamin Heber. *Revolution in Texas: How a Forgotten Rebellion and Its Bloody Suppression Turned Mexicans into Americans.* New Haven: Yale University Press, 2003.

Kelly, Louise. *Wichita County Beginnings.* Burnet, Tex.: Eakin Press, 1982.

Kens, Paul. "Don't Mess Around in Texas: Adultery and Justifiable Homicide in the Lone Star State." In *Law in the Western United States,* edited by Gordon Morris Bakken. Norman: University of Oklahoma Press, 2000.

King County Historical Society. *King County-Windmills and Barbed Wire.* Quanah, Tex.: Nortex Press, 1976.

Levy, Leonard W. *Origins of the Fifth Amendment.* London: Oxford University Press, 1968.

McCaslin, Richard B. *Tainted Breeze: The Great Hanging at Gainesville, Texas, 1862.* Baton Rouge: Louisiana State University Press, 1994.

McKanna, Clare V., Jr. *Homicide, Race, and Justice in the American West, 1880–1920.* Tucson: The University of Arizona Press, 1997.

Metz, Leon C. *Pat Garrett: The Story of a Western Lawman.* Norman: University of Oklahoma Press, 1974.

Moore, Kathleen Dean. *Pardons: Justice, Mercy, and the Public Interest.* New York: Oxford University Press, 1989.

Moretta, John Anthony. *William Pitt Ballinger: Texas Lawyer, Southern Statesman, 1825–1888.* Austin: Texas State Historical Association, 2000.

Morgan, Johnnie R. *The History of Wichita Falls.* Wichita Falls, Tex.: Nortex Press, 1971.

Nix, Evett Dumas. *Oklahombres.* St. Louis: Eden Publishing House, 1929.

O'Neal, Bill. *Cattlemen vs. Sheepherders.* Austin: Eakin Press, 1989.

O'Neal, Bill. *The Johnson County War.* Austin: Eakin Press, 2004.

Paine, Albert Bigelow. *Captain Bill McDonald, Texas Ranger.* Austin: State House Press, 1986.

Paulissen, May Nelson, and Carl McQueary. *Miriam: The Southern Belle Who Became the First Woman Governor of Texas.* Austin: Eakin Press, 1995.

Payne, Darwin. *As Old as Dallas Itself: A History of the Lawyers of Dallas, the Dallas Bar Associations, and the City They Helped Build.* Dallas: Three Forks Press, 1999.

Pickering, David, and Judy Falls. *Brush Men and Vigilantes: Civil War Dissent in Texas.* College Station: Texas A&M University Press, 2000.

Potts, Marisue Burleson. *Motley County Roundup: A Centennial History.* 2nd ed. Floydada, Tex.: Marisue Potts, 1991.

BIBLIOGRAPHY

Prassel, Frank Richard. *The Great American Outlaw: A Legacy of Fact and Fiction.* Norman: University of Oklahoma Press, 1993.

Randolph, H. C. *Panhandle Lawyers.* Amarillo, Tex.: Russell Stationery, 1931.

Rathjen, Frederick W. *The Texas Panhandle Frontier.* Lubbock: Texas Tech University Press, 1973.

Reid, John Phillip. *Chief Justice: The Judicial World of Charles Doe.* Cambridge: Harvard University Press, 1967.

Reid, John Phillip. *Policing the Elephant: Crime, Punishment, and Social Behavior on the Overland Trail.* San Marino, Calif.: Huntingron Library Press, 1997.

Rosa, Joseph G. *The Gunfighter: Man or Myth.* Norman: University of Oklahoma Press, 1969.

Rushing, Jane Gilmore, and Kline N. Nall. *Evolution of a University: Texas Tech's First Fifty Years.* Austin: Madrona Press, Inc., 1975.

Samuelson, Nancy B. *Shoot from the Lip: The Lives, Legends, and Lies of the Three Guardsmen of Oklahoma and U.S. Marshal Nix.* Eastford, Conn.: Shooting Star Press, 1998.

Shirley, Glenn. *Six-Gun and Silver Star.* Albuquerque: University of New Mexico Press, 1955.

Shirley, Glenn. *Temple Houston: Lawyer with a Gun.* Norman: University of Oklahoma Press, 1980.

Shirley, Glenn. *West of Hell's Fringe.* Norman: University of Oklahoma Press, 1978.

Singal, Daniel Joseph. *The War Within: From Victorian to Modernist Thought in the South, 1919–1945.* Chapel Hill: University of North Carolina Press, 1982.

Sonnichsen, C. L. *I'll Die before I'll Run: The Story of the Great Feuds of Texas.* Lincoln: University of Nebraska Press, 1951.

Smallwood, James M., Barry A. Crouch, and Larry Peacock. *Murder and Mayhem: The War of Reconstruction in Texas.* College Station: Texas A&M University Press, 2003.

Sullivan, W. J. L. *Twelve Years in the Saddle for Law and Order on the Frontiers of Texas.* Lincoln: University of Nebraska Press, 2001.

Tilghman, Zoe A. *Marshal of the Last Frontier: Life and Service of William Matthew (Bill) Tilghman.* Glendale: Arthur H. Clark Co., 1964.

Tilghman, Zoe A. *Outlaw Days: A True History of Early-Day Oklahoma Characters.* Oklahoma City: Harlow Publishing Co., 1926.

Traweek, Eleanor Mitchell. *Of Such As These: A History of Motley County and It's Families.* Wichita Falls, Tex.: Nortex Publications, Inc., 1973.

Tuller, Robert H. *"Let No Guilty Man Escape": A Judicial Biography of "Hanging Judge" Isaac C. Parker.* Norman: University of Oklahoma Press, 2001.

Utley, Robert M. *Billy the Kid: A Short and Violent Life*. Lincoln: University of Nebraska Press, 1989.

Webb, Walter Prescott. *The Texas Rangers*. Austin: University of Texas Press, 1935.

Williams, J. W. *The Big Ranch Country*. Wichita Falls, Tex.: Nortex Offset Publications, Inc., 1971.

Periodicals

Anderson, George S. "West Texas and It's Press as I Have Known Them." *West Texas Historical Association Year Book* 18, no. 3 (1942): 5.

Bass, Hank. "Temple Lea Houston: Gun-Toting, Bible-Quoting Lawyer of the Old West." *Texas Bar Journal* (January 2001): 64.

Carter, Keith. "The Texas Court of Criminal Appeals." *Texas Law Review* 11 (1933): 185–196.

Croy, Homer. "Where the Outlaws Hid," *True West Magazine* (Oct 1962).

Cunningham, J. F. "Experiences of a Pioneer District Attorney." *West Texas Historical Association Year Book* 8 (1923): 134–135.

Douthit, Ellis. "Some Experiences of a West Texas Lawyer." *West Texas Historical Association Year Book* 18 (1942): 42–46.

Hall, Michael. "And Justice for Some." *Texas Monthly* (November 2004): 153–157, 259–263.

Hall, Judge R. W. "The Prairie Dog Lawyers." *Texas Law Review* 48 (1929): 265–271.

Hatley, Allen G. "Cap Arrington: Adventurer, Ranger and Sheriff." *Wild West* (June 2001).

Holden, W. C. "Law and Lawlessness on the Texas Frontier, 1875–1890." *Southwestern Historical Quarterly* 44 (October 1940): 203.

Johnson, Corwin W. "Texas' Uncommon Laws." *UT Law: The Magazine of the University of Texas School of Law* 2, no. 2 (Summer 2003): 64.

King, Robert E. "Till the Drums Beat Again: The Fred Hoffman Story." Oklahoma City: Oklahoma State Archives (2002): 1–4, 40, 44.

McRill, Leslie. "Old Ingalls: The Story of a Town That Will Not Die." *Chronicles of Oklahoma* 36 (Winter 1958–1959): 441.

Mitchell, Billy. "Judge A. J. Fires, Childress Pioneer." *Panhandle-Plains Historical Review* 19 (1946): 27.

Rhea, John Bunyon. "Revenge." *Wichita Falls Heritage Magazine* (Spring 1990).

Samuelson, Nancy B. "Chris Madsen: Soldier, Oklahoma 89er, and Deputy U.S. Marshal." *Oklahomres Journal* 4 (1993): 4. http://www.oklahombres.org/madsen.htm (December 2001).

Sneed, Clara. "Because This Is Texas: An Account of the Sneed-Boyce Feud." *Panhandle-Plains Historical Review* 72 (1999): 1–99.

Turner, Thomas F. "Prairie Dog Lawyers." *Panhandle-Plains Historical Review* 2 (1929): 121–122.

Webb, Walter Prescott. "George W. Arrington: The Iron-Handed Man of the Panhandle." *Panhandle-Plains Historical Review* 8 (1935): 7–20.

Documents

Trial Court Cases

Fulcher v Fulcher, Cause No 23, Motley County, Texas, District Court (1894).

Jones v Jones, Cause No 532, Knox County, Texas, District Court (1904).

Mitchell v Mitchell, Cause No 146, King County, Texas, District Court (1916).

Mitchell v Mitchell, Cause No 1034, Knox County, Texas, District Court (1916).

State v Beckham, Cause No 35, Motley County, Texas, District Court (1893).

State v Blake, Cause No 108, Hemphill County, Texas, District Court (1894).

State v Blake, Cause No 939, Wilbarger County, Texas, District Court (1894).

State v Burnett, Cause No 1100, Baylor County, Texas, District Court (1912).

State v Davis, Cause No 608, Wichita County, Texas, District Court (1896).

State v Davis, Cause No 940, Wilbarger County, Texas, District Court (1896).

State v Douglas, Cause No 1027, 1028, Knox County, Texas, District Court (1916).

State v Fulcher, Cause No 50, Crosby County, Texas, District Court (1889).

State v Fulcher, Cause No 12, Motley County, Texas, District Court (1893).

State v Fulcher, Cause No 22, Crosby County, Texas, District Court (1887).

State v Fulcher, Cause No 32, 51, Motley County, Texas, District Court (1895).

State v Gafford, Cause No 318, 319, and 320, Foard County, Texas, District Court (1919).

State v Gafford, Cause No 1009, 1010 and 1011, Hardeman County, Texas, District Court (1919).

State v Hallum, Cause No 1113, Bowie County, Texas, District Court (1896).

State v Harbolt, Cause No 109, Hemphill County, Texas, District Court (1894).

State v Harbolt, Cause No 647, Donley County, Texas, District Court (1894).

State v Isaacs, Cause No 334, Hardeman County, Texas, District Court (1894).

State v Isaacs, Cause No 110, Hemphill County, Texas, District Court (1894).

State v McAdams, Cause No 24, Childress County, Texas, District Court (1890).

State v McAdams, Cause No 2482, Cooke County, Texas, District Court (1889).

State v McAdams, Cause No 1, Cottle County, Texas, District Court (1891).

State v McAdams, Cause No 1, King County, Texas, District Court (1891).

State v McAdams, Cause No 473, Wilbarger County, Texas, District Court (1890).

State v Mitchell, Cause No 1334, Baylor County, Texas, District Court (1916).

State v Mitchell, Cause No 1070, Knox County, Texas, District Court (1916).

State v Mitchell, Cause No 2312, Wilbarger County, Texas, District Court (1916).

State v Pettyjohn, Cause No 399, 406, 407, 436, Hardeman County, Texas, District Court (1895).

State v Pickett, Cause No 1099, Baylor County, Texas, District Court (1912).

State v Potter, Cause No 604, Wichita County, Texas, District Court (1896).

State v Potter, Cause No 3441, Cooke County, Texas, District Court (1896).

State v Quinn, Cause No 607, Wichita County, Texas, District Court (1896).

State v Quinn, Cause No 941, Wilbarger County, Texas, District Court (1896).

State v Sexton, Cause No 405, 437, Hardeman County, Texas, District Court (1895).

State v Shumate, Cause No 404, Hardeman County, Texas, District Court (1895).

State v Smith, Cause No 605, Wichita County, Texas, District Court (1896).

State v Smith, Cause No 943, Wilbarger County, Texas, District Court (1896).

State v Winter, Cause No 1073, 1074, Knox County, Texas, District Court (1916).

Territory v Chapman, Cause No 1, 70 D County, Oklahoma Territory Criminal Docket Book (1895).

Territory v Herring and Kopp, Cause No 1, 13 D County, Oklahoma Territory Criminal Docket Book (1895).

Territory v Moore, Cause No 1, 72 D County, Oklahoma Territory Criminal Docket Book (1895).

Territory v Pettyjohn, Cause No 1, 11 D County, Oklahoma Territory Criminal Docket Book (1894).

Territory v Yeager, Son, Son, McKinzie and Pettyjohn, Cause No 15, D County, Oklahoma Territory Second Judicial District Court (1895).

Appellate Court Decisions

Blake v State, 43 SW 107 (Tex.Ct.Crim.App. 1897).

Britain v State, 86 SW 2d 457 (Tex.Ct.Crim.App. 1935).

Brown v State, 38 SW 1008 (Tex.Ct.Crim.App. 1897).

Brown v State, 43 SW 986 (Tex.Ct.Crim.App. 1898).

Brown v United States, 256 US 335 (1921).

Commonwealth v McCann, 325 M 510, 515, 91 NE 2d 214, 217 (1950).

Crawford v Washington, 124 S Ct 1354, 158 L Ed 2d 177, 2004 WL 413301 (2004).

Dent v State, 65 SW 627 (Tex.Ct.Crim.App. 1901).

Fulcher v State, 13 SW 750, 751 (Tex.Ct.Crim.App. 1890).

Fulcher v State, 33 TCR 22 (Tex.Ct.Crim.App. 1893).

Gragg v State, 186 SW 2d 243 (Tex.Ct.Crim.App. 1945).

Harbolt v State, 40 SW 983 (Tex.Ct.Crim.App. 1897).

Harbolt, et al v State, 44 SW 1110 (Tex.Ct.Crim.App. 1898).

Isaacs v State, 38 SW 40 (Tex.Ct.Crim.App. 1896).

Jackson v State, 34 TCR 38, 28 SW 815 (Tex.Ct.Crim.App. 1894).

Jones v State, 26 SW 1082 (Tex.Ct.Crim.App. 1894).

Middleton v State, 25 SW 2d 614 (Tex.Ct.Crim.App. 1930).

Miranda v Arizona, 384 US 436, 86 S Ct 1602, 16 L Ed 2d 694 (US.Sup.Ct. 1966).

BIBLIOGRAPHY

M'Naghten's Case, 10 CL & F 200; 8 Eng Rep 718 (1843).
Northern v State, 203 SW 2d 206 (Tex.Ct.Crim.App. 1947).
Northern v State, 216 SW 2d 192 (Tex.Ct.Crim.App. 1948).
Son v Territory of Oklahoma, 5 OR 526, 49 P 923 (Okla.Sup.Ct. 1897).
United States v United Mine Workers, 330 US 258 (US.Sup.Ct. 1947).
Vaughan v State, 607 SW 2d 914 (Tex.Ct.Crim.App. 1980).

Newspapers

Abilene [Texas] Daily Reporter (1917)
Baylor County Banner (1904, 1934, 1999)
Cheyenne Sunbeam (1894)
Childress County [Texas] News (1938)
Childress Index (1938)
Crowell Index (1917)
Daily Oklahoman (1895, 1898)
Dallas Morning News (1896, 1898, 1919, 2002, 2003)
Dallas Semi-Weekly News (1896)
Foard County News (1917, 1919, 1920)
Fort Worth Gazette (1896)
Fort Worth Star-Telegram (1912, 1913, 1917, 1919, 1920, 1941)
Guthrie Daily Leader (1894)
Haskell Free Press (1904)
Jacksboro [Texas] Frontier Echo (1876)
Lawton News-Reporter (1903)
Lubbock Avalanche-Journal (1998)
Lubbock Morning Avalanche (1923, 1946)
Matador Tribune (1960)
McCracken [Kansas] Enterprise (1906)
Oklahoma Daily Press-Gazette (1894)
Oklahoma State Capital (1894).
Quanah Chief (1895)
Quanah Tribune-Chief (1919, 1920, 1931)
Taloga Advocate (1903)
Taloga Times (1906)
Taloga Times-Advocate (1941)
Taloga Tomahawk (1894)
University Daily (1969)
Wichita [Texas] Daily Times (1896, 1908, 1913, 1920, 1934, 1949, 1950, 1951, 1985)
Wichita Falls Record News (1944)
Wichita Falls Times (1895)

BIBLIOGRAPHY

Interviews

Betty B. McAdams, interviewed by the author, *in person* (December 1999).

Carol Morse, interviewed by the author, *telephone* (August 2004).

Clark Hitt, interviewed by the author, *in person* (February 2002).

district judge Clyde Whiteside, interviewed by the author, *in person* (April 2002).

Jack Jones, interviewed by the author, *in person* (April 2001).

James H. East, interviewed by J. Evetts Haley, *audiocassette*, Haley History Center, Midland, Texas (September 1927).

Jim Lois Gafford Johnson, interviewed by Judy Payne, *in person* (August 2001).

Judge John T. Forbis, interviewed by the author, *in person* (November 2001).

Judge Charlie Bell, interviewed by the author, *in person* (May 2001).

Patsy Smart, interviewed by author, *in person* (March 2003).

Ralph Powell, interviewed by the author, *telephone and fascimilie* (June 2005).

Robert E. King, interviewed by the author, *in person* (March 2003).

Theses

Clifford L. Gibbs. "The Establishment of Texas Technological College." (Master's Thesis) Texas Technological College, 1939.

Leroy Reeves. "The History of Childress County." (Master Thesis) West Texas State College, 1951.

Laws

Texas Penal Code, Sections 8.01, 9.31, 9.32.

Texas Penal Code, Article 562 (1857), Article 567 (1879), Article 597 (1895), Article 672 (1895), Article 1102 (1911), Article 1220 (1925).

Laws of Texas, Article 723, Vol 10, The Texas Code of Criminal Procedure; Gammel, comp., 25th *Tex Legis, sess. (1897) 17.*

Laws of Texas, H.B. 30, Vol 10, The Texas Code of Criminal Procedure; Gammel, comp., 25th Tex Legis, special sess., (1897), 1480.

Texas Code of Criminal Procedure, Article 46.02, 46.03.

Records

Governors Executive Records Book, Pardon No. 19573, *J W Brown*, [William J Dent] letters written: J W Brown to Gov Joseph Sayers, 13 July 1899, and W M C Hill to Gov Joseph Sayers, 8 July 1899, Austin: Texas State Archives.

Governors Executive Records Book, Pardon No 19573, 28 Aug 1899, *W J Dent*, letters: US district judge Jackson to Gov Joseph Sayers, 1 June 1899 and 26 July

BIBLIOGRAPHY

1899, and Gov. George W Atkinson to Gov. Joseph Sayers 2 June 1899 and 25 August 1899, Austin: Texas State Archives.

Governors Executive Records Book, Pardon No 28037, *Ruby Britain*, 1935, Austin: Texas State Archives.

Governors Executive Records Book, Pardon No 10, 654, May 16, 1911, W. J. Dent. Austin, Texas State Archives.

Public Record, 1, 385, Marriage License, 9 Dec 1918, Foard County, Texas.

Public Record, 1, 167, Death Certificate, 10 Feb 1919, Foard County, Texas.

Attorneys Ball and Burney to H H Campbell, 29 April 1889, letter in Matador Ranch Headquarters Correspondence, 1883–1889, Southwest Collections Library, Texas Tech University,

Dr. Robert J Chandler to author, 30 May 2002, email from Senior Research Historian, Historical Services, Wells Fargo Bank.

Knox County, Texas Deed Records, Vol 12, 245.

King County, Texas Deed Records, Vol 13, 32, Will of J J Mitchell (Sept 1916).

Texas Adjutant General's Correspondence Files, letter: Cap W J McDonald to Tx Adj Gen W H Mabry from, 4 April 1896, Austin: Texas State Archives.

Texas Prison Convict Record, No. 15,531, *George Isaacs*, Austin: Texas State Archives.

Texas Prison Convict Record, No. 16,314, *J W Brown*, Austin: Texas State Archives.

Texas Prison Convict Record, No. 20,538, *William J Dent*, Austin: Texas State Archives.

INDEX

INDEX